Lecture Notes in Business Information Processing 306

More information about this series at http://www.springer.com/series/7911

Ilan Oshri
Julia Kotlarsky
Leslie P. Willcocks (Eds.)

Global Sourcing of Digital Services

Micro and Macro Perspectives

11th Global Sourcing Workshop 2017
La Thuile, Italy, February 22–25, 2017
Revised Selected Papers

 Springer

Editors
Ilan Oshri
Loughborough School of Business
  and Economics
Loughborough University
Loughborough
UK

Julia Kotlarsky
Aston Business School
Aston University
Birmingham
UK

Leslie P. Willcocks
London School of Economics
London
UK

ISSN 1865-1348   ISSN 1865-1356 (electronic)
Lecture Notes in Business Information Processing
ISBN 978-3-319-70304-6   ISBN 978-3-319-70305-3 (eBook)
https://doi.org/10.1007/978-3-319-70305-3

Library of Congress Control Number: 2017957856

Printed on acid-free paper

This Springer imprint is published by Springer Nature
The registered company is Springer International Publishing AG
The registered company address is: Gewerbestrasse 11, 6330 Cham, Switzerland

Preface

This edited book is intended for use by students, academics and practitioners who take interest in outsourcing and offshoring of information technology and business services. The book offers a review of the key topics in sourcing of services, populated with practical frameworks that serve as a tool kit to students and managers.

The range of topics covered in this book is wide and diverse, offering micro and macro perspectives on successful sourcing of services. More specifically, the book examines sourcing decisions and management practices around digital services, giving specific attention to cloud-based services and innovation in sourcing. The book also explores new sourcing trends such as robotics process automation (RPA), which is gaining attention by academics and practitioners alike. Social aspects such as motivation and engagement received further attention in this book. Last but not least, multiple theoretical lenses have been applied across the studies, among them micro-foundations view of strategy, goal-framing theory, modularity, motivation and more.

The topics discussed in this book combine theoretical and practical insights regarding challenges that industry leaders, policy makers, and professionals face or should be concerned with. Case studies from various organizations, industries, and countries are used extensively throughout the book, giving it a unique position within the current literature offering.

The book is based on a vast empirical base brought together through years of extensive research by leading researchers in information systems, strategic management, international business, and operations.

September 2017

Ilan Oshri
Julia Kotlarsky
Leslie Willcocks

Organization

The Global Sourcing Workshop is an annual gathering of academics and practitioners.

Program Committee

Julia Kotlarsky	Aston Business School, UK
Ilan Oshri	Loughborough Centre for Global Sourcing and Services, UK
Leslie Willcocks	London School of Economics, London, UK

Contents

Services Offshoring: A Microfoundations Perspective

Ilias Gerogiannis[✉], Angelika Zimmermann, and Alex Wilson

School of Business and Economics, Loughborough University, Loughborough, UK
{I.Gerogiannis,A.Zimmermann,A.Wilson8}@lboro.ac.uk

Abstract. The objective of this paper is to shed light on the link between services offshoring strategy and its outcomes for the firm by developing a theoretical framework for examining the role of employee motivation in the implementation of services offshoring strategy. Our framework is built on two conceptual foundations: the Microfoundations view of strategy and Goal Framing theory. We analyze services offshoring in terms of (a) the attributes and (b) the outcomes of firm level offshoring strategies, and (c) the micro-level processes that are essential for realizing the outcomes. As part of these micro-level processes, we focus particularly on employee motivation for services offshoring strategy implementation. We argue that our framework should constitute the basis of future empirical research in services offshoring, as it aims to contribute a greater theoretical understanding and practical recommendations for the refinement of services offshoring strategies.

Keywords: Services offshoring · Microfoundations · Employee motivation · Goal framing theory

1 Introduction

For over a decade, the services offshoring phenomenon has attracted the attention of practitioners [1], scholars [2] and policy makers [3]. Services offshoring refers to the transnational transfer of service activities to foreign destinations in captive, collaborative or outsourced governance modes [4–7]. Compared to offshoring of production activities, services offshoring depends more on individual organizational members' knowledge, skills and competences (i.e. human capital) as sources of firm competitive advantage [8, 9].

Aiming for a better understanding of what drives the success of services offshoring initiatives, scholars have progressively investigated (a) services offshoring attributes (e.g. [5, 10, 11]), (b) services offshoring outcomes (e.g. [12–14]) and (c) micro-level processes (e.g. onshore and offshore employee motivational processes) that underlie the services offshoring strategy implementation [15, 16]. However, the focus of most extant research into services offshoring is pitched at the firm level of analysis rather than at individual actors and teams (i.e. the micro level of analysis), and we know little about the links between the micro and macro levels [6]. We therefore argue that a comprehensive synthesis is needed to understand the link between the macro and micro levels of analysis and to support our understanding of how micro-level processes aggregate into services offshoring strategy outcomes. We pay special attention to how a strategy

© Springer International Publishing AG 2017
I. Oshri et al. (Eds.): Global Sourcing 2017, LNBIP 306, pp. 1–18, 2017.
https://doi.org/10.1007/978-3-319-70305-3_1

is implemented at the micro level and thereby affects services offshoring strategy outcomes.

This paper situates the above argument within the Microfoundations (MFs) view of strategy. The MFs movement in strategy and organization theory provides the means to understand how micro-processes mediate relations between macro-variables (such as firm or business level strategy and firm/business level outcomes) [17]. In the same line, we hold that the macro-level phenomena of (a) services offshoring strategy and (b) its realized outcomes are linked to micro-level processes in terms of actions and interactions of individual organizational members (i.e. managers and employees) that work towards putting the strategy into effect (i.e. strategy implementation).

In this paper we pay particular attention to the role of employee motivation in the implementation of services offshoring strategy, in order to understand how the realized outcomes are generated. Services firms are seen to encounter several offshoring implementation challenges [18], some of which are tied to motivational processes amongst onshore and offshore employees [16]. Despite its apparent importance, the role of employee motivation in services offshoring strategy implementation has received little consideration among scholars until now [16]. We examine employee motivation through two theoretical lenses, the Microfoundations (MFs) perspective on strategy and Goal Framing theory (GFT).

The MFs literature suggests that micro-processes in the context of individual motivations and their behavior (i.e. actions and interactions) could be explored with the use of goal framing theory (GFT) [19, 20]. GFT suggests that in principle there are three overarching goals that individuals pursue: the hedonic and gain goals regarding personal needs and self-interest, and the normative goal concerning the need to work towards the realization of collective interests. GFT provides the lens through which to explore the microfoundations of strategy by using the concept of "joint production motivation". A joint production motivation is a motivation of individuals to contribute to a joint effort with their own "roles and responsibilities" and also with a shared understanding of "the relevant tasks, interdependencies, timing and possible obstacles to smooth coordination" [19, p. 89]. In other words, an employee/manager who pursues normative goals holds a joint production motivation. Based on these insights, we apply GFT to address employee motivations in services offshoring strategy implementation, and further suggest that joint production motivation can play a key role in the implementation of services offshoring strategy.

The rest of the paper is structured as follows: First we present a background description of the Microfoundations view of strategy and the use of GFT for MFs research. We then discuss firm-level attributes of services offshoring strategies and firm level outcomes of services offshoring in order to explore extant offshoring research from a macro/firm level perspective. Considering various levels of the services offshoring phenomenon, we next focus on previous insights into micro-processes of services offshoring strategy, and highlight blind spots and gaps in existing research on such micro-processes. We then propose a conceptual model for research on the microfoundations of services offshoring strategy. Following this, we elaborate on how GFT can be used to address the role of employee motivation in services offshoring strategy implementation. This leads to three propositions, concerning (1) how offshoring strategies can trigger joint production motivation and how this is a prerequisite for successful strategy implementation, (2) how the micro-processes of interpersonal relationships and relational signals impact on the micro-processes of employee motivation in services offshoring and (3) how joint production motivation may affect knowledge sharing (an essential condition for effective services offshoring outcomes). Finally, we highlight the managerial relevance of the proposed theoretical framework and identify possible directions for future research.

2   The Microfoundations View of Strategy and Goal Framing Theory

We build on the growing body of research that suggests a missing link between macro and micro aspects in strategy research [17]. Foss and Lindenberg [19] argue that this gap should be addressed through a focus on the cognitions and motivations of organizational members, using a 'micro-foundations of strategy' approach. The methodological perspective of MFs advocates that the micro level constitutes the basis, or the starting point, for the exploration of a collective phenomenon such as the central strategy aims of value creation and competitive advantage [17]. This approach points to individual(s)' actions and interactions as the ultimate possible element of analysis [17]. In this context, the explanatory role of macro-level variable(s) (including firm or business unit level strategy) is still considered present and significant. However, no direct macro-causation is deemed eligible for the explanation of collective phenomena without the presence of a micro-level mediation [17].

We adopt this MFs view of strategy in order to explore the role of employee motivation in the implementation of services offshoring. We assume that a services offshoring strategy is an aggregate phenomenon that takes place as a process across the macro/firm level and the micro/employee-team level. We therefore suggest that a MFs view of services offshoring strategy enables the inspection of employees' motivations to support offshoring and that certain actions and interactions of individuals drive the implementation of the offshoring strategy, which in turn affects firm-level outcomes.

According to GFT in turn, 'framing' is a cognitive process that governs human behavior, and frames are triggered by cues from the environment [19]. In the same line, we propose that an offshoring strategy provides cues that trigger the framing process in individuals. In detail, there are three overarching goals: the hedonic, the gain and the normative goals [19, p. 87]. The hedonic goal is linked to the desire for satisfaction (how one feels right now), the gain goal relates to the need to acquire and/or preserve one's own resources (or efficiency of resources) and the normative goal refers to the need to act appropriately and work collectively in relation to group goals and a joint production framework [19]. Such goals are "overarching", because they entail other relevant subgoals [19, p. 88].

GFT posits that when a situational cue triggers one of the main overarching goals, a frame (i.e. a specific state of mind) is created whereby one of the overarching goals is focal. However, overarching goals are interrelated: when one of the above three overarching goals is triggered and thereby becomes the focal goal, the remaining two background goals can still be influential. Thus, a frame can be stronger or weaker depending on the influence of its background goals [19]. Motivations can be mixed and heterogeneous since foreground and background goals are simultaneously operative [19].

3   Firm Level Services Offshoring Attributes and Outcomes

In the following section we summarize and discuss extant research on services offshoring as a macro-level construct. We review how extant research conceptualizes and empirically investigates: (a) firm level attributes of services offshoring, and (b) firm level services offshoring outcomes, and we point out how these two are interlinked. Following the MFs perspective, we then advocate that extant views on firm level services offshoring attributes and their outcomes provide only incomplete explanations. In particular, we hold that they need to be complemented by a focus on micro-processes that entail services offshoring strategy implementation.

3.1   Strategic Attributes of Services Offshoring

Several theories derived from various academic streams such as Strategic Management and International Business are relevant to the offshoring phenomenon as presented in the services offshoring and outsourcing literature (e.g. [4, 21–23]). The outsourcing literature is here relevant because it includes offshore outsourcing as a particular type of outsourcing. These theories can serve to describe certain strategic attributes of services offshoring in terms of motives or intended outcomes of services offshoring. Based on the concepts of competitive advantage and value chain [24], a services offshoring strategy is seen as a competitive strategy that aims at and potentially contributes to value creation and competitive advantage. To provide an example, Maskell et al.'s [25] empirical data from Danish firms in various industries and functions, including production of goods as well as services, suggest that the main three drivers for offshore outsourcing are cost reduction motives that can contribute to cost leadership, or quality-seeking motives and innovation motives that can create differentiation advantages.

According to the resource based view of the firm (RBV) in turn, offshoring and outsourcing decisions can be explained by a focus on strategic capabilities and resources that enable a sustained competitive advantage [26]. For example, the RBV provides a useful framework for the analysis of the role of internal firm capabilities (i.e. international and technical experience to deal with the offshoring process and leverage knowledge) for knowledge-seeking firms that offshore R&D activities [27, p. 18]. In the same vein, Manning et al. [7] hold that strategic firm capabilities including strategic talent management and collaborating effectively with external partners offshore can be considered as dynamic capabilities (see [28]) that allow the firms to face challenges (e.g. high turnover rates) and adapt to a dynamic offshoring environment (e.g. collaboration with new partners). The knowledge based view of the firm (KBV) emphasizes that offshoring is a firm strategy that aims at expanding the firm's knowledge resources. For example, in the case of advanced task offshoring, firms seek to leverage the knowledge assets of a skilled workforce (e.g. [10, 29]). Furthermore, transaction cost economics (TCE) can provide a basic explanation of offshoring decisions, based on cost efficiency and control choices over parts of the firm's value chain [30]. The OLI paradigm [31, 32] in turn provides a framework to explain offshoring/outsourcing strategic decisions in terms of a firm's motives (e.g. market seeking) [29].

Overall, scholars have identified various strategic attributes of service work offshoring, including cost efficiency, access to a skilled workforce, and access to new markets (see e.g. [5, 10, 11]). Whilst the prime and most commonly mentioned strategic attribute refers to cost motivations based on reduced labor costs (see [8]), scholars suggest that in the case of advanced services offshoring, the more central strategic firm goal is to foster international competitiveness through the expansion of knowledge resources and access to global talent pools [10, 11, 33].

3.2 Operational Attributes of Services Offshoring

Apart from their strategic attributes, offshoring strategies also have operational attributes including governance modes as well as functions, activities or tasks to be offshored [34]. As we propose later, these operational attributes impact on employee-level motivational processes in the implementation of services offshoring.

For example, offshoring strategies encompass mechanisms of formal and relational governance of offshoring relationships that aim to align and coordinate the goals, strategies, values and activities of the collaborating stakeholders [35]. Formal governance refers to the use of service level agreements (legal contractual agreements), key performance indicators and other formal control tools, whereas relational governance uses "softer" social control practices focusing on human relations [36]. Scholars have demonstrated the importance of various aspects of relational governance for successful outsourcing, including trust, commitment, open communication and mutual dependency between the outsourcing partners (see [36, pp. 506–508]). Researchers have also suggested that relational governance can substitute or complement formal governance (e.g. [36]). However, research on relational governance is generally limited to the actions and interactions of managers, and the possible role of lower-level employees in offshoring implementation is only implicit.

Furthermore, task interdependencies in distributed work may have a negative impact on firm performance [37]. In distributed work, coordination mechanisms such as task modularity, ongoing communication and tacit coordination mechanisms (i.e. pre-project familiarity, shared knowledge of work procedures and visibility of information across locations) are therefore likely to be required to ameliorate firm performance [37].

3.3 Services Offshoring Attributes and Firm Level Outcomes: The Missing View on Micro-Processes

Overall, existing research on strategic firm-level services offshoring attributes suggests that services offshoring includes many motives apart from cost reduction, especially where the need for a skilled workforce becomes paramount as in the case of advanced services offshoring. Accordingly, services offshoring outcomes can be classified into two subgroups by the outcomes sought: (a) organizational performance outcomes and (b) capabilities, resources and processes, as an aftermath of offshoring strategy implementation [6, 38]. These outcomes are relevant to the various strategic attributes of service offshoring discussed above, namely the motive to achieve cost efficiency, access to skilled work, or access to new markets, which can also be called intended outcomes. Overall, the named outcomes constitute the preconditions for firm competitive advantage and value creation. Various operational offshoring characteristics, including governance mechanisms and choice of activities to be offshored, are used to achieve intended offshoring outcomes.

Offshoring and outsourcing research does however not provide a clear view on how services offshoring strategies result in specific services offshoring outcomes. In other words, limited evidence is provided on the link between services offshoring strategy (i.e. strategic and operational attributes) and organizational outcomes such as performance, capabilities and resources. We hold that in particular, research is needed on the micro-level processes that underlie the link between services offshoring strategies and their outcomes.

A number of researchers have indeed demonstrated an association between services offshoring and certain firm level outcomes, but they have not considered the micro-level processes that underlie this association. Di Gregorio et al. [39] highlight that offshore outsourcing of administrative and technical services in SMEs has a positive effect on their international competitiveness (i.e. export performance), and Larsen et al. [12] report on cost estimation errors in services offshoring decisions. Furthermore, Jensen [13, 14] contends that offshoring capabilities evolve over time as the firms gain experience in services offshoring, and Manning [18] highlights in a more nuanced way how firm capability develops as a response to services offshoring implementation challenges, where offshoring firms decide to mitigate, tolerate or relocate depending predominately on their available resources.

These scholars examine services offshoring and its outcomes as independent and dependent variables at the firm or business (macro) level. They also examine the relationships between these macro variables, but without addressing the possible role of micro-level variables in this relationship. Only a few studies have explored micro-level processes within services offshoring. This set of studies has in turn not given a lot of consideration to macro level outcomes. In the following section, we will review this research with the aim to explore the role of micro-level processes in services offshoring strategy implementation.

4   Micro-Level Processes Linked with Services Offshoring

In the following section we summarize and discuss extant research on micro-level processes in services offshoring and outline its limitations. As we describe below, the term "micro-level processes" is an encompassing term pointing to individual (i.e. organizational members), team and small group level processes. We identify two different research foci in this micro-literature that involve various levels of analysis: (a) a focus on the impact of a macro (i.e. firm level)/meso (i.e. business unit level) services offshoring strategy on micro-level processes and (b) a focus on the role of micro-level processes in services offshoring strategy implementation that results in micro (i.e. team/small group) outcomes, meso (i.e. business unit) outcomes and macro (i.e. firm level) outcomes.

4.1 The Impact of a Services Offshoring Strategy on Micro-Level Processes

Regarding the first focus (i.e. how the services offshoring strategy impacts on micro-level processes), extant research explores how offshoring arrangements exert influence on the organizational members, responsible for the operational execution of the strategy. For example, Mattarelli and Tagliaventi [15] hold that a divergence between professional identity and offshore allocated tasks triggers job dissatisfaction among offshore employees, which can result in turnover or job crafting behaviours, depending on the organizational recognition of novelty and social support [15]. Similarly, Zimmermann and Ravishankar [40] discuss how an IT offshoring strategy reconfigures the employee professional role identities and career expectations, as a result of the allocated tasks and the required intercultural communication skills. Likewise, Zimmermann and Ravishankar [16] describe elements of an advanced tasks offshoring strategy that impact on onshore and offshore employee motivation. Such elements are "(a) the complexity and non-routineness of tasks, (b) the level of managerial responsibility allocated offshore and (c) the clarity of plans for distribution of tasks and the managerial responsibility onshore-offshore" [16, p. 554].

Furthermore, scholars focus on effective ways to coordinate globally distributed teams and discuss how a services offshoring strategy facilitates (or not) the cooperation between these teams. For example, Sidhu and Volberda [41], propose that an offshoring strategy that promotes (a) joint rewards between onshore and offshore teams, (b) project involvement of the offshore team at an early stage and (c) horizontal communication, has a positive impact on how geographically dispersed teams cooperate in captive offshoring. Conversely, they suggest that an offshoring strategy that enforces a homogeneous organizational identity and work context (similar to the one at the onshore organisation), may trigger negative emotions and confusion to offshore employees and result in deficient onshore – offshore task coordination.

4.2 The Role of the Micro-Level Processes in Services Offshoring Strategy Implementation

In relation to the second focus of the micro-literature, scholars maintain that the implementation of a services offshoring strategy is linked with the way individuals think, behave and feel (e.g. [15, 40]). In detail, extant research on micro-level processes of services offshoring strategies pertinent to strategy implementation touches primarily upon aspects of (a) the onshore and offshore employee collaboration, (b) the role of knowledge transfer in strategy implementation and (c) the links between micro-level processes, strategy implementation and the evolution of offshoring strategies.

The fruitful collaboration between geographically dispersed teams is commonly considered as a requirement for successful services offshoring (e.g. [42]). Hence, uncertainties about social order [43] and intergroup processes of informal status closure [44] are seen as reasons for problematic collaborations in geographically distributed teams working in services offshoring settings. Asymmetric power relations and status differentials in services offshoring project teams may even result in the "paradox of success", where onshore teams believe that they have more to lose than to benefit from the successful implementation of a project [43, p. 373, 44, p. 11]. In this situation, onshore employees can be reluctant to offshore advanced tasks (e.g. high-end IT tasks; [43]). Evidence also suggests that onshore employees perceive the services offshoring strategy differently depending on the complexity of their tasks [45]. In the case of simple routine tasks, services offshoring can be seen as a chance for professional and personal development (e.g. an opportunity for professional and intercultural learning), whereas in the case of more complex and advanced tasks, services offshoring may be perceived as a threat for their jobs and future career [45], as described above regarding the "paradox of success". Conversely, offshore employees can lack motivation to support the services offshoring strategy if they perceive offshored tasks to be insufficiently demanding [16].

Employees' active involvement in knowledge transfer is also important for the implementation of a services offshoring strategy, especially in the case of advanced tasks [45–48]. Zimmermann and Ravishankar [48] propose that knowledge senders' outcome expectations and efficacy beliefs, jointly with social capital, play a key motivational role in knowledge transfer processes. These psychological mechanisms are seen to constitute interlinked self-reinforcing motivational circles of "knowledge transfer success" that affect onshore employees' ability and willingness to transfer knowledge [48]. Interestingly, there are indications that the willingness of onshore employees to transfer their knowledge is less hindered by their job insecurity if they have strong personal relationships with the offshore employees [48].

Scholars also discuss how the services offshoring strategy changes and develops as a result of the successful (or not successful) implementation of the initial strategy [15, 16]. In detail, Mattarelli and Tagliaventi [15] discuss the impact of micro-processes (i.e. job crafting) on the evolution of firm services offshoring strategy based on employee new ideas. In a recent study, Zimmermann and Ravishankar [16] propose that the "offshoring system" comprises three interlinked organizational elements: the firm-level strategy and the employee motivations onshore and offshore. Bilateral interdependencies exist between the onshore and offshore motivational drivers, as well as between the services offshoring strategy and the motivational drivers in each site. As the authors contend, the motivational drivers for advanced task transfer onshore are formed by the employees' outcome expectations for their careers, their workload and the offshore task performance. For the offshore site, motivations include the levels of task ownership and career expectations. Firm-level strategy and micro-level motivational drivers for its implementation are therefore seen to be interdependent.

4.3 Research Gaps and Blind Spots Regarding Micro-Processes of Services Offshoring

Overall there is some theoretical and empirical support to show that services offshoring success rests on micro-level factors that underwrite or jeopardise its implementation.

However, research on this topic is still scarce, and theory building is in its beginnings (e.g. see [16, 48]). Furthermore, we contend that the analysis of strategy implementation in extant research is limited because of lacking operationalizations of the concepts of services offshoring strategy, its implementation and its outcomes, in terms of levels of analysis. Although extant research aims at exploring firm/business unit level offshoring strategies, its focus primarily is on the execution of the operational aspects of an offshoring strategy (e.g. transfer and execution of specific tasks), rather than incorporating outright explanations on the link between operational strategy outcomes and strategic firm/business unit level outcomes.

Therefore, while scholars discuss the effect of micro-processes on services offshoring implementation, there are limited explanations on consequences for macro-level offshoring outcomes in financial terms (i.e. organizational performance) or in non-financial terms (e.g. firm capabilities and resources). Jensen and Nardi [44] do consider such consequences, discussing how the problematic intergroup cooperation in an offshoring software development project resulted in partial reshoring and unexpected costs, but without analysing this effect in detail. Moreover, scholars discuss the impact of micro-processes on the evolution of operational aspects of firm offshoring strategy (e.g. transfer of new tasks or transfer of more advanced tasks) based on employee job crafting [15] or employee motivational processes [16], but without describing how employee-level motivational processes influence organizational performance outcomes or firm capabilities and resources. To conclude, we believe that more empirical and theoretical underpinning is needed to draw conclusions on how micro-level motivational mechanisms affect certain macro-level outcomes in services offshoring.

5 Conceptual Model for Services Offshoring Strategy Research

As mentioned before, based on the MFs perspective, we consider that the link between services offshoring strategy and its microfoundations still needs further exploration. In the following section we will use GFT to suggest how employee motivations are likely to be interlinked with a services offshoring strategy, its implementation and firm level outcomes, leading to specific propositions regarding these interlinkages. The propositions are incorporated in our theoretical model, shown in Fig. 1.

The core mechanism in GFT is that cues from the social environment can directly trigger the goal frames that an individual holds, or indirectly increase or decrease the relative strength of existing goal frames. We argue that a services offshoring strategy will provide cues that trigger the goal framing of individuals involved in the offshoring setting (see left hand arrow in Fig. 1). Importantly, to the degree that the strategy provides cues that trigger normative goal frames, employees' joint production motivation will be strengthened (see bottom left in Fig. 1). GFT can therefore help us investigate how employees are motivated to implement a services offshoring strategy, what the goals are that they want to pursue, what the prevailing goal frames are and what stabilizes these goal frames. Based on the MFs view of strategy, we further suggest that the individual goal frames direct employee and managerial actions and interactions and impact on strategy implementation (see bottom arrow in Fig. 1), which in turn affects the macro

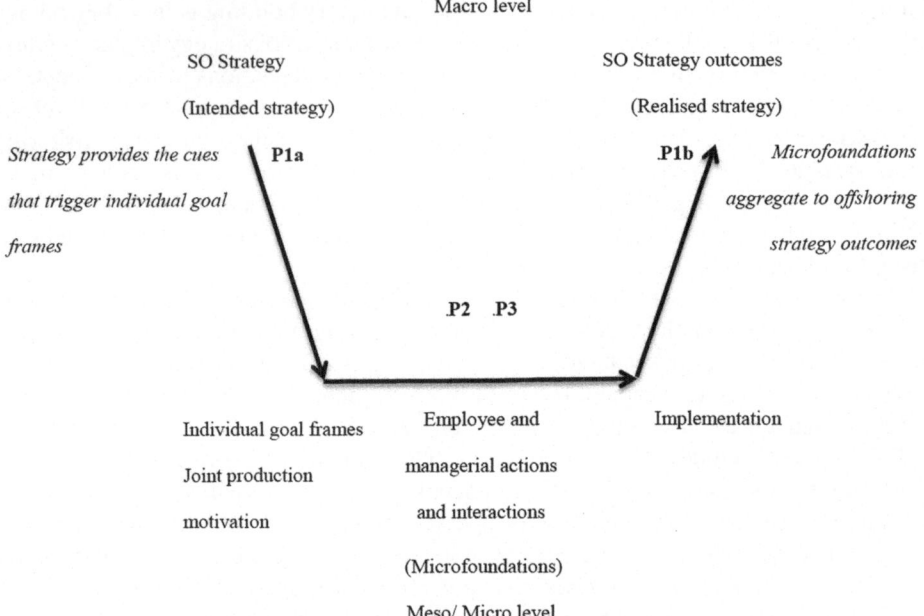

Fig. 1. Conceptual model for services offshoring (SO) strategy research

level outcomes of the services offshoring strategy (see right hand arrow in Fig. 1). On the whole, individual goal frames and actions/interactions together with strategy implementation constitute the microfoundations that aggregate into specific services offshoring outcomes (i.e. (a) organizational performance outcomes and/or (b) capabilities and resources. To conclude, the conceptual model describes the effect of a services offshoring strategy on its outcomes as a multi-level phenomenon. Its core key element is the employee motivation to implement the intended services offshoring strategy.

6 Goal Framing Theory and the Microfoundations of Services Offshoring Strategies

6.1 Services Offshoring Strategies that Trigger Joint Production Motivation

Foss and Lindenberg [19] suggest that GFT allows us to explore the cross-level connections between macro and micro levels of analysis, which is in line with the MFs perspective. In order to examine macro-level phenomena (here a services offshoring strategy and its outcomes), we need to focus on the actions and interactions of individuals (i.e. managers and employees). Therefore, we argue that the services offshoring strategy provides the cues that "frame" the goals of employees. Possible cues are (a) the strategy as articulated by a manager in terms of planning (processes and people involved in terms of organizational design and tasks) and (b) what this strategy aims at (e.g. cost savings) or entails, particularly for employees (e.g. the possibility for employees to engage in more interesting tasks). Such cues can trigger certain goal frames that support or do not support the services offshoring strategy implementation.

In detail, building upon extant literature on joint production motivation [19, 20] we propose that a services offshoring strategy based on transparent team and task structures, clear collective goals, and cognitive/symbolic management (i.e. vision/mission statements and relational signaling), directly supports the normative goal frames and initiates joint production motivation. To illustrate, transparent team and task structures, clear collective goals, and cognitive/symbolic management for both onshore and offshore employees will trigger normative goal frames and thereby incite employees to support the services offshoring strategy implementation and focus on acting appropriately towards the common benefit. This is likely to decrease the extent to which they will promote only their own individual financial and social status (e.g. financial rewards, career prospects) that would be in line with gain goals, or enjoyment (e.g. enjoyable tasks) which would be in line with a hedonic goal frame. In addition, rewards that are geared to joint goals are likely to stabilize the normative goals of employees and maintain the joint production motivation [20]. For example, Lindenberg and Foss [20] suggest that gain contingent rewards (e.g. career promotion) and hedonic contingent rewards (e.g. bigger offices) are necessary to keep normative goal frames from decaying. Likewise, we postulate that this could also be the case in a services offshoring setting. Furthermore, based on Foss and Milagres [49], we consider that joint production motivation of onshore as well as offshore employees can take place not only in the case of captive offshoring (i.e. intra-firm collaboration), but also in the case of offshore outsourcing (i.e. beyond the firm boundaries), if a shared offshoring purpose is established for onshore as well as offshore employees. This speculation is in line with a core assumption of Goal Framing theory: cues that convey the information that a social situation refers to a joint project will trigger a normative goal frame, conversely to cues that convey the information that a social situation is a "competitive" or an "economic" one and will thus trigger a gain goal frame [50, p. 672]. We therefore put forward the following proposition:

Proposition 1a (P1a)

A services offshoring strategy that provides cues for joint effort of offshore and onshore employees is more likely to contribute to a normative goal frame and thereby joint production motivation, compared to a services offshoring strategy that provides cues that trigger or stabilize gain or hedonic goal frames.

The reasons why a firm makes specific offshoring decisions (from cost efficiency to knowledge seeking motives), what these decisions entail (e.g. possible job reduction measures, organizational restructuring or transfer of specific tasks) and how these decisions translate into a services offshoring strategy, provide cues to the onshore employees that signal a prevailing firm gain. Thus, a prevailing firm gain can explain why onshore employees may express fears (e.g. possible loss of jobs) and are not willing to contribute to the implementation of the services offshoring strategy. Perceptions of job insecurity onshore may exist at all stages of services offshoring (e.g. [40, 44, 51]). As discussed above, the "paradox of success" has a negative impact on onshore employee motivation to transfer knowledge [40, 43] and collaboration [44]. When the services offshoring strategy as planned and executed does not signal managerial interest in employee concerns about losing their jobs, onshore employees try to feel better while dealing with frustration and uncertainty as the outcome of their prevailing hedonic goal frames, or focus primarily on their individual concerns on preserving their jobs/resources/tasks, while in a gain goal frame. For example, Zimmermann and Ravishankar [40] describe onshore employees who intentionally transferred tasks offshore without providing adequate support, in order to get the tasks back (i.e. gain goal frame) and unfairly blamed offshore employees for mistakes (i.e. hedonic goal frame).

Similarly, offshore firms (captives or external providers) may be dealing with high employee turnover rates (e.g. see [52, 53]) and job dissatisfaction (e.g. [15]). We suggest that turnover behaviors and job dissatisfaction may be the outcome of the prevailing firm gain and its impact on employees' individual goals, especially in the context of services offshoring strategy implementation. For example, if an offshore firm and its management are concerned with the implementation of a services offshoring strategy mainly in terms of good financial results and future contractual agreements, the cues towards offshore employees may suggest that their firm is in a gain goal frame. Thus, if the main concern of the offshore firms is to provide services with the minimum financial cost, cues will hinder employee normative goal frames and may foster their gain goal frames (e.g. leaving this company for another one that provides a better salary, status or career prospects) or even their hedonic goal frames (leading in some cases to sabotage or revenge behaviors). Likewise, we reason that when a services offshoring strategy does not involve the transfer of interesting tasks to the offshore employees (e.g. [40]), this may provide cues that will not support the offshore employees' normative goal frames, but would mostly trigger their gain goal frames, for example their focus on career progress, and hedonic goal frames, for example their need to feel better by lowering their expectations from their work.

Furthermore, based on GFT, scholars contend that the normative goal frame is linked with the highest levels of firm value creation (i.e. organizational performance characterized by productivity gains and innovativeness), since it can motivate organizational members to work in concert, in truly collaborative activities (i.e. joint production motivation) [19, p. 89]. Building on these insights, we argue that value creation is linked also to the successful implementation of services offshoring.

Moreover, Foss and Lindenberg [19, p. 89] contend that when a firm makes strategic decisions on what (new) resources to use and how to combine resources, the motivation of human resources plays a key role in how these resources are combined. Therefore, the motivation of organizational members is the starting point for the realization of higher level strategic goals (e.g. organizational performance). Moreover, they point out that organizational teams are forms of human cooperation, where joint production can take place. Thus cues for joint effort of offshore and onshore employees provide an essential normative goal frame for employees. This would help to avoid some of the conflicts of interests between onshore and offshore employees observed in previous research (e.g. [48, 54]).

Accordingly, what motivates individuals towards team-based cooperation is focal for the workings of joint production in a firm [55]. Following GFT, they contend that a "we-frame" instead of an "I-frame" is needed to gear collaborative activities in teams

[55, p. 374]. Similarly, we argue that a determinant for the successful implementation of a services offshoring strategy is the establishment of a "we-frame" among onshore and offshore employees. Moreover, when employees are in a normative goal frame, coordination costs (i.e. the need for planning and operational-level governance) are reduced, because they hold a shared understanding of actions and interactions in terms of collective goals [19, p. 91]. Along these lines, we suggest that joint production motivation will enable services offshoring firms to minimize coordination costs in offshoring arrangements and gain offshoring capabilities and resources.

Proposition 1b (P1b)

Joint production motivation in services offshoring is a prerequisite for strategy implementation and thereby for achieving the intended offshoring outcomes.

6.2 The Role of Interpersonal Relationships and Relational Signals in the Implementation of a Services Offshoring Strategy

GFT further suggests that interpersonal relationships play a role in goal framing. In detail, the goals that other people hold in one's social environment influence one's own goals [56, p. 64]. This mechanism is what Lindenberg refers to as "goal contagion" [50, p. 672]. In the context of services offshoring strategy implementation, when individuals engage in goal framing which will motivate them to carry out a particular strategy, the mental models of the interpersonal relationships will shape part of their goal framing. These relationships can be formal (e.g. with a manager) and/or informal (e.g. with a colleague). Moreover, the behaviors of others within hierarchical and cooperative relationships may stabilize (or not) the employee's goal frames (i.e. via relational signals).

Therefore, relational signals (i.e. the way employees interpret the actions of others) between onshore and offshore employees, as well as relational signals between managers and employees in each site, may play a role in stabilizing the normative goal frames or hindering gain and hedonic ones and thereby joint production motivations can support the successful implementation of a services offshoring strategy. For example, Zimmermann et al. [45] suggest that offshoring attitudes of onshore employees influence their relational behaviors towards offshore employees (e.g. treating them as colleagues instead of external suppliers) and that these behaviors feed back into their attitudes, by creating vicious or virtuous circles of offshoring collaboration. Moreover, Zimmermann et al. [45] advise that managers should also show positive offshoring attitudes and behaviors themselves. Hence, what Zimmermann et al. [45] describe is very similar to the outcomes of the contagion effect of goal frames based on relational signals.

Proposition 2 (P2)

Interpersonal relationships and relational signals can stabilize or hinder normative goal frames and thereby joint production motivation, which affects employee motivation to implement a services offshoring strategy.

Although scholars have already addressed the relevance of relational signals during services offshoring implementation, they have not gone so far as to provide a mechanism that explicitly links them with the realized strategy outcomes. Thus we strongly believe that future research will benefit from examining this link. Moreover our proposition has practical implications for governance in services offshoring. Relational positive performance feedback (formal or informal) is considered an effective mechanism for stabilizing normative goal frames [57, p. 53]. Therefore, we suggest that managers dealing with the services offshoring arrangements should plan and execute the strategy in a way that translates into structures and activities enabling both onshore and offshore employees to achieve an understanding of shared tasks, labor and rewards. Furthermore, managers should provide feedback clearly geared towards collective goals and provide rewards that support them.

6.3   Services Offshoring Strategies that Trigger Knowledge Sharing Behaviors

GFT can also provide the lens to explain motivational processes for knowledge sharing, which is one of the major issues that scholars have already addressed in services offshoring research [16, 45–47, 54]. In particular, Foss and Milagres [49] suggest that a joint production motivation enables knowledge transfer and knowledge integration. Based on this assumption, we suggest that if a services offshoring strategy triggers normative goal frames, knowledge sharing behaviors of onshore and offshore employees will increase.

Proposition 3 (P3)

A services offshoring strategy that triggers normative goal frames in employees will increase knowledge sharing behaviors between onshore and offshore employees.

As we reviewed, extant offshoring research suggests that knowledge seeking is one of the major firm level criteria for services offshoring decisions. In line with the KBV, knowledge resources are considered as important services offshoring strategy outcomes. However, within the context of services offshoring it is not clear how employees are motivated to share their knowledge and therefore contribute to macro-level strategy outcomes. We contend that the above research proposition provides the means to explore the link between "knowledge seeking" services offshoring firms and knowledge resources as a firm level construct.

Apart from implications for research, we hope that this proposition also offers guidance for governance tools in services offshoring. In detail we hold that an action of implementing the strategy involves knowledge sharing. For example, if tasks and rewards are linked to joint outcomes [49, 58], it is likely that (within services offshoring arrangements) onshore employees are not afraid of losing their jobs [cf. 46] and therefore, are motivated to share knowledge [45]. Similarly, shared goals, trust and good communication as determinants of knowledge sharing [47] are in line with a joint production motivation. Furthermore, building upon the model of knowledge transfer in IT offshoring by Zimmermann and Ravishankar [48], we believe that knowledge senders' outcome expectations (e.g. contribution to a common goal) and efficacy beliefs (e.g. the belief that an individual can contribute to shared knowledge) can be tied to a normative goal frame. When these are combined with social capital (e.g. through intensive communication, shared team identity, trust and a shared contextual understanding), they can lead to effective knowledge sharing in services offshoring.

7   Conclusions

In recent years, scholars have suggested that offshoring systematically entails more knowledge intensive, high value, innovative, non-routine activities in the services sector (see e.g. [10, 11, 29]). In this context, they explored various firm level criteria for services offshoring decisions that describe the initial firm motivations such as cost efficiency and knowledge seeking [34]. However, extant research on firm-level criteria for services offshoring decisions does not provide a clear view on how these decisions result in specific services offshoring outcomes. In parallel, researchers have addressed the role of micro-processes and especially the role of employee motivational processes in services offshoring implementation. Nevertheless, the corresponding micro-research does not provide comprehensive explanations of the links between employee motivational processes, services offshoring strategy implementation and its macro-level outcomes.

Understanding services offshoring implementation in terms of its realized outcomes is fascinating but challenging. We therefore proposed a conceptual model that focuses on employee motivation in implementing services offshoring strategies. In other words, the proposed model accounts for the employee-level microfoundations of services offshoring strategy. Its importance is its explanatory power. In detail, it links service offshoring strategy attributes and the realized outcomes of the strategy, with employee motivational processes that lead to actions and interactions and facilitate (or not) the implementation of the services offshoring strategy. Thus we contend that our proposed model can help to bridge the two complimentary streams of research that explore (a) firm level services offshoring attributes and outcomes and (b) micro-level processes linked with services offshoring. Furthermore, we developed three propositions to advocate that in order to investigate services offshoring outcomes, scholars and practitioners should use GFT to consider possible links of these outcomes with employee level processes in services offshoring. Hence, the model also offers a guiding tool for governance in services offshoring arrangements and introduces a new starting point for future empirical research.

References

1. Booth, T.: Here, there and everywhere-special report: Outsourcing and offshoring. Econ (2013)
2. Jensen, P.D.Ø., Larsen, M.M., Pedersen, T. (eds.): Developing Offshoring Capabilities for the Contemporary Offshoring Organization. Elsevier Science, Netherlands (2013). [Special issue]. J. Int. Manag. **19**
3. UNCTAD: World Investment Report 2004: The Shift Towards Services. United Nations, New York and Geneva (2004)
4. Doh, J.P.: Offshore outsourcing: implications for international business and strategic management theory and practice. J. Manag. Stud. **42**, 695–704 (2005)
5. Bunyaratavej, K., Doh, J., Hahn, E.D., Lewin, A.Y., Massini, S.: Conceptual issues in services offshoring research: a multidisciplinary review. Gr. Organ. Manag. **36**, 70–102 (2011)
6. Pisani, N., Ricart, J.E.: Offshoring of services: a review of the literature and organizing framework. Manag. Int. Rev. **56**, 385–424 (2016)

7. Manning, S., Massini, S., Lewin, A.Y.: A dynamic perspective on next-generation offshoring: the global sourcing of science and engineering talent. Acad. Manag. Perspect. **22**, 35–54 (2008)
8. Lewin, A.Y., Peeters, C.: Offshoring work: business hype or the onset of fundamental transformation? Long Range Plann. **39**, 221–239 (2006)
9. Lahiri, S., Kedia, B.L., Mukherjee, D.: The impact of management capability on the resource–performance linkage: examining Indian outsourcing providers. J. World Bus. **47**, 145–155 (2012)
10. Jensen, P.D.Ø., Pedersen, T.: Offshoring and international competitiveness: antecedents of offshoring advanced tasks. J. Acad. Mark. Sci. **40**, 313–328 (2012)
11. Lewin, A.Y., Massini, S., Peeters, C.: Why are companies offshoring innovation? the emerging global race for talent. J. Int. Bus. Stud. **40**, 901–925 (2009)
12. Larsen, M.M., Manning, S., Pedersen, T.: Uncovering the hidden costs of offshoring: the interplay of complexity, organizational design, and experience. Strateg. Manag. J. **34**, 533–552 (2013)
13. Jensen, P.D.Ø.: A learning perspective on the offshoring of advanced services. J. Int. Manag. **15**, 181–193 (2009)
14. Jensen, P.D.Ø.: A passage to India: a dual case study of activities, processes and resources in offshore outsourcing of advanced services. J. World Bus. **47**, 311–326 (2012)
15. Mattarelli, E., Tagliaventi, M.R.: How offshore professionals' job dissatisfaction can promote further offshoring: organizational outcomes of job crafting. J. Manag. Stud. **52**, 585–620 (2012)
16. Zimmermann, A., Ravishankar, M.N.: A systems perspective on offshoring strategy and motivational drivers amongst onshore and offshore employees. J. World Bus. **51**, 548–567 (2016)
17. Felin, T., Foss, N.J., Ployhart, R.E.: The microfoundations movement in strategy and organization theory. Acad. Manag. Ann. **9**, 575–632 (2015)
18. Manning, S.: Mitigate, tolerate or relocate? Offshoring challenges, strategic imperatives and resource constraints. J. World Bus. **49**, 522–535 (2014)
19. Foss, N.J., Lindenberg, S.M.: Microfoundations for strategy: a goal-framing perspective on the drivers of value creation. Acad. Manag. Perspect. **27**, 85–102 (2013)
20. Lindenberg, S., Foss, N.J.: Managing joint production motivation: the role of goal framing and governance mechanisms. Acad. Manag. Rev. **36**, 500–525 (2011)
21. Bunyaratavej, K., Hahn, E.D., Doh, J.P.: International offshoring of services: a parity study. J. Int. Manag. **13**, 7–21 (2007)
22. Hätönen, J., Eriksson, T.: 30 + years of research and practice of outsourcing – Exploring the past and anticipating the future. J. Int. Manag. **15**, 142–155 (2009)
23. Sako, M.: Outsourcing and offshoring of professional services. In: Empson, L., Muzio, D., Broschak, J., Hinings, B. (eds.) The Oxford Handbook of Professional Service Firms, pp. 327–347. Oxford University Press, Oxford (2015)
24. Porter, M.E.: The Competitive Advantage: Creating and Sustaining Superior Performance. Free Press, New York (1985)
25. Maskell, P., Pedersen, T., Petersen, B., Dick-Nielsen, J.: Learning paths to offshore outsourcing: from cost reduction to knowledge seeking. Ind. Innov. **14**, 239–257 (2007)
26. Gerbl, M., McIvor, R., Loane, S., Humphreys, P.: A multi-theory approach to understanding the business process outsourcing decision. J. World Bus. **50**, 505–518 (2015)
27. Martinez-Noya, A., Garcia-Canal, E., Guillen, M.F.: International R&D service outsourcing by technology-intensive firms: whether and where? J. Int. Manag. **18**, 18–37 (2012)

28. Teece, D.J., Pisano, G., Shuen, A.: Dynamic capabilities and strategic management. Strateg. Manag. J. **18**(7), 509–533 (1997)
29. Contractor, F.J., Kumar, V., Kundu, S.K., Pedersen, T.: Reconceptualizing the firm in a world of outsourcing and offshoring: the organizational and geographical relocation of high-value company functions. J. Manag. Stud. **47**, 1417–1433 (2010)
30. Mudambi, R., Venzin, M.: The strategic nexus of offshoring and outsourcing decisions. J. Manag. Stud. **47**, 1510–1533 (2010)
31. Dunning, J.H.: Location and the multinational enterprise: a neglected factor? J. Int. Bus. Stud. **29**(1), 45–66 (1998)
32. Dunning, J.H.: The eclectic (OLI) paradigm of international production: past, present and future. Int. J. Econ. Bus. **8**, 173–190 (2001)
33. Pisani, N., Ricart, J.E.: Offshoring and the global sourcing of talent: understanding the new frontier of internationalization. In: Proceedings of 2nd Annual Offshoring Research Network Conference and Workshop, Philadelphia, pp. 1–45 (2008)
34. Roza, M., Van den Bosch, F.A.J., Volberda, H.W.: Offshoring strategy: motives, functions, locations, and governance modes of small, medium-sized and large firms. Int. Bus. Rev. **20**, 314–323 (2011)
35. Oshri, I., Kotlarsky, J., Willcocks, L.P.: The Handbook of Global Outsourcing and Offshoring. Palgrave Macmillan, London (2015)
36. Lioliou, E., Zimmermann, A., Willcocks, L., Gao, L.: Formal and relational governance in IT outsourcing: substitution, complementarity and the role of the psychological contract. Inf. Syst. J. **24**, 503–535 (2014)
37. Srikanth, K., Puranam, P.: Integrating distributed work: comparing task design, communication, and tacit coordination mechanisms. Strateg. Manag. J. **32**, 849–875 (2011)
38. Schmeisser, B.: A systematic review of literature on offshoring of value chain activities. J. Int. Manag. **19**, 390–406 (2013)
39. Di Gregorio, D., Musteen, M., Thomas, D.E.: Offshore outsourcing as a source of international competitiveness for SMEs. J. Int. Bus. Stud. **40**, 969–988 (2008)
40. Zimmermann, A., Ravishankar, M.N.: Collaborative IT offshoring relationships and professional role identities: reflections from a field study. J. Vocat. Behav. **78**, 351–360 (2011)
41. Sidhu, J.S., Volberda, H.W.: Coordination of globally distributed teams: a co-evolution perspective on offshoring. Int. Bus. Rev. **20**, 278–290 (2011)
42. Levina, N., Vaast, E.: Innovating or doing as told? status differences and overlapping boundaries in offshore collaboration. MIS Q. **32**, 307–332 (2008)
43. van Marrewijk, A.: Situational construction of Dutch-Indian cultural differences in global IT projects. Scand. J. Manag. **26**, 368–380 (2010)
44. Jensen, R.E., Nardi, B.: The rhetoric of culture as an act of closure in a cross-national software development department. Paper presented at 22nd European Conference on Information Systems. AIS, Tel-Aviv, 9–11 June 2014
45. Zimmermann, A., Raab, K., Zanotelli, L.: Vicious and virtuous circles of offshoring attitudes and relational behaviours. a configurational study of German IT developers. Inf. Syst. J. **23**, 65–88 (2013)
46. Mahadevan, J.: Power/Knowledge in postcolonial settings: the case of IT Bangalore. Intercult. J. **10**, 61–81 (2011)
47. Rottman, J.W.: Successful knowledge transfer within offshore supplier networks: a case study exploring social capital in strategic alliances. J. Inf. Technol. **23**, 31–43 (2008)
48. Zimmermann, A., Ravishankar, M.N.: Knowledge transfer in IT offshoring relationships: the roles of social capital, efficacy and outcome expectations. Inf. Syst. J. **24**, 167–202 (2014)

49. Foss, N.J., Milagres, R.: Pro-social motivation beyond firm boundaries: the case of the genolyptus network. BAR - Brazilian Adm. Rev. **11**, 364–384 (2014)
50. Lindenberg, S.: Social rationality, semi-modularity and goal-framing: what is it all about? Anal. Krit. **30**, 669–687 (2008)
51. Cohen, L., El-Sawad, A.: Lived experiences of offshoring: an examination of UK and Indian financial service employees' accounts of themselves and one another. Hum. Relat. **60**, 1235–1262 (2007)
52. Dibbern, J., Winkler, J., Heinzl, A.: Explaining variations in client extra costs between software projects offshored to india. MIS Q. **32**(2), 333–366 (2008)
53. Lacity, M.C., Iyer, V.V., Rudramuniyaiah, P.S.: Turnover intentions of Indian IS professionals. Inf. Syst. Front. **10**, 225–241 (2008)
54. Metiu, A.: Owning the code: status closure in distributed groups. Organ. Sci. **17**, 418–435 (2006)
55. Foss, N.J., Lindenberg, S.: Teams, team motivation, and the theory of the firm. Manag. Decis. Econ. **33**, 369–383 (2012)
56. Lindenberg, S.: The cognitive side of governance. In: Buskens, V., Raub, W., Snijders, C. (eds.) The Governance of Relations in Markets and Organizations, Research in the Sociology of Organizations, pp. 47–76. Emerald Group Publishing Limited (2003)
57. Lindenberg, S.: Governance seen from a framing point of view: the employment relationship and relational signalling. In: Nooteboom, B., Six, F. (eds.) The Trust Process in Organizations: Empirical Studies of the Determinants and the Process of Trust Development, pp. 37–57. Edward Elgar, Cheltenham (2003)
58. Lindenberg, S.: Cognition and governance: why incentives have to take a back seat. In: Grandori, A. (ed.) Handbook of Economic Organisation - Integrating Economic and Organization Theory, pp. 41–61. Edward Elgar, Cheltenham (2013)

Motivation and Autonomy in Global Software Development

John Noll[1], Sarah Beecham[2], Abdur Razzak[2], Bob Richardson[3],
Ann Barcomb[2], and Ita Richardson[2(✉)]

[1] University of East London, Docklands Campus University Way, London, E16 2RD, UK
`john.noll@uel.ac.uk`
[2] Lero – the Irish Software Research Centre, University of Limerick, Limerick, Ireland
`{sarah.beecham,abdur.razzak,ann.barcomb,ita.richardson}@lero.ie`
[3] Ashling Microsystems Ltd., Limerick, Ireland
`bob.richardson@ashling.com`

Abstract. Global software development has become the norm rather than the exception for even the smallest companies. However, global software development is known to lead to numerous negative effects among distributed teams. This paper focuses on the effect of global software development on motivation. Specifically we ask: "Does increased autonomy, through the introduction of scrum, result in higher motivation among distributed developers?" We studied two distributed software development teams within one company headquartered in Ireland. Teams employ the scrum approach to software development which emphasizes, among other things, autonomy. We observed the teams during their scrum ceremonies, interviewed each team member and administered a motivation survey. We found that the difference in motivation levels before and after the introduction of scrum was slight and not statistically significant. Instead, there was a significant difference in the motivation levels of experienced team members, which were lower than less experienced members.

Keywords: Global software development · Agile software development · Scrum · Autonomy · Motivation

1 Introduction

As companies expand into new markets, acquire other companies in distant locations, and seek skilled staff in different locations, Global software development (GSD) has now become the norm rather than the exception. Even very small companies have developers and teams in remote locations.

Geographic separation, lack of timezone overlap, and cultural differences – collectively referred to as global distance – make the already complex task of software development even more complex. Geographic separation hinders informal communication that co-located teams use to clarify ambiguities and gaps in specifications and other formal documents. Lack of timezone overlap introduces communication delays that can slow progress, and in the extreme case prevents any kind of synchronous communication during normal working hours [1]. Cultural differences can introduce misunderstandings

© Springer International Publishing AG 2017
I. Oshri et al. (Eds.): Global Sourcing 2017, LNBIP 306, pp. 19–38, 2017.
https://doi.org/10.1007/978-3-319-70305-3_2

as a result of different interpretations of requirements and other documents, and may cause mistrust due to misperceptions of different cultural norms. Organizations need to be aware of the negative impact that fear of losing control and jobs can have on the motivation of teams, thus decreasing the sharing of knowledge and levels of trust that can exist between colleagues [2].

Different organizational models have emerged to implement GSD, such as outsourcing, in-sourcing, near-shoring, off-shoring, etc. [3, 4]. Each of these approaches has specific needs for autonomy of the "remote" teams. Organizational boundaries, as exist for example in outsourcing arrangements, may require explicit contractual arrangements defining who can make what decisions about the project. However, other models also require good governance, because global distance renders conventional project management less effective [5, 6]. For example, a remote team in a distant timezone may experience substantial delays if they have to wait for the home office to make decisions. Through previous research in GSD, we observed that the different levels of autonomy were, somehow, presenting a difficulty for team members. This was supported by previous researchers in other disciplines. For example, in the Management literature, [7–9] have identified that a mismatch between an individual's need for autonomy, and the degree of autonomy someone actually has, can cause problems and may have an impact on motivation levels. We note from the Organisational Behaviour literature that motivation is viewed as a social process that defines how people join, remain part of, and perform adequately in, a human organization [10]. Motivation tends to be overlooked in project management since it is difficult to measure and control [11] due to its complex nature, yet motivation is shown to have an impact on the quality of work produced [12], productivity [13] and on employee retention [14]. Given that autonomy is strongly associated with job satisfaction [15], we postulate that members of teams who have less autonomy than they perceive to be necessary are less motivated. Furthermore, we are interested in the effect the introduction of scrum has on motivation. Given that scrum is expected to also increase autonomy within teams [16], our research question is: "Does increased autonomy, through the introduction of scrum, result in higher motivation among distributed developers?" We studied the motivation of members from two distributed project teams in a single company. This was undertaken within a larger software process improvement study in a medium-sized company in Ireland, where team members had made a transition from plan-driven to agile development (specifically scrum) just prior to our investigation.

This paper expands on research previously presented by [17] presented at the Global Sourcing Workshop, and by [18] at the Evaluation and Assessment in Software Engineering Conference, both in 2017. The paper is organized as follows: in the next section we give a brief background to Motivation theory in a global context, and reflect on changing software engineer characteristics. We discuss how GSD and Agile software development affects the software engineer, which motivates our research question. In Sect. 3 we present the case study, including our data collection and analysis methods. In Sect. 4 we present our qualitative and quantitative results. Section 5 discusses how our results address our research question. We conclude the paper in Sect. 6, with a summary of our findings, our limitations and plans for future work.

2 Background

There are numerous theories that try to explain the conscious or unconscious decisions people make to expend effort or energy on a particular activity [19]. These theories provide insight into what motivates software engineers to engage fully in their tasks, commit to the organization's goals, produce higher quality software [11], and stimulate innovation [20]. Conversely, a demotivated workforce can lead to project failure [21].

Table 1. Software engineer motivation factors [24]

Motivator	Type
Rewards and incentives	Extrinsic
Development/training needs addressed	Intrinsic
Variety of work	Intrinsic
Career Path	Intrinsic
Empowerment/responsibility/shared leadership	Intrinsic
Good Management	Extrinsic
Sense of belonging/team spirit	Extrinsic
Work/life balance	Extrinsic
Working in successful company	Extrinsic
Employee participation	Intrinsic
Feedback	Extrinsic
Recognition	Intrinsic
Equity	Intrinsic
Trust/respect	Intrinsic
Technically challenging work	Intrinsic
Job security/stable environment	Extrinsic
Identify with the task	Intrinsic
Autonomy	Intrinsic
Appropriate working conditions/infrastructure	Extrinsic
Making a contribution/task significance	Intrinsic
Sufficient resources	Extrinsic
Team quality	Extrinsic
Creativity/Innovation	Intrinsic
Fun (playing)	Intrinsic
Professionalism/setting standards	Extrinsic
Having an ideology	Extrinsic
Non-financial benefits (availability of rewards)	Extrinsic
Penalty Policies	Extrinsic
Good relationship with users/customers	Intrinsic
Recognition of cultural differences	Intrinsic
Recognition of individuality	Intrinsic
Construction/delivery/completion	Intrinsic

Of particular relevance to this study is Self Determination Theory, in which [15] postu-late that to be self-motivated, employees require three innate psychological needs to be satisfied: the need for competence, autonomy, and relatedness.

2.1 Motivation in Software Engineering

Three reviews covering over 150 empirical studies of software engineer motivation [11, 22, 24] together with one case study [24] yield an inventory of 32 motivation factors for software engineers (Table 1). Among these are Problem Solving, Team Working, Change, Challenge, and Benefit. In addition, nine separate studies in the SLR undertaken by [11] on Software Engineer motivation identified autonomy to be an important factor.

2.2 Motivation and Agile

Traditionally, GSD has followed a plan-driven, structured, waterfall approach, where tasks are allocated according to where they appear in the software lifecycle [25]. It was considered that agile methods, envisaged for small projects and co-located teams with informal processes [26, 27], would be a poor fit for distributed development approaches [28] which relies on formal mechanisms. Yet, there is a growing trend for companies engaged in GSD to adopt agile methods [29, 30]. Adopting agile practices such as short iterations, frequent builds, and continuous delivery all pose challenges to configuration management and version management [31]. But, practices such as short iterations increase transparency of work-in-progress, and provide a big picture of project progress to stakeholders [32]. However, setting up an agile team is usually motivated by benefits such as increased productivity, innovation, and employee satisfaction [33].

Introducing agile methods can change the culture in a company - developers need to have more autonomy as well as decision-making power to implement agile practices [16]. Sutherland [34] states that autonomy is a key indicator that scrum is working, where "the scrum team is (and feels) totally responsible for their product and no outside agency impacts the work inside a sprint", while [35] have also found evidence of autonomy in the scrum teams whom they studied. Through frequent communications and meetings (i.e.; daily stand-ups), agile team members can motivate and influence each other's behavior [36], but little is known about motivation in an agile context [37, 38].

2.3 Motivation and Global Software Development

Some of the issues introduced by GSD [39] may be addressed by meeting the motiva-tional needs of software engineers. For example, GSD projects have been shown to suffer from high staff turnover [40, 41] whereas high levels of motivation can have a positive effect on staff retention [14]. The review conducted by [22] and the case study by [23] looked at motivation of GSD software engineers. Both found that the GSD practitioner has specific and new needs, such as recognition of cultural differences and individuality, and the need to see how their work contributes to a complete and finished product.

2.4   Demotivation and Herzberg's Two Factor Theory

According to Herzberg's two factor theory [42], extrinsic motivators (also called hygiene factors) have the power to demotivate if absent, but when present do not trigger the long term desired impetus and positive energy of intrinsic motivators. Software engineers working in a multi-site team are likely to face many demotivating factors, which in turn can cause difficulties [43]. Among these are:

- Motivation and Autonomy in GSD;
- Inequity, where remote working causes training, growth and promotion opportunities to be missed, inequitable holiday allowances are given, and they may need to work anti-social hours to communicate with colleagues;
- Interesting work going to other parties, as complex tasks are retained at the home site, while less rewarding tasks such as maintenance go to the remote teams;
- Unfair reward system, which may happen if the remote software engineer is only noticed when there is a problem;
- Poor communication such as poor feedback, and loss of direct contact with other team members and management;
- Bad relationship with users and colleagues, where lack of face to face contact can result in mistrust and difficulty in building relationships with colleagues;
- Poor working environment, when being physically separated from the rest of the team, or the home site, is considered demotivating;
- Role ambiguity, which can occur when working in remote teams where each member is expected to take on many different roles, providing variety and challenge, but often resulting in overstretching the individual;
- Lack of influence, for example when senior management from the head office discusses issues with the client without involving the on-site project manager.

De-motivators, as listed above, are not necessarily the opposite of motivators, and so should be treated separately. For example role ambiguity is found to be de-motivating, but someone with a fixed job description may not be motivated. Sometimes, one factor can be both motivating and demotivating depending on context, e.g. working on maintenance tasks [11].

2.5   GSD Environmental Impact on Software Engineer Characteristics

A review of the literature found that in nearly three-quarters (73%) of the cases software engineers form a distinct identifiable occupational group [11]. Most cited characteristics were "growth oriented," "introverted," and "need for independence" indicating that these occur across many contexts. The view that software engineers are introverted reflects findings from [44] in their Job Diagnostics Survey. This view is not universal as some studies characterize software engineers as sociable people [11].

Although some research suggests that the needs of a global software engineer are similar to those of the general population of engineers [24, 45], speculated in their empirical study on software engineer motivation that this may be changing – in that working in distributed teams, the need to travel and less need for a work/life balance is attracting a different type of personality. In the same study, those engineers working in a GSD environment did not mention the following factors as attracting them to, or keeping in the software engineering field: development practices, autonomy, empowerment and responsibility, trust and respect, recognition of individuality. Of note here is that *autonomy* is not mentioned as important to the small sample of engineers in [24]. This distinguishing feature may be due to personality and "individual differences in their tendencies toward autonomous functioning across specific domains and behaviors" [46].

2.6 Is Autonomy Still an Important Factor?

We define autonomy as a feeling of independence, freedom and control (or self-determination) [7]. Autonomy has been identified in earlier studies as an important motivator for software engineers [11], and is also a core concept in self-determination theory [15, 47, 48]. [46] reason that the more autonomy one feels, the more intrinsically motivated one becomes. It might be that the global software engineer profile is changing as discussed in Sect. 2.4. This may reflect Deci and Ryan's Cognitive Evaluation Theory (CET) [7] that specifically addresses social and environmental external factors which facilitate or undermine intrinsic motivation. Taking this argument forward, and given that many environmental factors are inevitable when working in GSD (such as having to meet colleagues virtually, fitting in with hours of remote teams in different timezones, and travel), [24] suggest that those engineers who remain working in GSD teams for the long term are resilient to the demotivating factors that are inherent in GSD.

In this study, we focus on one factor, as picked up in [24] and ask whether autonomy affects motivation of software engineers working in GSD. Because autonomy is a crucial component of agile development, as well as important for software engineers' motivation, but potentially difficult to satisfy within the context of GSD, we examined the extent to which autonomy affects the motivation of two GSD teams within a company who were introducing scrum. Our research question is expressed as: "Does increased autonomy, through the introduction of scrum, result in higher motivation among distributed developers?" The research method is discussed in the next section.

3 Research Methods

As part of a larger software process improvement study, we studied two distributed software development teams: the first comprising six members in 3 locations in Wales, England and Ireland and the second with nine members in three locations in Ireland, Canada and USA. Both projects included teams comprising former employees of companies acquired by the current parent company. We observed team planning, review meetings, and daily "scrums," over a period of ten months for one team and fifteen months for the second team. We also interviewed each team member, and asked them to rate their motivation on a five likert point scale. Finally, we asked all members of each team to complete a short motivation survey.

3.1 The Case

The company we studied, which we shall call OptiManage, is a medium-sized Irish-based software company that develops practice management software for the optical industry. The business model which the company has been using is to acquire small companies worldwide. When companies are acquired, they become part of the global software team, thus integrating their software processes with that of OptiManage. The software developed by the acquired company is supported by OptiManage until it is either absorbed into the main product or phased out completely. This has resulted in OptiManage having a headquarters in Dublin, Ireland employing approximately 50 software engineers, and many small GSD teams. Teams hold face-to-face meetings at least twice per year, conducting their global, often daily, interactions through means such as video conferencing, e-mail and messaging.

We studied two teams, each of which is involved in different aspects of OptiManage's business. Team A is responsible for maintaining the core software for their product line. They also maintain and enhance the retail product for the Irish, UK, Canadian, and Mexican markets. Finally, they perform maintenance on a legacy product resulting from an acquisition that also brought four of Team A's team members to the company. Team A's members are located in England, Wales, and Ireland. Two of Team A's members work primarily from home in England, the other members are distributed equally between the head office in Ireland and an office in Wales. For this team, they are working in similar time zones and, as everyone speaks English, they do not have to deal with language barriers. Team B is distributed between Ireland, and the west coasts of Canada and USA. Within each of these countries the members are co-located. Their responsibility is to tailor the company's product for a large customer in North America. While there is no language barrier – all team members speak English as their native language, this team have to cope with up to eight hours difference in timezones. Team Composition (Table 2) shows the distribution of members of both teams. Both teams use Agile Software Development methods, holding scrum "ceremonies" including daily stand-up, sprint planning and retrospective meetings. The Project Manager also plays role of Scrum Master.

3.2 Data Collection

Two of the authors acted in a participant-observer role by sitting in on each team's scrum "ceremonies". Team A was observed from November, 2015 to June, 2016, and Team B was observed from January, 2016 to March, 2017. Due to the team being global, they held video conferences for daily standups, sprint planning, backlog grooming, and sprint retrospectives. The observer also conducted semi-structured interviews with each member of the team (see Appendix A). The interview protocol was based on that used by [49], and was extended in this project to include questions triggered during the participant-observation sessions within OptiManage.

Table 2. Case study team composition

Country		Number
Team A		**6**
Ireland	Software developer	2
Wales	Scrum master	1
	Product owner	1
England	Quality assurance	1
	Senior Developer	1
Team B		**9**
Ireland	Product owner	1
	Software developer	3
	Quality assurance	1
Canada	Scrum master	1
	Product owner	1
	Developer	1
USA	Senior developer	1

All respondents were asked to describe their backgrounds, roles on the team, and development processes. They were asked to rate his or her motivation on a five point interval scale - definitely low (1), somewhat low (2), neither low nor high (3), somewhat high (4) and definitely high (5). In addition, as participant-observers, each researcher kept a journal of the daily ceremonies, which was retained in note form for future reference. The interviews were recorded and later transcribed.

Finally, we held a workshop in early 2016, in which all Team A members attended in person. It was based in Dublin, at the head office. During this workshop Team A completed a short motivation survey (see Appendix A – A.4). Team B completed the survey via e-mail. We have administered this survey with other software development companies operating across geographic boundaries, see, for example, the case study described in [24]. The survey is an adaptation of questions created by [50] designed specifically to reveal what motivates practicing software engineers.

3.3 Data Analysis

We used a mixed methods analysis approach, where quantitative methods were used to rate and aggregate the levels of motivation, and qualitative methods were applied to explore themes in the semi-structured interview data, observations, and in the responses to the open questions in the motivation survey.

Quantitatively, results were aggregated across individuals and teams based on a 5 point Likert scale to gain a measure of motivation. We also aggregated the responses to the motivation questions in the survey. Qualitatively, we took an inductive approach, and analyzed the responses to the open questions in Sections A3–A5 of the survey, grouping the survey responses into themes using content analysis [51]. We also took a deductive approach, by looking specifically for themes coming from the semi-structured interviews and observations that related to autonomy.

4   Results

We first present results of team members' self-reported motivation. As mentioned in the previous section, at the end of each interview, interviewees were asked to rate their motivation on a five-point interval scale (see Table 3). There is little difference of motivation between roles. Two developers reported "definitely high" motivation, two reported "somewhat high" motivation, and four reported "neither low nor high" motivation. One product owner reported "definitely high" motivation, the other two "neither low nor high" motivation. The two scrum masters and the two quality assurance team members reported either "neither low nor high" or "somewhat high" motivation. Developers seem to be more motivated after the introduction of scrum. However, once again the Wilcoxon Signed-Rank test does not show this difference to be significant (p-value = .24). Location seems to favor the home office or the most remote locations in North America (Canada and USA): each had a median motivation rating of "somewhat high", while North America also had a mode of "somewhat high". Similarly, the home office and North America both appear to have slightly increased motivation after the introduction of scrum, but the Wilcoxon Signed-Rank test does not show this difference to be significant (p-value = .5 and .68 respectively).

Table 3. Team member motivation by role

Country	Number	Minimum	Maximum	Median	Mode
Scrum master /Project manager	2	3	4	3.5	3&4
Product owner	3	3	5	3	3
Developer	8	3	5	3.5	3
Quality assurance	2	3	4	3.5	3&4

Table 4 summarizes the results from before and after the introduction of scrum. (Note: three additional team members were hired after scrum was introduced). The range of reported motivation ranges from "neither low nor high" to "very high" motivation, both before and after scrum introduction - no-one reported low motivation. The most common motivation level before the introduction of scrum was "neither low nor high", while after the introduction of scrum, motivation levels were evenly distributed among "neither low nor high," "somewhat high," and "definitely high," with some team members reporting higher motivation, others reporting lower, and some reporting no difference. This suggests that introducing scrum had a positive effect on motivation (see Fig. 1). However, comparing the before and after results using the Wilcoxon Signed-Rank test for differences between populations shows no statistically significant difference (p-value = .4) between the motivation levels of team members that were present before and after the introduction of scrum.

Table 4. Team member motivation by location, before and after introduction of scrum

Location/Scrum stage	Rating	Total	Median	Mode
	3 4 5			
Ireland/before	2 1 2	5	4	3&5
Ireland/after	1 3 3	7	4	4&5
UK/before	2 2 0	4	3.5	3&4
UK/after	3 0 1	4	3	3
Nth America/before	1 1 1	3	4	3,4,5
Nth America/after	1 2 1	5	4	4

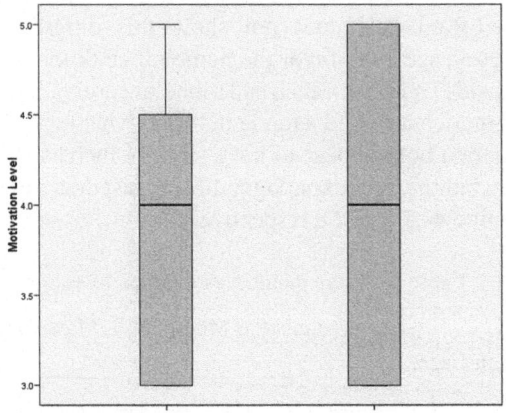

Fig. 1. Individual motivation before (left) and after (right) the introduction of scrum

Finally, experience does seem to affect motivation: the highest motivation scores were reported by the team members with less than ten years' experience (Tables 5 and 6, Fig. 2). Comparing these less experienced developers to their peers with ten or more years' experience, the Wilcoxon Signed-Rank test does not show any difference in motivation before the introduction of scrum. However, after the introduction of scrum, the less experienced developers did have significantly higher motivation (p-value = .04 for the unpaired Wilcoxon test[1] (Fig. 2).

Table 5. Team member motivation by experience

Years of Experience	Number	Minimum	Maximum	Median	Mode
<5 years	2	3	4	3.5	3&4
5–9 years	5	3	5	3.5	3
10–19 years	5	3	5	3	3
20+ years	3	3	5	3.5	3

---

[1] We used the unpaired Wilcoxon test to compare two different samples, rather than pairs of results from the same sample.

Table 6. Team member motivation by experience, before and after introduction of scrum

Experience/Scrum stage	Rating	Total	Median	Mode
	3 4 5			
<10 years/before	2 1 1	4	3.5	3
<10 years/after	0 4 3	7	4	4
10+ years/before	3 3 2	8	4	3&4
10+ years/after	5 1 2	8	3	4

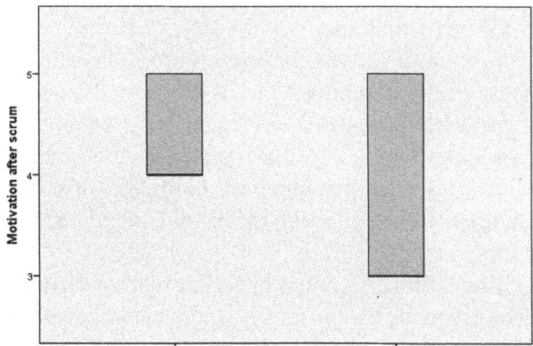

Fig. 2. Individual motivation after scrum implementation showing less than 10 years' experience (left) and greater than ten years' experience (right).

5 Discussion

Examining our qualitative responses, looking at motivation levels, some participants divided their level of motivation according to current role and current project. Three gave a measure of their personal level of motivation: two stating it was 'very high' (Respondents 1 & 4), and one 'somewhat high' (Respondent 6). In contrast when rating their motivation on current project, three responded 'somewhat high' (Respondents 1, 5 and 6). This shows a slight shift from 'very high' personal motivation, to lower motivation in this particular project. The two that gave a general overall level of motivation, stated their motivation level was 'neither high nor low' (Respondents 2, and 3).

One of the attributes presented as a positive for agile software development, within which scrum is a technique, is that teams have more autonomy than in plan-driven e.g. waterfall development [16]. In our study, we observed that less experienced developers ('Developers' in tables in Sect. 4) have increased levels of motivation – each one returning a 'somewhat high' (4) or 'definitely high' (5) level. The numbers are small, and there is no significant difference in motivation levels before and after the introduction of scrum. However, if we observe the more experienced engineers, we note that the majority returned "neither low nor high" (3) levels of motivation after scrum introduction. We also note that the Ireland/England/Wales teams registered lower levels of motivation than the Ireland/Canada/USA team.

One possible reason for the lower motivation among the more experienced developers might be due to these developers having less autonomy than would normally be found in an agile environment. Our findings showed hints of issues concerning autonomy in responses from two more experienced respondents. They described issues like "*being overruled by seniors*" and "*team decisions disregarded by higher management.*" This may be GSD, location, company or scrum-specific. In their paper, in which they studied a different global company, [24], noted that 'autonomy' was not a motivator expressed in survey responses. This may also be the case here, and warrants further investigation to understand whether GSD software engineers demonstrate different motivators than those working in co-located situations.

In contrast, the more junior members were comfortable with their dependence on senior developer inputs in the planning. One of the Canadian developers on Team B reported that all of his code had to be reviewed by a senior developer in Dublin, suggesting a lack of autonomy. Yet the same developer said that "*checks and balances*" and "*more communication*" which are hallmarks of scrum, result in a "*better product at the end of the sprint*", suggesting that he did not perceive a mismatch between his ideal and actual autonomy.

This reflects a healthy attitude as noted in earlier work with a high performing agile team where decisions were made by consensus, and when asked about what drives down performance, the high performing team members responded "developers wanting to do things the way they want to and not listen to anyone else" [53]. Developers in our sample were exhibiting similar behaviour to those developers in the high performance team.

Another factor regarding motivation within scrum teams is the customer. One developer, based in Wales, stated that she feels "*very motivated now*", despite difficulties due to customer dynamics as they "*sometimes neglects the important tasks at hand*". Another developer who rated their motivation as "somewhat high" was concerned that he had to "*humour every single request no matter how obscene*". The participants who rated their motivation as "neither low nor high" liked the idea that they do not have to deal with customers, and so possibly enjoyed a level of autonomy where they were allowed to focus their own programming activities.

Other reasons for high motivation were cited, for example, a senior developer in Dublin mentioned intellectual challenge "*To be honest as long there is new stuff to do or new task to do it [the process] doesn't matter. So, it's very high.*"

Finally, a comment from one experienced Team A member sheds light on what might be the true reason for some of his lack of motivation. Describing Team A's role as maintainers of the core codebase, this person said: "*It has to be done, but nobody else wants to do it.*" Maintenance tasks have been found to be de-motivating [11], and may even be overlooked in process improvement activities [52].

These results support our hypothesis that software engineers in GSD teams do not perceive a lack of autonomy nor reduced motivation stemming from it even when they appear to have less autonomy than is generally expected in an agile environment. It also supports the idea that engineers who persist with GSD are less negatively affected by aspects of GSD than other engineers [24].

Clearly these observations are based on limited evidence, and there may be several other factors that are influencing the levels of motivation that we are not currently measuring, or may not be able to measure. However, our study starts to build a hypothesis where the global software engineer has an awareness of the dependence they have on their team members and management, and are not so concerned with a lack of autonomy.

It could be that autonomy alone is not sufficient, and that it needs to be matched by creativity, identity and variety. Perhaps the more experienced software engineers in our sample were not able to be creative, and their work lacked variety. Identity in terms of recognition for a task well done can lack visibility outside the team, a problem we identified in an earlier study when analysing motivation in a high performing team [37]. This also supports the findings in [24] in which creativity, construction, and making a contribution was by far the most prevalent motivation factor mentioned across the sample of experienced engineers. Do these results support our hypothesis that software engineers characteristics are changing? If our hypothesis is correct, then, in addressing our research question, a perceived lack of autonomy may be less important to the global software engineers in our study.

It could also be that the level of autonomy which exists in co-located scrum is not evident in GSD teams. [24] also identified in their previous study that 11 software engineering motivation factors did not exist in the GSD team they studied. One of these was autonomy. The study presented in this paper is also pointing in this direction. However, amongst the many answers to the open motivation and de-motivation questions, very few related to autonomy. The participants who rated their motivation as neither high nor low liked the idea that they do not have to deal with customers and possibly enjoyed a level of autonomy, where they were allowed to get on with their own programming activities. But this is just conjecture at this stage. What it does say is that we need to re-structure our motivation questionnaire to focus on those factors which may not be present as motivators for GSD software engineers.

Our motivation survey results for Team A reveal further potential reasons for their lower levels of motivation. Firstly, focusing on the second section of the survey "What motivates you?", some respondents slightly misunderstood question 6, in that they divided their motivation levels according to their current role (personal level), and the motivation in working on the project. This error was actually revealing, and suggests that we need to re-design the survey in future. The motivation in working on the project was slightly lower than their personal levels of motivation (this is consistent with the semi-structured interview findings), supporting the idea that they don't get intrinsic motivation from undertaking maintenance tasks (which is core to their work) or that there are certain pressures on the current project that is reducing their motivation. Looking at the responses to the open questions on what motivates this group, their answers support previous research, in that intrinsic motivations are what attract them to software engineering as a profession. Factors include making a difference, problem solving, constructing something from nothing, and learning something new.

The participant, who gave a very high level of motivation rating, noted that the Team and Support were important to them. Respondent (5), was very aware of the dependence on senior developer inputs into the planning – and found this de-motivating since a lack of input in planning breaks the sprint. This respondent was suggesting that they needed more support from the senior developer, rather than working alone. This is re-iterated when they suggest that involving other senior developers into the sprint grooming planning was an issue. Respondent 5 had a 'somewhat high' level of motivation.

We are aware that in previous studies, e.g. [54], there has been some discussion around scrum and agile methods offering "no advice on how shared leadership could be implemented". There is a possibility that these teams need guidance on how this should happen within the context of agile implementation. Indeed, in their research, [55] concluded that there is a need for team leaders to have development programs "aimed at developing capabilities for adaptive switching of achievement priorities, and for effectively communicating changing goal priorities". The introduction of scrum in the versatile business and software development environment in which OptiManage operates.

5.1 Threats to Validity

We note that our study has limitations which threaten the validity of our conclusions. Our 5-point measure for motivation was only used once during the study period. However, we asked 15 team members at different levels, and have supplemented their answers with qualitative research which has given insight into why those studied presented the specific answers.

Also, we did not have a direct measure of autonomy. Because scrum implementation is expected to introduce autonomy into teams [16], we assumed this would work also for global software development teams. This, of course, raised the additional question for us to study – in global software development teams, does scrum provide autonomy to team members? We also note that the study participants were from one company, and therefore, this factor may be company related. However, our research to date provides no evidence to support this. Given that our study consisted of only fifteen subjects, we have not generalized our findings.

6 Conclusion

Prior research has shown that software engineers who are motivated deliver higher quality software [11], are more innovative [19], more successful [20] and less prone to attrition [14]. Companies, including those with GSD teams, are adopting agile methods [56] in an effort to realize benefits such as increased productivity, innovation, and employee satisfaction [32]. However, agile methods were originally designed for small, co-located teams [25, 26], and require significant autonomy to be fully deployed [16].

Following this study, we have identified a number of questions which we need to consider:

Why are there apparent differences in motivation between the two teams? To uncover this, we intend to administer the motivation survey developed by [50] to all project groups (currently only Teams A and B have completed the survey). We would like to identify whether this effect is company specific, or whether there is a possibility that the autonomy expected from scrum implementation is lessened when it is implemented in global software development teams.

Could gender difference be a factor in motivation? We have not split the results by gender, but 33% of Team A was female developers and 22% of Team B were female. While this is a higher percentage than often seen in software development teams globally (~10%), given that it is now realized that women have different requirements than men in work situations, it would be interesting to investigate this further.

Are the software engineer motivation factors identified in [24] different for software engineers who are co-located and software engineers working GSD teams? This requires the distribution of motivation surveys developed by [50] to co-located and GSD teams in multiple countries. In doing this, there needs to be account taken of other potential factors, such as type of work being completed, culture and responsibility of the person completing the survey.

When implemented in GSD, does autonomy exist to a lesser extent than when implemented in co-located teams? Again, a detailed study is needed, supported by the development of a measure of autonomy to compare against motivation level.

Our study has found little evidence to suggest there is a difference in motivation between members of agile teams, and those in teams employing plan-driven development. Our research has shown that motivation differences related to experience, intellectual challenge and contributing to a valuable product.

Scrum emphasizes "self-organizing teams" that decide among themselves the best way to achieve their objectives. As such, we expected that motivation would be higher after the introduction of scrum due to higher autonomy. We found, however, that the difference in motivation levels before and after the introduction of scrum was slight and not statistically significant. Instead, there was a significant difference in the motivation levels of experienced team members, which were lower than less experienced members. We speculate that this is due to the absence of other motivators that are important to senior-level software engineers. We conclude that, while autonomy is an important motivator, it is not sufficient on its own, and that the implementation of scrum within GSD may not provide the autonomy level expected and seen in co-located teams.

Acknowledgments. We thank the members of Team A and Team B for their generous and thoughtful collaboration on this study, and OptiManage, for allowing us to study their software development efforts. This work was supported, in part, by Science Foundation Ireland grants 10/CE/I1855 and 13/RC/2094 to Lero - the Irish Software Research Centre (http://www.lero.i.e). This work was supported, in part, by Enterprise Ireland and the European Development Fund through grant IR20130022.

Appendix A: Interview Protocol

A.1 Demographics

(1) Time at OptiManage.
(2) Time on current project.
(3) Current position.
(4) Current location.
(5) Previous position & company.

(6) Total development experience.
(7) Total domain experience.
(8) Education and formal qualifications.
(9) Gender.
(10) Nationality.

A.2 Motivation Rating

For the next two questions, rate your motivation on the following scale: Very low, Somewhat low, Neither low nor high, Somewhat high, Very high

(1) How would you rate your motivation now?
(2) How would you rate your motivation prior to introduction of Scrum?

A.3 Project

(1) How would you describe your current project?
(2) How would you describe your project's current domain?
(3) What is your role?
(4) Have you met any of your remote colleagues?
(5) Does geographic separation hinder the project?
(6) Why do you think OptiManage is employing distributed devel-opment for this project?
(7) Have you had any training in Agile methods?
(8) Have you had any training in distributed development?

A.4 Process

(1) Describe your dev process.
    (a) How do devlopers test changes?
    (b) How are builds created for QA?
    (c) Is build machine a bottleneck?
    (d) How does "outside of sprint" work?
    (e) Are there separate QA tasks?
    (f) Are spikes time-boxed? How is effort accounted for?
    (g) Is sprint too short?
    (h) Does the Product Owner ever make estimates?
    (i) What is the [important customer] button?
    (j) Who is [Chief Architect]?
(2) Does the application domain restrict the process in any way?
(3) How would you describe the previous process (before Scrum)?
(4) What advantages does Scrum offer over that process?
(5) What advantages did the previous process have over Scrum?
(6) What is working well with Scrum?
(7) What is not working well with Scrum?
(8) What obstacles exist that prevent Scrum from working well?
(9) What is the best aspect of Scrum?
(10) What is the worst aspect of Scrum?

(11) If there was one thing you could change, what would it be?

A.5 Motivation

1. What aspects of your work in software engineering do you get most satisfaction from?
2. What makes you stay working in software engineering?
3. What factors attracted you to work in software engineering?
4. What makes software development worthwhile to you?
5. What do you plan to do when you have completed your current project?
6. On a scale of 1 – 5 how motivated are you in your current role and project? (1 = very low, 2 = somewhat high, 3 = neither high nor low, 4 = somewhat high, 5 = very high).
7. If you didn't answer 5 to the previous question, what do you think could improve your motivation?
8. Are there any aspects of your job that you find de-motivating? If so, please list the top three here.
9. Please add any ideas you have here about motivating or de-motivating aspects of your job. (Note: motivating aspects of your job relate to things that you do for reasons of personal fulfillment. De-motivating aspects are constraints that are external to you and outside your immediate control).

References

1. Casey, V., Richardson, I.: Practical Experience of Virtual Team Software Development, European Software Process Improvement Conference, Industrial Proceedings, Trondheim, Norway, pp. 3–D.9-13-D.15, 9–11 November 2004
2. Casey, V., Richardson, I.: Virtual teams: understanding the impact of fear, special issue on global software engineering, J. Softw. Evol. Process **13**, 511–526 (2008)
3. Smite, D., Wohlin, C., Galvin, Z., Prikladnicki, R.: An empirically based terminology and taxonomy for global software engineering. Empirical Softw. Eng. **19**(1), 105–153 (2014)
4. Vizcaiıno, A., Garcıa, F., Piattini, M., Beecham, S.: A validated ontology for global software development. Comput. Stand. Interfaces **46**(2016), 66–78 (2016)
5. Noll, J., Beecham, S., Richardson, I., Nic Canna, C.: Global teaming for global software development governance: a case study. In: International Conference on Global Software Engineering. IEEE, Irvine (2016)
6. Deshpande, S., Richardson, I.: Management at the outsourcing destination – global software development in india. In: 4th IEEE International Conference on Global Software Engineering, Limerick, pp. 217–225, 16–19 July 2009
7. Deci, E.L., Ryan, R.M.: Cognitive Evaluation Theory Intrinsic Motivation and Self-Determination in Human Behavior, pp. 43–85. Springer, US (1985). doi:10.1007/978-1-4899-2271-7_4
8. Ferratt, T.W., Harvey, G.E., Prasad, J.: Instrument validation for investigating a model of employment arrangement fit for IT professionals. In: Proceedings of the 2003 SIGMIS Conference on Computer Personnel Research: Freedom in Philadelphia–leveraging Differences and Diversity in the IT Workforce (SIGMIS CPR 2003). ACM, New York, pp. 168–178 (2003)

9. Porter, L.W., Pearce, J.L., Tripoli, A.M., Lewis, K.M.: Differential perceptions of employer's inducements: implications for psychological contracts. J. Organ. Behav. **19**(1998), 769–782 (1998)

10. Huczynski, A., Buchanan, D.: Organizational Behaviour: An Introductory Text. (1991)

11. Beecham, S., Baddoo, N., Hall, T., Robinson, H., Sharp, H.: Motivation in software engineering: a systematic literature review. Inf. Softw. Technol. **50**(9), 78–860 (2008)

12. Boehm, B.W.: Software engineering economics, vol. 197. Prentice-hall Englewood Cliffs (NJ) (1981)

13. Law, A., Charron, R.: Effects of agile practices on social factors. In: ACM SIGSOFT Software Engineering Notes, vol. 30. ACM, pp. 1–5 (2005)

14. Hall, T., Beecham, S., Verner, J., Wilson, D.: The Impact of staff turnover on software projects: the importance of understanding what makes software practitioners tick (refilling the pipeline: meeting the renewed demand for information technology workers). In: ACM-SIGMIS CPR 2008 Conference. Charlottesville, Virginia, 3-5 April 2008

15. Ryan, R.M., Deci, E.L.: Self-determination theory and the facilitation of intrinsic motivation, social development, and well-being. Am. Psychol. 55(1), 68–78 (2000) http://dx.doi.org/10.1037/0003-066X.55.1.68

16. Fowler M.: Using an agile software process with offshore development. Capturado em, May 2006 http://martinfowler.com/articles/agileOffshore.html

17. Noll, J., Richardson, B., Razzak, M.A., Barcomb, A., Richardson, I., Beecham, S.: "Motivation and Autonomy in Global Software Development." The 11th Global Sourcing Workshop in La Thuile, Italy (2017)

18. Noll, J., Razzak, M.A., Beecham, S.: Motivation and autonomy in global software development: an empirical study. In: Proceedings of the 21st International Conference on Evaluation and Assessment in Software Engineering (EASE 2017). ACM, New York, pp. 394–399 (2017) https://doi.org/10.1145/3084226.3084277

19. Petri, H.L., Govern, J.M.: Motivation: Theory, Research, and Application -, 6th edn. Wadsworth Publishing, Belmont (2012)

20. Frey, B.S., Osterloh, M.: Successful Management by Motivation: Balancing Intrinsic and Extrinsic Incentives. Springer-Verlag, Berlin (2002). doi:10.1007/978-3-662-10132-2

21. Verner, J.M., Babar, M.A., Cerpa, N., Hall, T., Beecham, S.: Factors that motivate software engineering teams: a four country empirical study. J. Syst. Softw. **92**, 115–127 (2014)

22. França, A.C.C., Gouveia, T.B., Santos, P.C.F., Santana, C.A., da Silva, F.Q.B.: Motivation in software engineering: a systematic review update. In: 15th Annual Conference on Evaluation Assessment in Software Engineering (Ease 2011), pp. 63–154 (2011). doi: 10.1049/ic.2011.0019

23. de, Farias, Jr., I.H., Duarte, L., de, Oliveira, J.P.N., Dantas, A.R.N., Barbosa, J.F., de, Moura, H.P.: Motivational factors for distributed software development teams. In: 2012 IEEE Seventh International Conference on Global Software Engineering Workshops (ICGSEW), pp. 49–54. IEEE (2012). doi:10.1109/ICGSEW.2012.17

24. Beecham, S., Noll, J.: What Motivates Software Engineers Working in Global Software Development?, pp. 193–209. Springer International Publishing, Berlin, Heidelberg (2015). doi:10.1007/978-3-319-26844-6_14

25. Estler, H.C., Nordio, M., Furia, C.A., Meyer, B., Schneider, J.: Agile vs. structured distributed software development: a case study. Empirical Softw. Eng. **19**(5), 224–1197 (2014)

26. Kahkonen, T.: Agile methods for large organizations-building communities of practice. In: Agile Development Conference, pp. 2–10. IEEE, 22 Jun 2004

27. Abrahamsson, P., Conboy, K., Wang, X.: Lots done, more to do': the current state of agile systems development research. Eur. J. Inf. Syst. **18**(4), 281 (2009)

28. Ramesh, B., Cao, L., Mohan, K., Xu, P.: Can distributed software development be agile? Commun. ACM **49**(10), 6–41 (2006)
29. Hanssen, G.K., Šmite, D., Moe, N.B.: Signs of agile trends in global software engineering research: a tertiary study. In: 2011 Sixth IEEE International Conference on Global Software Engineering Workshop (ICGSEW), pp. 17–23. IEEE, 15 Aug 2011
30. Fitzgerald, B., Stol, K.J., O'Sullivan, R., O'Brien, D.: Scaling agile methods to regulated environments: an industry case study. In: 2013 35th International Conference on Software Engineering (ICSE), pp. 863–872. IEEE, 18 May 2013
31. Paasivaara, M., Lassenius, C.: Could global software development benefit from agile methods?. In: International Conference on Global Software Engineering, ICGSE 2006, pp. 109–113. IEEE 2006
32. Paasivaara, M., Lassenius, C.: Using iterative and incremental processes in global software development. In: 3rd International Workshop on Global Software Development, pp. 42–47, 24 May 2004
33. Šmite, D., Moe, N.B., Ågerfalk, P.J.: Fundamentals of agile distributed software development. In: Agility Across Time And Space 2010, pp. 3–7. Springer, Berlin (2010)
34. Sutherland, J.: Future of scrum: parallel pipelining of sprints in complex projects. In: 2005 Proceedings of Agile Conference. IEEE (2005)
35. Monteiro, C.V., da Silva, F.Q., dos Santos, I.R., Farias, F., Cardozo, E.S., do A Leitão, A.R., Pernambuco Filho, M.J.: A qualitative study of the determinants of self-managing team effectiveness in a scrum team. In: Proceedings of the 4th International Workshop on Cooperative and Human Aspects of Software Engineering, pp. 16–23. ACM, May 2011
36. Das, T.K., Teng, B.S.: Trust, control, and risk in strategic alliances: an integrated framework. Organ. stud. **22**(2), 83–251 (2001)
37. Beecham, S., Sharp, H., Baddoo, N., Hall, T., Robinson, H.: Does the XP environment meet the motivational needs of the software developer? an empirical study. In: Agile Conference (AGILE), pp. 37–49. IEEE 13 Aug 2007
38. McHugh, O., Conboy, K., Lang, M.: Motivating agile teams: a case study of teams in Ireland and Sweden. In: International Research Workshop on IT Project Management 2010
39. Noll, J., Beecham, S., Richardson, I.: Global software development and collaboration: barriers and solutions. ACM inroads **1**(3), 66–78 (2010)
40. Holmstrom, H., Ó Conchúir, E., Ågerfalk, P.J., Fitzgerald, B.: Global software development challenges: a case study on temporal, geographical and socio-cultural distance. In: International Conference on Global Software Engineering ICGSE 2006, pp. 3–11. IEEE (2006)
41. Ebert, C., Murthy, B.K., Jha, N.N.: Managing risks in global software engineering: principles and practices. In: IEEE International Conference on Global Software Engineering (ICGSE 2008), pp. 40–131. IEEE (2008)
42. Herzberg, F., Mausner, B., Snyderman, B.B.: Motivation to Work, 2nd edn. Wiley, New York (1959)
43. Beecham, S.: Motivating software engineers working in virtual teams across the globe. In: Wohlin, C., Ruhe, G. (eds.) Software Project Management in a Changing World, pp. 82–255. Springer, Germany (2014). doi:10.1007/978-3-642-55035-5_10
44. Couger, J.D., Zawacki, R.A.: Motivating and Managing Computer Personnel. Wiley, New York (1980)
45. El Khatib, V., Trang, S., Reimers, K., Kolbe, L.: The role of motivational factors in distributed software development teams: an empirical investigation. In: ECIS, p. 221 (2013)

46. Ryan, R.M., Deci, E.L.: Self regulation and the problem of human autonomy: does psychology need choice, self determination, and will ? Journal of Personality, 74:6. Blackwell Publishing, Inc. DOI:10:1111/j.146-6494.2006.00420.x. (2006). http://www.intrinsicmotiva tion.net/SDT/documents/2006_RyanDeci_Self-RegulationProblemofHumanAutonomy.pdf
47. Deci, E.L., Ryan, R.M.: Intrinsic Motivation and Self-Determination in Human Behavior. Plenum Press, New York (1985). doi:10.1007/978-1-4899-2271-7
48. Gagne, M., Deci, E.L.: Self.-determination. theory work. motivation. J. Organ. Behav. **26**, 331–362 (2005). John Wiley and Sons Ltd
49. Beecham, S.: Motivating software engineers working in virtual teams across the globe. In: Ruhe, G., Wohlin, C. (eds.) Software Project Management in a Changing World, pp. 255–277. Springer, Heidelberg (2014). doi:10.1007/978-3-642-55035-5_10
50. Sharp, H.: "What Motivates Software Engineers: A Workshop Report." Overload Project Management, p. 99 (2010). http://accu.org/index.php/journals/1703
51. Krippendorff, K.: Content Analysis: an Introduction to Its Methodology, 2nd edn. Sage Publications, Beverly Hills (2004)
52. Hall, T., Rainer, A., Baddoo, N., Beecham, S.: An empirical study of maintenance issues within process improvement programmes in software industry. In: IEEE Conference Soft Maintenance, Florence, Italy, pp. 422–423, 7-9 November 2001
53. Beecham, S., Sharp, H., Baddoo, N., Hall, T., Robinson, H.: Does the XP environment meet the motivational needs of the software developer an empirical study. In: Agile Conference (AGILE 2007), pp. 37–49. IEEE (2007)
54. Moe, N.B., Dingsøyr, T., Dybå, T.: A teamwork model for understanding an agile team: a case study of a scrum project. Inf. Softw. Technol. **52**(5), 480–491 (2010)
55. Alexander, L., Van Knippenberg, D.: Teams in pursuit of radical innovation: a goal orientation perspective. Acad. Manag. Rev. **39**(4), 423–438 (2014)
56. Hanssen, G.K., Smite, D., Moe, N.B.: Signs of agile trends in global software engineering research: a tertiary study. In: Sixth IEEE International Conference on Global Software Engineering Workshop (ICGSEW), pp. 17–23. IEEE (2011)

Outsourcing 2.0: Towards an Innovation-Driven Process Model for Client-Vendor Relationships in Information Technology Outsourcing

Robert Linden[✉], Nikolaus Schmidt, and Christoph Rosenkranz

University of Cologne, Albertus-Magnus-Platz, 50923 Cologne, Germany
{robert.linden, nikolaus.schmidt,
christoph.rosenkranz}@wiso.uni-koeln.de

Abstract. While most ITO deals focused on cost-reduction through out-sourcing of already matured services, tasks and systems, many ITO engagements are moving into new directions – the joint identification and exploiting of innovative, IT-based ideas to generate additional value for the organization and strengthen its market competitiveness. This paper proposes to investigate how the client-vendor relationship need to be modelled, structured, and managed to foster innovations within ITO. To answer our research questions, we conducted an explorative field study by interviewing 16 ITO experts from both client and vendor organizations. Our research results in an enhanced client-vendor relationship process model consisting of five process steps as well as corresponding categories describing management actions focusing on innovation generation within ITO client-vendor relationships. The contribution of our study is the development of an innovation-focused model for managing such relationships and the extension of our understanding of ITO management in times of increased digital innovation.

Keywords: Information technology outsourcing · Innovation · Innovation through outsourcing · Client-Vendor relationship · Process model

1 Introduction

Information technology outsourcing (ITO) continues to be an important part of contemporary organizations' information technology (IT) strategy [1, 2]. Current market analysts estimate the global market for ITO with the total volume of $303 bn. USD in 2016, with an additional expected growth rate of 5.9% for 2017 [3]. While, so far, most ITO deals focussed on cost-reduction through outsourcing of already matured services, tasks and systems to an external provider, many ITO engagements currently are moving into a new direction – the joint generation of innovation [4]. While these ITO engagements still partially focus on cost reduction, the main goal is the identification and exploiting of innovative, IT-based ideas, which can be used in the client organization's (IT) products, services, or processes, in order to generate additional value for the organization and strengthen its market competitiveness [5]. One example for such

© Springer International Publishing AG 2017
I. Oshri et al. (Eds.): Global Sourcing 2017, LNBIP 306, pp. 39–64, 2017.
https://doi.org/10.1007/978-3-319-70305-3_3

an innovation-focussed ITO engagement is the long-term, ongoing partnership between the German car manufacturer Audi and the US-based technology company Google. Within this outsourcing partnership, Google adapts specific functions of their Google Maps and Google Earth platform for usage within the Audi connect car entertainment system, for example, point-of-interest search functions as well as Google Earth-based map display [6, 7].

The ITO client-vendor relationship is well acknowledge for being a key success factor for overall ITO success [8–10] as well as for the generation of innovation through ITO engagements [11]. The body of knowledge about the client-vendor relationship is rich, and different elements have been investigated such as control or trust [12], or formal contracts and the concept of relational governance [13]. Several authors summarized the status quo in the literature and developed different models of the ITO relationship [e.g., 14, 15, 16]. Unfortunately, so far, all existent ITO relationship models try to explain the traditional, cost-based success of an ITO engagement without focusing on additional goals such as innovation generation (anonymous for review).

Hence, building upon the amount and diversity of past studies about client-vendor relationship models [17, 18] and upon calls for further research on the topics of innovation in ITO relationships [19–21], our study aims at extending the existent ITO client-vendor relationship models by adding an innovation lens. Hereby, our research focuses on the following research question:

RQ. How does the client-vendor relationship need to be modelled, structured, and managed to foster innovation generation within information technology outsourcing?

To answer our research question, we conducted an explorative field study by interviewing 16 experts from both client and vendor organizations involved in ITO. We build on existing client-vendor relationship models as our theoretical framework, especially in terms of data categorization, and augment them with insights for innovation generation. Our research results in an enhanced client-vendor relationship process model consisting of five process steps as well as corresponding categories describing management actions focusing on innovation generation within ITO client-vendor relationships. The contribution of our study is the development of an innovation-focused model for managing ITO client-vendor relationships and therefore the extension of our understanding of ITO management in times of increased digital innovation.

The remainder of this paper is organized as follows. In Sect. 2, we provide a summary of existing ITO client-vendor relationship frameworks, which are building the cornerstone for our data analysis and model development. Section 3 provides an overview about our research design including data collection and data analysis. Section 4 summarizes our results by describing an innovation-driven process model for client-vendor relationships in information technology outsourcing. Within Sect. 5 we discuss our results, provide future research directions as well as implications for practice while Sect. 6 concludes our research endeavor.

2 Related Work and Theoretical Background

2.1 Client-Vendor Relationship Models in Information Technology Outsourcing

One of the salient concepts that have emerged to describe the ITO process is the client-vendor relationship. A *client-vendor relationship* in ITO is defined as "an ongoing, long term linkage between an outsourcing vendor and customer arising from a contractual agreement to provide one or more comprehensive IT activities, processes, or services with understanding that the benefits attained by each firm are at least in part dependent on the other" [17]. It is a key success factor for achieving a positive and therefore successful outsourcing outcome [9, 20]. The importance of developing and maintaining a successful client-vendor relationship is particularly valid for long-term ITO engagements due to the fact that contracts "often cannot respond to a dynamic business environment" [22] and "it is not possible to address all facets of a relationship in a formal, written contract" [23]. This is especially true in today's increasingly turbulent and dynamic business environment, which intensifies the need for appropriate resource management in organizations [24].

Building upon an extensive literature review of the ITO client-vendor relationship (anonymous for review), we identified 20 papers explaining the ITO client-vendor relationship based on models and frameworks. Hereby, we identified three distinct research streams: (1) research focusing on explaining parts of the ITO client-vendor relationship models (e.g., the antecedents of formal control), (2) research focusing on developing a comprehensive ITO client-vendor relationship model for predicting quality and success as well as (3) research focusing on developing process models for explaining the different phases of an ITO client-vendor relationship. Table 1 summarizes existing studies in the ITO client-vendor relationship in all three streams.

Research within the first research stream generally focusses on explaining integral parts of the ITO client-vendor relationship. For example, building upon transaction cost economics theory [25], Rustagi, King [26] evaluate how task characteristics in terms of task uncertainty and degree of core competency involvement as well as client knowledge in terms of technical knowledge and relationship management knowledge affect the amount of formal control applied within an ITO client-vendor relationship. Gopal and Koka [13] focus their research on the topic of relational flexibility in ITO client-vendor relationships. Specifically, on the one hand, they show the positive influence of exchange hazards and relational factors such as prior projects with the client on relational flexibility within the relationship. On the other hand, their research shows that, within fixed price contracts, relational flexibility positively affects vendor profitability, while within- time and material contracts relational flexibility leads to higher service quality.

The second research stream takes a broader perspective. Instead of evaluating one part of the ITO client-vendor relationship in detail, research within this stream focusses on developing a comprehensive ITO client-vendor relationship model. One of the most cited articles within this research stream is the partnership quality model by Lee and Kim [15]. The model describes how partnership quality, defined by the constructs of trust, business understanding, benefit and risk share, conflict, and commitment, positively

Table 1. Research on the ITO client-vendor relationship

#	Article	Description	Applied Data
(1) Research focusing on explaining parts of the ITO client-vendor relationship models			
1	Rustagi, King [26]	Analyze the influence of task characteristics, client knowledge and trust on formal control	Quantitative
2	Gopal and Koka [13]	Appraisal of relational flexibility (exchange hazards and relation factors) to the descendant's vendor profitability and quality influenced by the type of contract	Quantitative
3	Håkansson and Group [30]	Exploring ITO relationships in terms of the interaction of industrial market and purchasing group (using organizational and individual aspects) surrounded by the environment (like market structure and social system)	Quantitative
4	Goo, Kishore [31]	The model on service level agreements helps to analyze the influence of the formal contract (foundation characteristics like service level objectives or process ownership; change characteristics like future demand management and feedback process; governance characteristics like communication and measurement charter) and the relational governance to the commitment	Quantitative
5	Fjermestad and Saitta [32]	Identify the synergies and success factors (like govern, align to business strategy, management support and as a key factor the economics like cost and quality)	Quantitative
6	Gregory, Beck [33]	The process model, based on control balancing, consists of the two parts "control balancing and evolution in ISD offshoring" (like authoritative control, coordinated control and trust-based control) and "evolution of ISD offshoring client-vendor shared understanding" (like shared understanding deterioration or shared understanding development)	Quantitative
7	Koh, Ang [34]	Appraisal of the supplier obligation (like clear authority structure and taking charge) and the customer obligation (like clear specification and prompt payment) on the perceived outsourcing success	Quantitative
8	Zimmermann and Ravishankar [35]	Analyze the relations of social capital (different dimensions: structural like tie strength; relational like trust; cognitive like shared contextual understanding; efficacy like knowledge transfer efficacy; and outcome expectations like performance) to ability and willingness to transfer knowledge	Quantitative

(continued)

Table 1. (*continued*)

#	Article	Description	Applied Data
9	Søderberg, Krishna [36]	Enhancing the understanding of intercultural collaboration and boundary spanning by trust and transparency, commitment and identification, and cultural understanding and sensitivity	Qualitative
(2) Research focusing on developing a comprehensive ITO client-vendor relationship model			
10	Lee and Kim [15]	Evaluation of several determinants (dynamic factors like participation and information sharing; static factors like age of relationship; contextual factors like top management support) of partnership quality and outsourcing success	Quantitative
11	Paravastu [37]	Building upon trust using the social exchange theory, the author develops a model on the effect of trust and risks on outsourcing constructs including relationship quality and outsourcing success	Quantitative
12	Goles and Chin [17]	Analyze the relationships on interdependence between 11 constructs (six attributes like commitment, consensus, and cultural; and five processes like communication, conflict resolution, and coordination) using the relational exchange theory	Quantitative
13	Blumenberg, Beimborn [27]	Based on the social exchange theory, on the relational exchange theory and on IT business alignment, the model consists of 11 dimensions of relationship quality (interaction determinants like strategic fit; structural determinants like shared benefits/risks, and control mechanisms; contractual determinants like contract completeness; and contextual determinants like interdependence, and service specificity) and 15 relationship quality determinants results (like overall trust, influence and conflict)	Quantitative
14	Galbraith, Downey [38]	The Star model consists of the three components Strategy, Structure, and Process on which the company can based its design choices	Qualitative
15	Kern and Willcocks [14]	Building upon social exchange theory and social contract theory, the authors develop and empirically test an outsourcing relationship model including the categories context, relationship focus (including contract and structure), interactions (between the involved parties) as well as behavior (of the involved parties)	Qualitative

(continued)

Table 1. (*continued*)

#	Article	Description	Applied Data
(3) Research focusing on developing ITO client-vendor relationship process models			
16	Alborz, Seddon [29]	Analyze the influence to outsourcing success as perceived by stakeholders by stages (like pre-contract stage, contract stage and post-contract stage) and operationalization (like outsourcing strategy, due diligence, or contract development)	Quantitative
17	Heiskanen, Newman [12]	Evaluation of the Client-Vendor relationship using the three categories: Trust, Equivocation, and Control	Quantitative
18	Dwyer, Schurr [28]	Estimate the deepen of a relationship (between vendor and client) in four stages (Awareness, Exploration, Expansion, and Commitment) and five sub processes (attraction, Communication and Bargaining, Power, Norms, and Expectations)	Qualitative
19	ISO [39]	The ISO 37500 outsourcing life cycle model, which is one of the major models used in ITO practice, contains 4 phases (outsourcing strategy analysis; initiation and selection; transition; deliver value) as well as one overarching outsourcing governance phase overlapping all four phases	Not applicable

affects outsourcing success. Moreover, the model explains how specific determinants such as participation, information sharing, age of the relationship, and cultural similarity affect the development of partnership quality in general. Building upon this work as a cornerstone, other studies showed how interaction determinants such as strategic fit and communication, structural determinants such as knowledge sharing routings, contractual determinants such as contract completeness, or contextual determinants such as interdependence and service complexity affect relationship quality [27].

The third research stream took a different road. Instead of explaining the ITO client-vendor relationship and it's building blocks, studies within this research stream considered the procedural nature of an ITO engagement. In general, all ITO engagements follow a specific process [28]. This process generally starts with a strategy phase, wherein the client organization defines the goal of the ITO as well as the ITO object ('what to outsource'). Afterwards, the client chooses the vendor organization for the engagement and negotiates a corresponding contract. After a transition and transformation phase, wherein the vendor takes over the IT service, the following steady state (or delivery) phase includes the service delivery of the outsourced IT service by the vendor. Studies taking such a process view on the ITO client-vendor relationship, for example, develop specific knowledge in terms of how each of the phases need to be operationalized (e.g., in terms of governance approach, contract development techniques, etc.) [29].

Our analysis of existing ITO client-vendor relationship models shows the already extensive knowledge on this topic. Nevertheless, none of the existing research explaining the ITO client-vendor relationship integrates innovation-focused aspects such as management activities as well as contextual factors required for innovation generation into their respective model. Building upon current research on innovation in ITO [19–21], we argue that to generate innovation in ITO client-vendor relationships, all phases as well as aspects of an ITO engagement needs to be considered. Therefore, as the cornerstone for our data categorization and analysis, we use the different models and frameworks explaining the ITO client-vendor relationship.

2.2 Innovation in Information Technology Outsourcing Relationships

The traditional goal of ITO is the reduction of the client's overall IT costs [40, 41]. But in the past years, organizations tried to use such outsourcing contracts and client-vendor relationships for gaining and developing new products or services or for optimizing their processes. This so-called *innovation through outsourcing* aims to deliver added value and helps to generate new ideas for organizations with external client-vendor relationships [2, 20].

Surprisingly – and even though it is increasingly acknowledged as an increasingly important topic [1, 2, 42] –, innovation through outsourcing is seldom mentioned as an explicit research gap or phenomenon of interested. However, it is mentioned as a relevant topic in the outsourcing research community, but mostly under the umbrella of other topics. For example, Lacity, Khan [20] identified ITO outcome, especially the strategic outcome of an ITO relationship, as a research topic, which includes innovation through outsourcing engagements [19]. Moreover, a current literature review highlights that innovation serves as an enabler for ITO success as well as an ITO outcome itself [2].

While we know that the client-vendor relationship is important for ITO success in terms of cost reductions [e.g., 15], it also has been shown that the client-vendor relationship has a positive impact on the likelihood of achieving innovations [11, 43]. However, we know next to nothing about what antecedents and factors positively affect such a relationship in order to enable and foster innovation in ITO engagements [43], or if these are the same or different than for cost reduction and more traditional ITO settings.

2.3 IT Outsourcing Relationship Process Model

What we know is that innovations are often understood as a process in organizations [44, 45]. New ideas run through several phases before being implemented. Our research uses these process perspectives as well as the existing models and frameworks explaining the ITO client-vendor relationship quality as a baseline and 'theoretical lens' for data analysis and structuring. Building upon Alborz, Seddon [29] and ISO [39], we apply the process view of an ITO engagement as our high-level structuring element. Specifically, we are using the phases (1) outsourcing strategy, (2) contracting, (3) transition, (4) service delivery and (5) outsourcing governance as the procedural building blocks of our model, which are described briefly in Table 2.

Table 2. Phases of the ITO Relationship Process Model

#	Description	Applied data
1	Outsourcing strategy	The first phase is about the initiation and evaluation of outsourcing opportunities and the establishment of an outsourcing strategy, which meets the business requirements. The result of this phase is the set-up of an outsourcing project
2	Contracting	The second phase is about specification of the requirements for proposed services to outsource, the selection of adequate vendors, and about the establishment of outsourcing contracts
3	Transition	The third phase is about the transition of the services to outsource to the vendor and the enablement of the vendor to establish the delivery capabilities
4	Service delivery	The fourth phase is about the operative business between client and vendor and about the sustainment of the value of the outsourcing engagement
5	Outsourcing governance	The fifth phase is an overarching phase containing the processes, policies and structures between client and vendor. The governance phase is critical for the success of an outsourcing engagement as well as in the client-vendor relationship as it enables the joint leadership to make effective decisions and react to changing business requirements

Figure 1 summarizes the resulting process model including the five structuring elements.

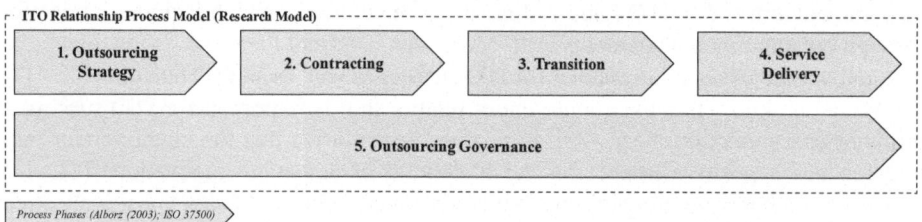

Fig. 1. ITO relationship process model

3   Research Design

3.1   Data Collection

To tackle our research question (*"How does the client-vendor relationship needs to be modelled, structured and managed to foster innovation generation within information technology outsourcing?"*), we apply a mainly qualitative research design building on expert interviews. Our data collection process is twofold: (a) we conducted a systematic literature review to identify innovation-driving factors and (b) we conducted semi-structured interviews with client and vendor experts in ITO to verify existing and identify new innovation-driving factors.

As our baseline for our study, we conducted a concept-driven systematic literature review based on Webster and Watson [46]. Our review included articles from 19 peer-reviewed journals in the years 2001 to 2011. We reviewed each publication by reading their titles and abstracts. We read those articles in detail that deal with innovation, IT innovation, or knowledge sharing. After the forward and backward search, we identified 13 articles, which contain 33 factors innovation-promoting factors in ITO projects.

In the next step, we defined our sampling requirements for the interview partners regarding our research objective and research question. The interview partner must have experiences with ITO projects, especially with a focus on innovation, and our interview partners should belong to one part of a relationship, either client or vendor. Based on our established contacts to practice partners, we identified 16 interview partners. They all have experiences with ITO projects and work either for the client or vendor side. The position and role of the interview partners varied between analysts and directors of the company. Table 3 provides an overview about all interview partner including their position and role, their working experience, and the size of the projects they worked for. The interview lasted between 45 and 120 min. All interviews were tape-recorded, anonymized, and transcribed.

Table 3. Overview about the interview partners

ID	Current position	Experience	Projects
1	Manager (V)	6	9
2	Analyst (V)	1	2
3	Senior Manager (V)	1	4
4	Manager (V)	8	4
5	Divisional Director (C)	20	6
6	Manager (V)	7	2
7	Principal Project Manager (V)	20	4
8	Manager (V)	7	5
9	Project Manager (V)	20	12
10	Consultant (V)	3	3
11	Technology Solution Architect (V)	15	6
12	Director (V)	12	10
13	Service Manager (C)	9	20
14	Manager (V)	5	2
15	Manager (V)	6.5	3
16	Director (V)	16	10

Legend: *Experience* = Years of professional experience | *Projects* = # of ITO projects participated | *C* = Client | *V* = Vendor

All interviews were based on a pre-defined guideline following five consecutive steps. In step 1, we started with a brief introduction of the research project and general information about the interview. In step 2, we explained definitions as well as used concepts to reach a same understanding. Step 3 marks the beginning of the main part of the interview. We described a fictional situation from a project and ask for their opinion about each innovation-promoting factor for verification. The interview partner described their view about each factor and pertained the relevance of the factors by rating them on a 7-point Likert scale (total disagreement – total agreement). Furthermore, we asked each interview partner to explain their relevance rating where possible. In step 4 we asked the interview partners to proposed addition innovation-promoting factors based on their project experience. In step 5, the interview was closed with a brief investigation about the participant's background as well as with a general debriefing for explaining the next steps of the research project.

3.2 Data Analysis

Our data analysis process consists of four working steps including verification of existing innovation-driving factors, ranking of innovation-driving factors, and identification of new innovation-driving factors.

The first step addresses the verification of existing innovation-driving factors identified during the literature review. During the interviews with our study participants, we asked for more information and project experience on each factor. The participants could answer these questions on an optional basis. The additional information and project experiences help to analyze the value of the innovation-driving factors in a real project scenario. For example, one factor ('Geographically and technological distance') has caused some confusion for the interview partners because of the different meaning of geographically and technological meaning. Therefore, we decided to split this factor into two separate ones.

The second step ranks the innovation-driving factors. Each study participant was asked to rate the importance of each factor collected from the literature on a 7-point Likert scale (factor is important: 1: total agreement – 7: total disagreement). We aggregated all results and set up a ranking for all factors as well as for each process phase based on the score of the factors. The ranking represents the relevance of the factors for the study participants to foster innovation in ITO engagements.

The third step is about the identification of new innovation-driving factors, which have not been identified in the literature review. During the interview, the study participants could bring up new factors, which might be relevant in practice from their point of view. We used the descriptive coding based on Miles, Huberman [47] to identify new factors. We consolidated the new factors to gain a redundant-free list of innovation factors. The interviews resulted in three additional innovation-driving factors. We did not identify additional factors during the last five interviews. Hence, we presume that we achieved result saturation [48].

In the fourth step, we assigned all factors into phases of the ITO Relationship Process Model. Two researchers coded the complete data set independently of each other to ensure a high intercoder reliability of 85,6%. We discussed every discrepancy and agreed on a phase for every factor of the list. The outcome is a final list of 37 factors assigned to phases of the process model.

4 Findings

4.1 An Innovation-Driven Process Model for Client-Vendor Relationships in Information Technology Outsourcing

Based on our data collection and data analysis, we developed an innovation-driven process model for ITO client-vendor relationships model composed of five phases. Based on the conducted interviews we identified 37 distinct management factors for driving innovation generation within each phase of the ITO engagement.

While Fig. 2 provides an overview of the process model including the innovation-driving management factors, the remainder of this section provides an overview about each phase including a detailed explanation of the corresponding innovation-related activities.

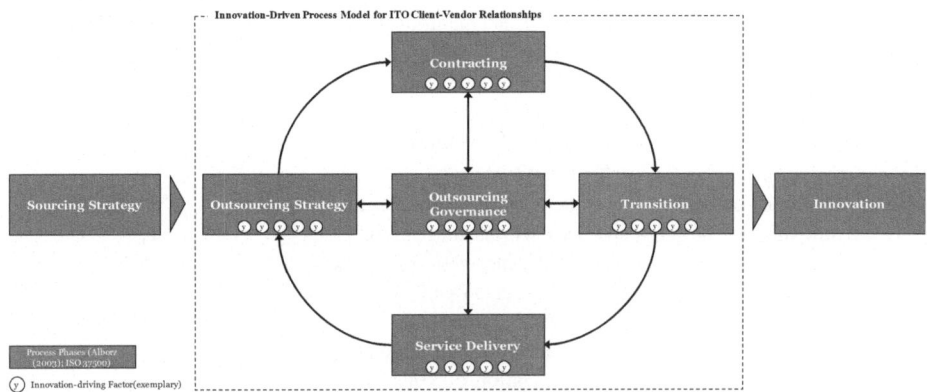

Fig. 2. Innovation-driven process model for ITO client-vendor relationships

4.2 Driving Innovation Within the Outsourcing Strategy Phase

The outsourcing strategy phase is the first phase within an ITO engagement. Within this phase, the client organization develops their outsourcing plan including strategy as well as the definition of the outsourcing target. Table 4 provides an overview of the activities assigned to the outsourcing strategy phase including factor name, description, importance score (based on the interviewee assessment) as well as relevant literature sources.

Within our data collection and analysis, we identified 12 innovation-driving factors associated to the outsourcing strategy phase. These factors generally describe contextual conditions of an ITO engagement. For example, several study participants mentioned the importance of a compatible corporate culture (ID 1.1) between client and vendor for ITO innovation generation. Hereby, a certain corporate culture compatibility is especially important for innovation generation in terms of goal alignment:

Table 4. Outsourcing strategy phase: innovation-driving factors

ID	Factor	Description	Score	References
1.1	Compatibility of corporate cultures	Compatibility of the client and provider's corporate cultures is critical for achieving both parties outsourcing objectives	1.7	Whitley and Willcocks [49]
1.2	Communication between business and IT	Communication between the business and the IT fosters the IT's understanding of the organizational requirements. Hence, lack of communication will make it hard to define a outsourcing project generating innovation and thus business value	2.1	Westerman and Curley [50]
1.3	Strategic portfolio planning	Clear portfolio planning of IT innovations and management of the client's investments positively effects the motivation to generate innovation within outsourcing projects	2.1	Whitley and Willcocks [49], Cui and Loch [51]
1.4	Existence of an innovation outsourcing strategy	A strategy within the client specifies which innovations / parts of the innovation processes should be outsourced. It is important for the client organization to stay targeted in their innovation outsourcing endeavors in the long term	2.3	Cui and Loch [51]
1.5	Tendency to innovate	Provider's tendency to appreciate and stimulate the generation of innovation	2.3	Quinn [52]
1.6	Experience in innovation outsourcing	The client's experience with innovation outsourcing projects. With growing experience, the company develops a concept of how to measure innovation and how to interact effectively with its providers	2.4	Calantone and Stanko [53]
1.7	Complementarity of the knowledge	Complimentary knowledge of the client's and the provider's employees results in greater cooperation and therefore fosters innovation	2.7	Bandyopadhyay and Pathak [54]
1.8	Geographically distance	The degree of interaction and understanding between the client and the provider tends to	3.2	Cui and Loch [51], Kimble, Grenier [55]

(continued)

Table 4. (*continued*)

ID	Factor	Description	Score	References
		increase with the decline in the geographical distance		
1.9	Technological compatibility	The degree of interaction and understanding between the client and the provider tends to increase with the decline in the technological compatibility	3.2	Cui and Loch [51], Kimble, Grenier [55]
1.10	Focus on innovation	Clear focus on innovation, rather than costs, within the outsourcing project	3.3	Willcocks [56]
1.11	IT's contribution to organizational performance	Perception of the IT as a department that contributes to the overall organizational performance within the client company and not just as a cost center	3.4	Westerman and Curley [50]
1.12	Company size	The company's size has a positive impact on the number of innovations. The larger the company, the higher the number and scope of innovations	5.3	Patrakosol and Olson [57]

Legend: *Score* = Ranking on a 7-point Likert scale (1: total agreement – 7: total disagreement) | *Sorting*: Factors are sorted by the score, from 1 to 7

> *"For example, if I have an organization which is listed on the stock market. These organizations tend to think in very short terms, for example the next quarter. This can generally harm innovation [especially if the other involved organization is more long-term focused]."* (Interview 1)

Another important factor describing a contextual condition for generating innovation within ITO engagements is the communication between the business and IT departments (ID 1.2) within the client organization. Several study participants mentioned this type of internal client communication to be of upmost important for innovation generation within an ITO project, especially because of an increased business-IT alignment and therefore an increased understanding of the current business focus within the organization:

> *"The better the IT department is informed about was is going on within the business departments, the better it could channel innovations into the right direction. For example, by providing [IT-driven] innovations, which support value creation and improvements within the core activities [of an employee /department]."* (Interview 2)

In summary, all innovation-driving factors assigned to the outsourcing strategy phase describe contextual conditions, either solely on the client and vendor side or on both sides. It is therefore especially important to notice that to drive innovation within an ITO engagement, the client and vendor organization need to check their own set-up in terms of innovation-readiness prior to conducting an innovation-focused ITO project.

4.3   Driving Innovation Within the Contracting Phase

The contractual relationship between client and vendor is designed and implemented in the contracting phase of an ITO project. Although the development and management of contracts have been well investigated in the past [34, 58, 59], only few studies focus on contracts in regards to innovations [19]. In Table 5 we present an overview about the assigned innovation-driving factors including descriptions, importance scores (based on the interviewee assessment) as well as relevant literature sources.

We identified six innovation-driving factors associated to the contracting phase. The highest ranked one is the 'development of a common vision' (ID 2.1). Several study participants mentioned the importance of a joint vision of how innovations will be generated:

"I think that client and vendor have to agree on a common vision and a common goal. Otherwise, both parties work against each other instead of together." (Interview 11)

Closely connected is the factor 'existence of an innovation agenda' (ID 2.4), which has been identified as a new one during the interviews. The innovation agenda is a written contractual document, which details the common vision and make it visible for client and vendor. It supports both parties to stick to the defined innovation goals in the later phases of the projects.

"[... the common vision] is really important. This would be a kick-off for an innovation agenda, which tells us what to implement for the service delivery. The innovation agenda includes meeting guidelines as well as other guidelines what both parties have to do." (Interview 1)

Another two factors, which are closely related to each other, are 'contract-based risk and rent sharing' (ID 2.2) and the novel factor 'win-win situation' (ID 2.6). [19] showed in a broad study that different types of contracts have a positive influence on the likelihood to achieve innovations in ITO engagements, but all included a joint venture of the client and vendor. Our study participants ranked the contract-based risk and rent sharing as an important innovation-driving factor, which is one way to imitate a joint venture contract:

"[...] the service provider tries to stay as innovative as possible to deliver better services if there are penalty costs or bonus payments." (Interview 15)

Furthermore, a win-win situation in such contracts avoids unforeseen imbalances between both parties.

To sum up, we identified new innovation-driving factors assigned to the contractual phase, which extend the literature. Our study shows that the contractual basis is an important factor for fostering innovations in ITO engagements. Our findings

Table 5. Contracting Phase: Innovation-Driving Factors

ID	Factor	Description	Score	References
2.1	Development of a common vision	A common vision of how innovation will be generated between the client and the provider is necessary to promote an atmosphere of innovation among the employees	2.1	Quinn [52]
2.2	Contract-based risk and rent sharing	A contractual tool allowing risks and rewards of innovation- focused outsourcing projects to be shared and regulated among the parties involved	2.6	Whitley and Willcocks [49], Westerman and Curley [50], Willcocks [56]
2.3	New forms of contract setting	Usage of new contractual elements incentivizing the provider to generate innovation (e.g., an agreement to share knowledge and best practices across outsourcing partners)	2.6	Weeks and Feeny [21], Whitley and Willcocks [49]
2.3	Compatible "Innovation Roadmap"	The "Innovation Roadmap" defines the goals for generating innovation and explains how to reach them (e.g., in which technologies a company is going to invest). If the "Innovation Roadmap" of the client and the provider coincide, innovation is likelier to occur	3.1	Whitley and Willcocks [49]
2.4	Existence of an innovation agenda	(Contractual) agreement between client and provider which defines how innovation will be generated (e.g., monthly innovation workshops)	New	Interview ID #1
2.5	Use of an evaluation catalogue	Usage of an evaluation catalogue compromising innovation-related selection criteria	New	Interview ID #1

Legend: *Score* = Ranking on a 7-point Likert scale (1: total agreement – 7: total disagreement) | *Sorting*: Factors are sorted by the score, from 1 to 7 complement the results of Oshri, Kotlarsky [19] and show that transparent, fair and rewarding contracts are potential factors to drive innovations.

4.4   Driving Innovation Within the Transition and Service Delivery Phase

The ITO relationship model distinguishes between the transition phase and the service delivery phase. The border between those two phases is fluent and the combination is often titled as a post-contract stage [29]. During our coding process, we were not able to assign factors to one specific phase (transition or service delivery). Instead, we realized that several factors could be assigned to both phases. Therefore, we combine the transition and service delivery phase. We provide a brief overview about the assigned factors including the descriptions, importance scores (based on the interviewee assessment) as well as relevant literature sources in Table 6.

We identified eight innovation-driving factors for the transition and service delivery phase. The factors support the client and vendor in their operative project business and support the drive for innovations during operative processes. In the following, we present more details on the three highest ranked factors.

First, our study participants rated the capacity to absorb knowledge (ID 3.1) as one of the top factors in total and as the highest one in this category. It was mentioned that both client and vendor need to be able to absorb knowledge to foster innovations:

> "That is an important factor. We say we need to change it towards this way and it will get better afterwards but the customer tells us that they do it like they always did and nothing changes. No innovation can be generated like this. I belief that both parties have to be open minded." (Interview 1)

A recent study showed similar results using the lens of absorptive capacity and a knowledge-based model for radical innovations [60].

Second, the network and collaboration of the vendor to other clients have been highly ranked as an important factor. This seems a bit obvious as the vendor can profit from experiences with other clients and use their network for developing new ideas. But our study participants mentioned the importance of this factors several times.

Third, Innovations are something new and the more a vendor propose new ideas about any processes, services or products without any requests, the more ideas can be developed into potential innovations. One study participants mentioned that proactivity (ID 3.3) is closely related to flexibility. Both attributes help both client and vendor to work with an outside-the-box thinking.

> "That is what we summarize as flexibility. The employees should question the outside-in-view after 5 years." (Interview 3)

The focus should stick on the development of new ideas instead of just maintaining the status-quo.

Summarized, the operative business in the transition and service delivery phase is a source for driving innovation in ITO engagements. Especially the daily collaboration between client and vendor and the ability to absorb knowledge from each other is a key process. The knowledge exchange and the proactivity are the focus of this phase and play an important role in the whole innovation process.

Table 6. Transition & Service Delivery Phase: Innovation-Driving Factors

ID	Factor	Description	Score	References
3.1	Capacity to absorb knowledge	The ability to recognize the value of new external information, to process this information and to apply it. This process facilitates, for instance, contribution to discussions and development of new ideas	1.6	Weeks and Feeny [21]
3.2	Network and collaboration of the provider	The degree of the vendor's connection to other clients. The higher the degree of the provider's connections, the greater the ability to innovate	1.9	Weeks and Feeny [21]
3.3	Proactivity	A proactive provider is able to anticipate changes in the client's business. It proposes new ideas in order to help the client while taking available resources and costs into account	1.9	Whitley and Willcocks [49]
3.4	Flexible and adaptive relationship	A relationship characterized by flexibility and adaptively allows the employees to think and act out of the box. In order to allow for more flexibility, the client might set goals for the provider but may not determine how to reach these goals	2.1	Willcocks [56]
3.5	Provision of IT-enabling infrastructure	Provision of a certain infrastructure (e.g., innovation centers) has a positive impact on the degree of innovation within outsourcing projects	2.4	Westerman and Curley [50], Quinn [52]
3.6	Continuous information sharing and project execution	Information sharing and project execution on a three-point contact system: (1) Development of vision and strategy, as well as continuous realignment of strategy at the top management level, (2) information sharing with the employees whose careers depend on the relationship's success, and (3) information sharing on an operational level	2.5	Quinn [52]
3.7	"Brokers" to facilitate interaction	Mediators between the client and the provider that translate, coordinate and align the different	3.0	Kimble, Grenier [55]

(*continued*)

Table 6. (*continued*)

ID	Factor	Description	Score	References
		perspectives and the different knowledge of the groups and thus help create a mutual understanding		
3.8	Client's strong leadership	Client's strong leadership is characterized by the ability to handle adaptive challenges, which require changing values, behaviors, beliefs, relationships, and approaches to work	3.6	Willcocks [56]

Legend: *Score* = Ranking on a 7-point Likert scale (1: total agreement – 7: total disagreement) | *Sorting*: Factors are sorted by the score, from 1 to 7

4.5 Driving Innovation Within the Outsourcing Governance Phase

The outsourcing governance phase is related to the whole ITO engagement and addresses all parties and not only the organization of the customer or service provider. It is an overarching phase and the innovation-enabling activities enable both client and vendor to foster innovations in the project without focusing on a specific project phase. Table 7 provides a brief overview about the factors including description, importance score (based on the interviewee assessment) as well as relevant literature sources.

The governance of IT projects is one of the key factors for a successful project implementation [17, 18]. Especially IT projects with an innovation focus rely on a governance model, which consist of a partnership development instead of a strict contractual view [21]. Moreover, the relationship focusses on the exploration of new ideas in order to generate an improved outcome of the projects [21].

We identified 11 innovation-driving activities for the governance phase in total. The three highest ranked ones are 'high level of trust' (ID 5.1), 'top management support' (ID 5.2), and 'establish interfirm and multifunctional teams' (ID 5.3). According to our interview partners from the practice, these activities are the most relevant ones for improving the governance of ITO projects in order to generate innovations. In the following, we will describe and explain the them in detail.

First, our study participants mentioned two situations in which the level of trust (ID 5.1) is especially important: (a) innovations will trigger major changes in the organization and (b) the collaboration of client and vendor is based on differences in cultural patterns. A high level of trust is a key factor for generating innovation in ITO engagements.

> "[...] the customer has to trust us because we dig in deep in the processes or the organization and the customer has to trust us that this is really correct approach we propose. If the customer only thinks that we want to get a follow-up order than it could not work." (Interview 1)

The fact that the 'high level of trust' is the highest ranked factor in our study underlines the importance and key impact on the project governance.

Table 7. Governance Phase: Innovation-Driving Factors

ID	Factor	Description	Score	References
5.1	High level of trust	Innovation outsourcing projects are much more disposed to risk than clearly defined cost-focused outsourcing projects, since the outcome is less specific. Therefore, a high level of trust is a prerequisite for collaborative innovation	1.5	Whitley and Willcocks [49], Bandyopadhyay and Pathak [54], Panteli and Sockalingam [61], Park, Im [62]
5.2	Top management support	Top management support during the entire outsourcing project's life cycle	1.9	Weeks and Feeny [21], Westerman and Curley [50]
5.3	Establish interfirm and multifunctional teams	Teams consisting of client and provider staff, as well as including individuals working in different functional areas, will tend to generate more innovations	1.9	Whitley and Willcocks [49]
5.4	Project closure and evaluation of provider	Evaluation of the provider at the end of the outsourcing project and identification of areas for improvement	2.1	Boehm, Michalik [63]
5.5	Measurement & tracking of IT innovations	This process includes measuring, tracking and publishing of innovations, fosters continuous improvement, supports sustained innovation, and encourages recognition of innovation	2.2	Westerman and Curley [50]
5.6	Innovation trainings	Training programs provide the employees with tools that facilitate an efficient innovation generation process. The training could consist of techniques to moderate and to promote creativity within workshops, aiming to generate new ideas	2.4	Westerman and Curley [50]
5.7	Internal "masters of process"	Individuals or groups of internal employees with specific knowledge and expertise of the company's processes, who are specialized in identifying the best outsourcing partners	2.5	Quinn [52]

(continued)

Table 7. (*continued*)

ID	Factor	Description	Score	References
5.8	Use of boundary objects	A boundary object is an object such as a technology or a set of rules, which serves as a common agreement between the client and the provider. They provide a common understanding, allow for coordination between the groups and might be conjointly developed further	3.3	Kimble, Grenier [55]
5.9	Strategic knowledge management	Utilization of strategic knowledge management systems, which includes processes or infrastructure. The aim of this initiative is to gain, generate and interchange knowledge, in order to formulate a strategy or to take appropriate strategic decisions	3.3	López-Nicolás and Meroño-Cerdán [64]
5.10	Agreed guidelines of interaction (knowledge exchange)	Definition of formal guidelines of interaction (type and extent of knowledge exchange) in order to facilitate the knowledge exchange between the outsourcing partners	3.7	Bandyopadhyay and Pathak [54]
5.11	Effective conflict management	Implementation of flexible conflict escalation and resolution processes to strengthen trust and learning within the relationship, as well as maintain knowledge and innovation generation	3.9	Cui and Loch [51], Panteli and Sockalingam [61]

Legend: *Score* = Ranking on a 7-point Likert scale (1: total agreement – 7: total disagreement) |
Sorting: Factors are sorted by the score, from 1 to 7

Second, the top management support (ID 5.2) is another factor, which enable ITO projects being innovative. Due to our interviews, most ITO projects have a focus on cost reduction instead of innovation topics. The top management supports selected projects to develop innovations overall.

"If budget gets cut and there is a short-term view no innovation can be generated." (Interview 1)

Another aspect which profits from a top management support is the standing of the project in an organization. There are projects with an innovative focus, which differentiate from other projects. Project members need the support to further work in these projects with an open-minded view and without any negative influences from outside the project. The top management support help to project such projects.

Third, multiple interview partners confirmed that interfirm and multifunctional teams (ID 5.3) have a positive effect on the generation of innovation in ITO projects:

"The establishment of interfirm and multifunctional teams lead to more innovation in IT sourcing projects." (Interview 8)

Most interview partners mentioned that the exchange of ideas and experiences is key for being innovative. Both forms interfirm and multifunctional could force this exchange.

In contrast to the most relevant innovation-driving factors, the effective conflict management (ID 5.11) has been ranked as the weakest one. Several interview partners mentioned that the conflict management is more generic process for the governance of IT projects without having a focus on innovations.

"This holds in general. An effective and flexible conflict management is a prerequisite for a working souring project. But I do not see the lever how this is directly connected with innovations." (Interview 5)

To sum up, the governance phase plays an important role in managing an ITO project successfully, especially for projects with an innovation focus. The high level of trust, the top management support as well as interfirm and multifunctional teams have been identified as key aspects to improve the governance of such projects. Both researcher and practitioners should focus on them in order to foster innovations.

5 Discussion

5.1 Contribution to Research

Building on our research question *"How does the ITO client-vendor relationship need to be structured and managed to foster innovation generation?"* we developed an innovation-focused client-vendor relationship model based on existing ones from the literature. Using the results from a literature review as well as our empirical data from interviews, we enhance our knowledge on the creation of innovation within ITO client-vendor relationships by several means.

First, by identifying innovation-driving factors within ITO client-vendor relationships. In total, we identified 37 factors which drive innovation within such relationships. While some of these factors (e.g. *1.1 Compatibility of Corporate Cultures; 2.1 Development of a Common Vision*) are already known in literature [49, 52], other factors were, for the first time, identified within our research project (e.g. *2.4 Existence of an Innovation Agenda*). The identified factors describe how organizations involved in ITO can increase their innovation outcome from ITO client-vendor relationships within each phase of the relationship. To the best of our knowledge, this overview of innovation-driving factors (and activities) is amongst the first available overviews on this important topic. Hence, our identified factor list promotes future research in several ways. On the one hand, we would like to emphasize other researchers to take our innovation-driving factor list as a groundwork and evaluate particular aspects and factors in more detail, for example, by evaluating how the capacity to absorb knowledge (factor 3.1) needs to be shaped in detail to enable innovation generation within ITO client-vendor relationships. On the other hand, future research could also take a broader perspective and evaluate further, based on our factor list, how the set-up of an innovation-focused ITO client-vendor relationship differs from a more cost-focused relationship.

Second, by integrating the identified factors into one comprehensive innovation-driven process model for ITO client-vendor relationships with five different phases. To the best of our knowledge, this is the first model, which focusses on explaining innovation generation within ITO client-vendor relationships. Building upon already existing models (e.g. [14, 39]), we assigned the identified factors into the five outsourcing relationship phases from strategy to delivery. By integrating the identified factors into an overarching model, we provided a preliminary model for explaining the generation of innovation within ITO relationships end-to-end. This model can be used as a groundwork for future research aiming at the development of indigenous ITO theories [20]. As already explained in the introduction and theoretical background part of this paper, driving innovations within ITO relationships is becoming increasingly important for today's organizations. Hence, developing an innovation-driving theory for ITO is an important future research direction for our community. We would like researchers to take our innovation-driving model as a valuable input and enhance as well as detail it through further research. For example, future research could focus on evaluating the relationships between the phases and factors and identify dependencies between the concepts. Furthermore, future research could develop an overarching theoretical framework on how to innovate within relationships based on our overview model.

5.2   Contribution to Practice

In terms of practice, our study provides interesting insights for both client as well as vendor organizations involved in innovation-focused ITO relationships. We developed an integrated, end-to-end model describing the management of innovation within such relationship based on 37 distinct and detailed factors (as well as activities). The implementation of these factors into the ITO relationship management structure and processes could help the client and the vendor to increase the overall innovation generation within the ITO client-vendor relationships.

5.3   Limitations

Although we are confident that our study achieved its pre-defined target and furthermore provides a degree of generalization, our study contains limitations, which are based on both the chosen research method as well as the results from our data collection and analysis.

First, we need to consider the research approach used within our study in general and the level of generalizability. Due to the exploratory nature of our study, we chose a strictly interview-based data collection method. Based on this approach, we could identify a suitable list of innovation-driving factors including descriptions, indications in regards to their effect as well as a preliminary importance ranking. Nevertheless, due to the small sample size within our study, we cannot assume that the identified factors are complete or exhaustive. Hence, to develop a comprehensive and complete list of innovation driving factors including dependencies and relationships between these factors, further research is required.

Second, we need further empirical and conceptual research to enable sufficient theory development. Our findings are mostly descriptive in nature (with some tentative explanations based on inductive reasoning). Therefore, explanatory, and predictive theory needs to be generated. For example, we do not know interaction effects between the factors and phases, or how strong they are. As this study is part of an overarching research project on innovation in ITO client-vendor relationships, the goal of this research project is solely the identification of innovation-driving factors in ITO client-vendor relationships and thereby extending our foundational knowledge related to this important phenomenon. Based on the study results, we are confident that the identified factors permit a certain degree of generalizability. Nevertheless, to enable sufficient theory development, the generalizability of our results needs to be extended by conducting further empirical research.

6 Conclusion

To the best of our knowledge, our study is amongst the first evaluating factors and activities leading to increased innovation within ITO client-vendor relationships. By identifying 37 innovation-driving factors, our study provides an important groundwork for explaining the generation and management of innovation within ITO client-vendor relationships. Furthermore, by categorizing the 37 identified factors into an overarching ITO relationship innovation model, we provided a suitable guideline for driving innovation within each phase of an ITO relationship. This knowledge can be used as an important input for developing indigenous theories on ITO innovation.

References

1. Gartner, I.: Forecast: IT Services, Worldwide, 2013–2019, 2Q15 Update. IT Services Worldwide (2015). https://www.gartner.com/doc/3075522. Accessed 25 Nov 2015
2. Lacity, M.C., Khan, S.A., Yan, A.: Review of the empirical business services sourcing literature: an update and future directions. J. Inf. Technol. (2016). doi:10.1057/jit.2016.2
3. Gartner, I.: Forecast: IT Services, Worldwide, 2014–2020, 3Q16 Update. IT Services Worldwide (2016). https://www.gartner.com/doc/3352451/. Accessed 10 Nov 2016
4. Gartner, I.: Sourcing Strategy Imperatives for 2011: Deliver High Business Value, Leverage Low-Cost IT Services (2012). http://www.gartner.com/id=1537314. Accessed 27 Nov 2015
5. Loch, C.H., DeMeyer, A., Pich, M.: Managing the Unknown: A New Approach to Managing High Uncertainty and Risk in Projects. Wiley, New York (2011)

6. Bloomberg: Google Teams With GM, Honda, and Audi to Bring Android to Cars (2014). https://www.bloomberg.com/news/articles/2014-01-06/google-teams-with-gm-honda-and-audi-to-bring-android-to-cars. Accessed 07 Dec 2016

7. Audi: Google Teams With GM, Honda, and Audi to Bring Android to Cars (2014). https://www.audiusa.com/newsroom/news/press-releases/2014/01/new-roads-ahead-android-open-automotive-alliance. Accessed 07 Dec 2016

8. Ang, S., Straub, D.W.: Production and transaction economies and is outsourcing: a study of the us banking industry. MIS Q. 535–552 (1998)

9. Levina, N., Ross, J.W.: From the vendor's perspective: exploring the value proposition in information technology outsourcing. MIS Q. 331–364 (2003)

10. Pannirselvam, G.P., Madupalli, R.: Antecedents of project success: the perception of vendor employees. Q. Manag. J. **18**(3), 7–20 (2011)

11. Oshri, I., Kotlarsky, J.: Innovation in outsourcing. a study on client expectations and commitment (2011). Warwick Business School and Rotterdam School of Management

12. Heiskanen, A., Newman, M., Eklin, M.: Control, trust, power, and the dynamics of information system outsourcing relationships: a process study of contractual software development. J. Strateg. Inf. Syst. **17**(4), 268–286 (2008)

13. Gopal, A., Koka, B.R.: The asymmetric benefits of relational flexibility: evidence from software development outsourcing. MIS Q. **36**(2), 553–576 (2012)

14. Kern, T., Willcocks, L.: Exploring information technology outsourcing relationships: theory and practice. J. Strateg. Inf. Syst. **9**(4), 321–350 (2000)

15. Lee, J.-N., Kim, Y.-G.: Effect of partnership quality on IS outsourcing success: conceptual framework and empirical validation. J. Manag. Inf. Syst. **15**, 29–61 (1999)

16. Kern, T.: The Gestalt of an information technology outsourcing relationship: an exploratory analysis. In: Proceedings of the Eighteenth International Conference on Information Systems. Association for Information Systems (1997)

17. Goles, T., Chin, W.W.: Information systems outsourcing relationship factors: detailed conceptualization and initial evidence. ACM SIGMIS Database **36**(4), 47–67 (2005)

18. Kern, T., Willcocks, L.: Exploring relationships in information technology outsourcing: the interaction approach. Eur. J. Inf. Syst. **11**(1), 3–19 (2002)

19. Oshri, I., Kotlarsky, J., Gerbasi, A.: Strategic innovation through outsourcing: the role of relational and contractual governance. J. Strateg. Inf. Syst. **24**(3), 203–216 (2015)

20. Lacity, M.C., et al.: A review of the IT outsourcing empirical literature and future research directions. J. Inf. Technol. **25**(4), 395–433 (2010)

21. Weeks, M.R., Feeny, D.: Outsourcing: From cost management to innovation and business value. Calif. Manag. Rev. **50**(4), 127–146 (2008)

22. Chengxun, T., Siew Kien, S.: Managing flexibility in outsourcing. J. Assoc. Inf. Syst. **7**(4), 179–205 (2006)

23. Jin Kim, H., Shin, B., Lee, H.: The mediating role of psychological contract breach in IS outsourcing: inter-firm governance perspective. Eur. J. Inf. Syst. **22**(5), 529–547 (2013)

24. Sirmon, D.G., Hitt, M.A., Ireland, R.D.: Managing firm resources in dynamic environments to create value: looking inside the black box. Acad. Manag. Rev. **32**(1), 273–292 (2007)

25. Williamson, O.E.: The Economic Institutions of Capitalism. Simon and Schuster, New York (1985)

26. Rustagi, S., King, W.R., Kirsch, L.J.: Predictors of formal control usage in IT outsourcing partnerships. Inf. Syst. Res. **19**(2), 126–143 (2008)

27. Blumenberg, S., Beimborn, D., Koenig, W.: Determinants of IT outsourcing relationships: a conceptual model. In: Proceedings of the 41st Annual Hawaii International Conference on System Sciences. IEEE (2008)

28. Dwyer, F.R., Schurr, P.H., Oh, S.: Developing buyer-seller relationships. J. Mark. 11–27 (1987)
29. Alborz, S., Seddon, P., Scheepers, R.: A model for studying IT outsourcing relationships. In: PACIS 2003 Proceedings, p. 90 (2003)
30. Håkansson, H., IMP Group: International Marketing and Purchasing of Industrial Goods: An Interaction Approach. Wiley, New York (1988)
31. Goo, J., et al.: The role of service level agreements in relational management of information technology outsourcing: an empirical study. MIS Q. **33**(1), 119–145 (2009)
32. Fjermestad, J., Saitta, J.A.: A strategic management framework for IT outsourcing: a review of the literature and the development of a success factors model. J. Inf. Technol. Case Appl. Res. **7**(3), 42–60 (2005)
33. Gregory, R.W., Beck, R., Keil, M.: Control balancing in information systems development offshoring projects. MIS Q. **37**(4), 1211–1232 (2013)
34. Koh, C., Ang, S., Straub, D.W.: IT outsourcing success: a psychological contract perspective. Inf. Syst. Res. **15**(4), 356–373 (2004)
35. Zimmermann, A., Ravishankar, M.: Knowledge transfer in IT offshoring relationships: the roles of social capital, efficacy and outcome expectations. Inf. Syst. J. **24**(2), 167–202 (2014)
36. Søderberg, A.-M., Krishna, S., Bjørn, P.: Global software development: commitment, trust and cultural sensitivity in strategic partnerships. J. Int. Manag. **19**(4), 347–361 (2013)
37. Paravastu, N.: Effect of trust and risk on IT outsourcing relationship quality and outsourcing success. Drexel University (2007)
38. Galbraith, J., Downey, D., Kates, A.: Designing dynamic organizations: a hands-on guide for leaders at all levels. In: AMACOM Division of the American Management Association (2001)
39. ISO: International Standard 37500 "Guidance on Outsourcing". International Standards Organization. Geneva (2014)
40. Hoecht, A., Trott, P.: Innovation risks of strategic outsourcing. Technovation **26**(5), 672–681 (2006)
41. Loh, L., Venkatraman, N.: Diffusion of information technology outsourcing: influence sources and the Kodak effect. Inf. Syst. Res. **3**(4), 334–358 (1992)
42. Liang, H., et al.: IT outsourcing research from 1992 to 2013: a literature review based on main path analysis. Inf. Manag. (2015)
43. Kotlarsky, J., et al.: Editorial: Understanding strategic innovation in IT and business process outsourcing. J. Strateg. Inf. Syst. (2015)
44. Tushman, M.L.: Special boundary roles in the innovation process. Adm. Sci. Q. **22**(4), 587–605 (1977)
45. Gassmann, O.: Opening up the innovation process: towards an agenda. R&D Manag. **36**(3), 223–228 (2006)
46. Webster, J., Watson, R.T.: Analyzing the past to prepare for the future: writing a literature review. Manag. Inf. Syst. Q. **26**(2), 13–23 (2002)
47. Miles, M.B., Huberman, A.M., Saldaña, J.: Qualitative Data Analysis: A Methods Sourcebook, 3rd edn. SAGE Publications Inc., Thousand Oaks (2014)
48. Guest, G., Bunce, A., Johnson, L.: How many interviews are enough? An experiment with data saturation and variability. Field methods **18**(1), 59–82 (2006)
49. Whitley, E.A., Willcocks, L.: Achieving step-change in outsourcing maturity: toward collaborative innovation. MIS Q. Executive **10**(3), 95–107 (2011)
50. Westerman, G., Curley, M.: Building IT-enabled innovation capabilities at Intel. MIS Q. Executive **7**(1), 33–48 (2008)
51. Cui, Z., Loch, C.: A strategic decision framework for innovation outsourcing. Int. J. Innov. Manag. **15**(05), 899–930 (2011)

52. Quinn, J.B.: Outsourcing Innovation: The New Engine of Growth. Sloan Management Review (2000)
53. Calantone, R.J., Stanko, M.A.: Drivers of outsourced innovation: an exploratory study. J. Prod. Innov. Manag. **24**(3), 230–241 (2007)
54. Bandyopadhyay, S., Pathak, P.: Knowledge sharing and cooperation in outsourcing projects—a game theoretic analysis. Decis. Support Syst. **43**(2), 349–358 (2007)
55. Kimble, C., Grenier, C., Goglio-Primard, K.: Innovation and knowledge sharing across professional boundaries: political interplay between boundary objects and brokers. Int. J. Inf. Manage. **30**(5), 437–444 (2010)
56. Willcocks, L.: The next step for the CEO: moving IT-enabled services outsourcing to the strategic agenda. Strateg. Outsourcing Int. J. **3**(1), 62–66 (2010)
57. Patrakosol, B., Olson, D.L.: How interfirm collaboration benefits IT innovation. Inf. Manag. **44**(1), 53–62 (2007)
58. Gopal, A., Koka, B.R.: The role of contracts on quality and returns to quality in offshore software development outsourcing. Decis. Sci. **41**(3), 491–516 (2010)
59. Schermann, M., et al.: The role of transaction cost economics in information technology outsourcing research: a meta-analysis of the choice of contract type. J. Strateg. Inf. Syst. **25**(1), 32–48 (2016)
60. Carlo, J.L., Lyytinen, K., Rose, G.M.: A knowledge-based model of radical innovation in small software firms. MIS Q. **36**(3), 865–869 (2012)
61. Panteli, N., Sockalingam, S.: Trust and conflict within virtual inter-organizational alliances: a framework for facilitating knowledge sharing. Decis. Support Syst. **39**(4), 599–617 (2005)
62. Park, J.Y., Im, K.S., Kim, J.S.: The role of IT human capability in the knowledge transfer process in IT outsourcing context. Inf. Manag. **48**(1), 53–61 (2011)
63. Boehm, A.-L., et al.: Innovate on purpose–factors contributing to innovation in IT outsourcing. In: 2014 47th Hawaii International Conference on System Sciences (HICSS). IEEE (2014)
64. López-Nicolás, C., Meroño-Cerdán, Á.L.: Strategic knowledge management, innovation and performance. Int. J. Inf. Manage. **31**(6), 502–509 (2011)

Understanding the Modularization of Business Services: The Maturity of Firms in Bundling Services

Albert Plugge[(✉)] and Harry Bouwman

Faculty of Technology, Policy and Management, Delft University of Technology,
Delft, The Netherlands
a.g.plugge@tudelft.nl

Abstract. Sourcing literature reveals that large firms bundle or unbundle existing business services by means of modularization to achieve organizational agility. However, one may assume that firms need some degree of maturity to manage the complexity that comes along with bundling modularized services. The aim of our research is to understand how modularization interrelates with firm maturity when bundling business services, a topic that has been given limited attention in sourcing literature. Based on an exploratory research amongst 110 firms we found evidence for the relevance of influencing factors on firm maturity in bundling services. The findings provide evidence that the number of business services and the size of the firm correlate with the maturity of the firm. More specifically, our analysis identified that the type of market in which a firm acts (i.e. private or public) and adding the Marketing business function to a bundle does not increase firm maturity. Our empirical research contributes to sourcing literature as we expanded previous research by taking a more in-depth view on business services while providing up-to-date insights.

Keywords: Bundled business services · Modularization · Outsourcing · Maturity

1 Introduction

Sourcing research reveals that large firms apply various sourcing strategies over time to cater for business demands effectively [1, 2]. These sourcing strategies relate to common used business services, such as Finance and Accounting, Procurement, Human Resources, R&D, and Information Technology [3–5] to respond quickly to changing market circumstances [1, 6]. During the past decade firms extended existing sourcing strategies, for example by selecting multiple providers (i.e. multisourcing) or bundling multiple services [1, 7] to achieve organizational agility. However, existing business services can be bundled and unbundled by means of modularization. By bundling various modules (e.g. business services) internally or with an external provider firms are able to achieve their sourcing objectives more effectively, while mitigating the degree of organizational complexity. As a result, modularization can be perceived as a prerequisite to adapt to changing circumstances, while bundling complementary and supplementary services offers advantages in management and governance. When dealing with bundled business services, firms need a certain degree of maturity to manage the complexity that comes along with modularization

© Springer International Publishing AG 2017
I. Oshri et al. (Eds.): Global Sourcing 2017, LNBIP 306, pp. 65–80, 2017.
https://doi.org/10.1007/978-3-319-70305-3_4

and bundling consequences. As this topic has been given limited attention in sourcing literature [1, 8], we need to understand how modularization interrelates with firm maturity when bundling business services. Despite the prominence of bundled business services, a greater understanding is required of the interrelation with firm maturity. As such, the research objective of this paper is to study the interrelation between modularization, bundling services and firm maturity. The contribution of this study is twofold. First, since empirical research on the bundling of modularized business services is scarce, our approach to study modularization endeavors on bundling vis-à-vis firm maturity. Second, this study also contributes to IT sourcing practitioners by increasing the awareness of firms of the relevance of bundling business services and its relation with maturity. Consequently, firms have the opportunity to assess their sourcing strategy and modularization in combination with an assessment of their maturity in managing bundled business services.

2   Literature Background

In an effort to adapt to dynamic circumstances, today, large firms apply a service perspective and transform themselves into a service-oriented enterprise (SOE). [9, p. 39] argue that a SOE 'can be viewed as a particular kind of sourcing arrangement', that comprise both in-house services, which are often established as service services, and outsourced services. The goal of a service-oriented enterprise is to cater for changes effectively that may relate to market, organizational, and technological developments [10, 11]. [5] review of sourcing literature reveals that firms use various sourcing models to provide services (i.e. in-house, shared services and outsourcing) extending [9] from information technology (IT) to business services. The choice to select a sourcing model, however, is affected by the characteristics of a firm, such as their business strategy, degree of risk aversion and internal capabilities, and market attractiveness. As a result of sourcing motivations and transaction attributes firms decide to keep specific functions or tasks in-house so the staff of the firms consciously focus on critical services.

2.1   Modularization

In response to creating organizational agility firms are unbundling their business processes by means of modularization and explore new sourcing arrangements [12]. [13] argues that the concept of modularization is considered as a generic concept, which can be viewed from a content perspective as well as an organization perspective. Some components of a module can be hidden and can be changed or adapted without affecting other modules. Other components of a module need to be visible and might be subject to change as they are interconnected with other modules. In this paper we use the definition of [14] who state that 'a module is a unit of whose structural elements are powerfully connected among themselves and relatively weakly connected to elements in other units'. [15] explored lessons for modularity that were drawn from the outsourcing of knowledge-intensive business services. Their research show that intangibility of services exacerbates the conflicts between clients and service providers, which may hinder innovation initiatives. Advantages of organizational modularity are studied by [16], who focus on the role of dedicated core initiative teams and 'loose coupling' by using rather simple coordination mechanisms. By implementing standardized modules the integration of group tasks and specialization of dedicated teams may create focus and flexibility to cater for changing capabilities. Ultimately, the goal of modularization is threefold: manage organizational complexity, enable parallel work and improvements, and limit the degree of uncertainty. From a SOE perspective, various business functions such as F&A, HR and IT, are supported by services [17]. Therefore, by means of modularization firms are able to bundle and unbundle business services and as such manage organizational complexity [18].

2.2 Bundled Services

[19] argue that firms business functions are bundled in modules in which each module represent a service. For example, the business function Finance and Accounting is modularized and exists of various services such as: Procure to Pay, Order to Cash and Record to Report. Next, services can be bundled or unbundled and subsequently organized internally or outsourced to the market. However, despite the fact that bundling services will contribute to manage complexity, the effort to govern such arrangements will increase significantly as bundling outcomes may vary within and across BPO and ITO services [20]. We define bundled services as 'a combination of business services and IT services that can be organized internally or outsourced to one or multiple service providers to achieve joint value creation and/or cost efficiencies' [based on 7]. A study conducted by [8] reveals that IT infrastructure, IT applications, and accounting are bundled and outsourced to the market representing 70% of the bundling activity. Bundled business processes like billing, finance, and accounting represents 15% of bundling activity. A comprehensive study conducted by [21] underpinned the importance of bundled services, which was reconfirmed in their 2016 study. [7] studied goals of firms in the period 2003–2008 to bundle business functions. Their study shows that based on the bundle '*Application outsourcing and Business process outsourcing*' and the bundle '*Application, IT infrastructure, and business process*' outsourcing firms select a second service provider to deliver services. The sourcing decision to bundle services is influenced by both the characteristics of a firm (e.g. organizational and technological factors), and market circumstances (e.g. regulatory and innovation factors). Taking these factors into account the strategic intent to bundle services is influenced by the experience, skills, and knowledge of a firm to bundle and unbundle business functions. Therefore, we assume that the maturity level of a firm can be seen as being related to the capability to manage bundled services.

2.3 Organizational Maturity

In management literature the organizational context is perceived to be a key determinant for business maturity and performance [22, 23]. Scholars have studied the degree of maturity in management and outsourcing research and identified various key influencing factors, namely: focus on core or non-core activities [24], risk strategies [25], IT and business orientation relationship management [26], governance [27], integration potential [28], and sourcing capabilities [29]. As the performance of an organization is affected by the staff's behavior and quality we may assume that their degree of maturity may differ. As a result, process readiness and business management readiness, which affect organizations' capability to manage business functions, may differ too. A firm's methodological capability is defined as an organization's level of maturity in terms of technical or process-related standards and best practices [30]. We draw on the definition of [31] who define organizational maturity as 'growth stages that are based on the assumption of predictable patterns (conceptualized in terms of stages) that exist in the growth of organizations..., and the diffusion of information technology, p. 280'.

Organizational maturity to bundle or unbundle services will be influenced by the characteristics of a firm. Examples relate to: number and type of business services, type of responsibility (local, regional, global), and geographical reach. Since various business functions including F&A, HR, and Procurement are interwoven with IT, the complexity to manage various type of business functions increases. Hence, clear coordination mechanisms are required to achieve a certain degree of organizational maturity in managing business services. [32] state that organizations do not necessarily demonstrate change by means of a linear sequence of maturity levels, but rather that observed configurations of problems, strategies, structures, and processes will determine a firm's progress. [33] argues that an important feature of maturity levels and their manifestations is to identify transition points that can be used to improve the quality of organizations. Notably, a firm's organizational culture also influences the behavior of an organization [34] and consequently the maturity of an organization.

2.4 Framework of the Study

As prior research on bundling business services is limited [1], a straightforward research model was used for investigating characteristics of a firm and their effect on maturity. The research model, as depicted in Fig. 1, consists of five interrelated constructs. The first

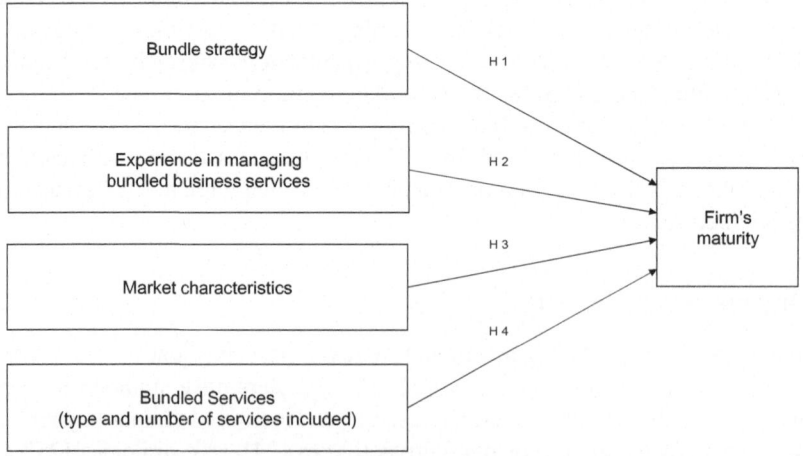

Fig. 1. Research model

embedded element is formed by a firm's bundle strategy. Our basic assumption is that a firm's decision to bundle modularized business services must be derived from a conscious strategy as the type and number of services effects organizational complexity. Therefore, we argue that firms who aim to bundle business services need to be mature in order to be ultimately capable to manage the complexity of bundled business services. [35] argue that business processes, organizational structures, and souring have to be redesigned to create a fit with existing business functions. Thus, we may expect that firms have the experience to manage organizational complexity, which can be considered as a characteristic that impacts the strategic intent of firms to bundling decisions. Consequently, the experience of a firm in managing bundled business services is related to their maturity, which is represented by the second embedded element. Moreover, we may expect that market characteristics influence the ability of a firm to bundle and manage business services effectively. Literature [36] suggests that managers in the public sector are more skillful in handling complex business services, compared to managers in the private sector. Since market characteristics (private or public) determine the degree of competition and cooperation between firms, it is important to understand if market characteristics influence firm maturity in bundling services. When considering bundled services it is assumed that both the type of service (e.g. F&A, HR, IT) and the number of services have an impact on organizational complexity. As such, the type of bundling combination and an increase of the number of services that are bundled may impact firm maturity.

The hypotheses, listed in Table 1, are derived from the research model and the reviewed literature. The hypotheses claim that there is a significant difference in maturity between firms.

The research model will be tested, based on empirical data. We will explain the way we collected data in the next section.

Table 1. Core hypotheses overview

Core constructs	Hypotheses
Bundle strategy	Hypothesis 1: There is a difference in maturity between firms who bundle business services and firms who does not bundle business services.
Experience in managing bundled services	Hypothesis 2: There is a difference in maturity between firms that are more experienced in managing bundled business services and firms that has less experience.
Market characteristics	Hypothesis 3: There is a difference in maturity between firms that act in the private sector and firms that act in the public sector.
Bundled related constructs	Hypotheses
Finance and Accounting as part of a bundle	Hypothesis 4a: There is a difference in maturity between firms that include Finance and Accounting in a bundle and firms that exclude Finance and Accounting.
IT as part of a bundle	Hypothesis 4b: There is a difference in maturity between firms that include IT in a bundle and firms that exclude IT.
HR as part of a bundle	Hypothesis 4c: There is a difference in maturity between firms that include HR in a bundle and firms that exclude HR.
Procurement as part of a bundle	Hypothesis 4d: There is a difference in maturity between firms that include Procurement in a bundle and firms that exclude Procurement.
Marketing as part of a bundle	Hypothesis 4e: There is a difference in maturity between firms that include Marketing in a bundle and firms that exclude Marketing.
Data Analytics as part of a bundle	Hypothesis 4f: There is a difference in maturity between firms that include Data Analytics in a bundle and firms that exclude Data Analytics.

3   Research Method

In order to fathom the maturity of a firm in bundling business services we followed a research approach that focusses on a number of case-firms. Within each case we used a questionnaire to collect data. There are no existing scales to measure our core concepts, so we use the concepts only in an exploratory way. First, we will explain the selection of the cases and the selection of respondents, after which we will discuss the questionnaire used, as well as the way in which the constructs were measured, and the data analysed. The selection criteria were based on the constructs modularization and maturity. First, the variance of business services, i.e. type and number, were taken into account when selecting the firms. Next, we selected firms that started after 1999 in providing services. The selected firms met all criteria. Identifying distinctions between the firms result in valuable observations. Next, we started to execute interviews in the selected firms.

Selection of Respondents
The data was collected on the basis of in-depth face-to-face interviews supported by a web questionnaire that was sent to the interviewees afterwards. The questionnaire was refined during several pre-tests and accompanied by a short cover letter that explained the purpose of the study. The data was collected between 2013 and early 2016. The interviewees that participated in the questionnaire are all responsible for managing multiple services. In total, 110 interviews were conducted, to explain the questionnaire addressing the selected firms on senior management level. Interviewees held positions in the firms like CEO, CIO, CFO, Head of business services, (Senior) Vice President, and director. A small number of respondents had an alternative function description. Their responsibility regarding business services varies, ranging from regional to global responsibility for a varying number of bundled services. Interviews varied from 60 to 90 min in length. Table 2 shows some descriptive data about the selected cases. The international firms under study are acting in a wide range of industries, such as: Pharma, Energy and Utilities, Financial Services, Logistics, Manufacturing, Food and Beverages and Consumer Products. Nine business functions were studied including Finance and Accounting (F&A), Information Technology (IT), Human Resources (HR), Procurement, Marketing, Analytics, Master Data Management (MDM), Customer Care (CC) and Manufacturing.

Web Questionnaire
The questionnaire consisted of four sections, and was sent to the interviewees directly. The questionnaire was accompanied by a short cover letter which summarized the purpose of the study. The first section addressed the organizational context including the organizational structure of business services (e.g. centralized, decentralized, or federative) and reporting lines how business services are managed in practice. The second section investigated the geographical reach in which business services were provided: domestic, regional or global. The third section studied the type and number of business services while the fourth section addressed the driver for bundling services. The questionnaire was refined during several pre-tests. While a vast majority of the questions are identical, minor modifications were made to the questionnaire to fit

Table 2. Example - descriptive information about the selected cases

Case	Industry	Sector	Country	Employees	Number of Business Services	Type of Business Services	Start year Business Services	Geographical reach
Firm 1	Pharmaceutical	Private	USA	500 to 1,000	3	Finance & Accounting, IT, HR	2014	North America, Europe, South America, Asia Pacific
Firm 2	Professional services	Private	Finland	1,001 to 5,000	3	Finance & Accounting, IT, HR	2009	Western Europe
Firm 3	Hospitality	Private	Brazil	5,001 to 10,000	3	Finance & Accounting, HR, Other SG&A	2014	South America, Europe
Firm 4	Chemicals	Private	Brazil	5,001 to 10,000	3	Finance & Accounting, HR, Other SG&A	2009	North America, South America
Firm 5	Energy & Utilities	Private	South Africa	1,001 to 5,000	4	Finance & Accounting, HR, Procurement / Supply Chain,	2010	Middle East & Africa
Firm 6	Education	Public	Netherlands	5,001 to 10,000	5	Finance & Accounting, IT, HR, Procurement / Supply Chain	2012	Europe
Firm 7	Publishing	Private	Netherlands	10,001 to 20,000	5	Finance & Accounting, IT, HR, Procurement / Supply Chain	2009	North America, Europe, Asia Pacific
Firm 8	Manufacturing	Private	Mexico	10,001 to 20,000	3	Finance & Accounting, Procurement / Supply Chain	2009	North America
Firm 9	Government	Public	Netherlands	10,001 to 20,000	5	Finance & Accounting, IT, HR, Procurement / Supply Chain	2014	Europe
Firm 10	Energy & Utilities	Private	USA	20,001 to 75,000	2	Procurement / Supply Chain	2006	South America, Asia Pacific
Firm 11	Diversified Conglomerate	Private	Norway	10,001 to 20,000	3	Finance & Accounting, IT, HR	2007	Europe
Firm 12	Diversified Conglomerate	Private	Panama	10,001 to 20,000	3	Finance & Accounting, Procurement / Supply Chain	2005	South America
Firm 13	Logistics	Private	Australia	1,001 to 5,000	2	Finance & Accounting, IT	2014	Asia Pacific
Firm 14	Energy & Utilities	Private	United Kingdom	10,001 to 20,000	2	Finance & Accounting, HR	2007	Europe, Asia Pacific
Firm 15	Financial Services	Private	Switzerland	5,001 to 10,000	4	Finance & Accounting, HR, Procurement / Supply Chain	2011	North America, Europe, South America, Asia Pacific, Middle East &
Firm 16	Chemicals	Private	Peru	1,001 to 5,000	3	Finance & Accounting, IT, HR	2009	South America

particular departments, terminology and practices. These changes did not affect the basic intentions of the items used. Moreover, considering the need for clarity, and preventing the terminology from being interpreted differently, an explanation of the questions was included, relating to the topics. In addition, maturity infographics were added to the questionnaire to improve the interviewees' understanding. The maturity items were rated on 5-point Likert scales, ranging from: very low (1), below average (2), average (3), above average (4), very high (5).

Data Analyses

All the data is screened on their normal distribution, based on the Kolmogorov-Smirnov and the Shapiro-Wilk tests, and homogeneity of variance based on the Levene's test. Depending on the measurement level of the concepts, a specific statistical test is used. In the case of data that does not meet assumptions of normality we used Mann Whitney tests, in other cases we used t-tests or regression analysis, making use of SPSS.

4   Results

We tested the research model as depicted in Fig. 1. Some hypothesized effects were found significant while other were rejected. With regard to hypothesis 1 our results indicate that the maturity of firms that bundle services consciously as part of their strategy (mdn = 3,00) is significantly higher, compared to firms that do not bundle business services (mdn = 2,30) $U = 460,50$, $Z = -3,724$, $p < 0,001$, $r = -0,33$. This means that the hypothesis was supported. With regard to hypothesis 2, the results show that the maturity of firms that have more than 6 years of experience in managing bundled services (mdn = 3,00; $U = 146,50$; $Z = -0,828$ $p < .03$, $r = -0,21$) is significantly higher than firms that have less experience (mdn = 2,10). Consequently, our hypothesis can be accepted. Furthermore, the analysis show that the maturity of firms that act in the private sector (mdn = 3,10), which relate to hypothesis 3, is similar to firms that act in the public sector (mdn = 300; $U = 673,50$; $Z = -2,237$, ns, $r = -0,09$). Consequently, our hypothesis is rejected. When considering the relationship between the Finance and Accounting function and bundles (hypothesis 4a) we found that the maturity of firms that included F&A in a bundle (mdn = 3,00) is significantly higher compared to firms that excluded F&A (mdn = 2,30; U = 596,50; Z = −3,908, p < .001, r = −0,34). As such, we find evidence for the support of our hypothesis. In contrast our analyses of hypothesis 4b indicate that there is no difference in maturity between firms that included (mdn IT = 2,90) or excluded the IT function in a bundle (mdn = 2,80, U = 1810,00; Z = − 1,501, ns, r = −0,13), which result in the rejection of our hypothesis. With regard to hypothesis 4c we found that the maturity of firms that included HR in a bundle (mdn = 3,10) is significantly higher compared to firms that excluded HR (mdn = 2,60, U = 1333,50; Z = −3,531, p < .001, r = −0,31). Thus, our hypothesis is accepted. Moreover, our analysis of hypothesis 4d show that firms that include their Procurement function in a bundle (mdn Pro = 3,20) are significantly more mature, compared to firms that exclude Procurement in a bundle (mdn = 2,60, U = 1185,00; Z = −4,420, p < .001, r = − 0,39). Hence, our hypothesis is accepted. Furthermore, the results of hypothesis 4e indicate that there is a significant difference between firms that included their Marketing function in a bundle (mdn = 3,10) and firms which excluded Marketing (mdn = 2,85, U = 603,00; Z = −0,473, p < .001, r = −0,04). This means that the hypothesis was accepted. Finally, when addressing hypothesis 4f, our analysis show that firms which included Data Analytics as part of a bundle (mdn = 3,20) are significantly more mature compared to firms that excluded Data Analytics (mdn = 2,80, U = 541,00; Z = −2,380, p < .002, r = −0,21). Consequently, this hypothesis is accepted. The results of the research model is shown in Table 3.

Table 3.   Core relations as tested

Core constructs	Hypotheses	Company maturity (Mann Whitney test)	Effect on difference in maturity
Bundle strategy	Hypothesis 1: There is a difference in maturity between firms who bundle business services and firms who does not bundle business services.	Mdn, = 3.00 vs mdn = 2.30; U =460.50; Z= -3.724, p < .001, r = -0.33	Yes
Experience in managing bundled services	Hypothesis 2: There is a difference in maturity between firms that are more experienced in managing bundled business services and firms that has less experience.	Mdn, = 3.00 vs mdn = 2.10; U = 146.50; Z = -0.828 p < .03, r = -0.21	Yes
Market characteristics	Hypothesis 3: There is a difference in maturity between firms that act in the private sector and firms that act in the public sector.	Mdn, = 3.10 vs mdn = 3.00; U =673.50; Z= -2.237, ns, r = -0.09)	No

Bundled related constructs	Hypotheses	Company maturity (Mann Whitney test)	Effect on difference in maturity
Finance and Accounting as part of a bundle	Hypothesis 4a: There is a difference in maturity between firms that include Finance and Accounting in a bundle and firms that exclude Finance and Accounting.	Mdn F&A= 3.00 vs. mdn non F&A = 2.30; U = 596.50; Z= -3.908, p <.001, r =-0.34	Yes
IT as part of a bundle	Hypothesis 4b: There is a difference in maturity between firms that include IT in a bundle and firms that exclude IT.	Mdn IT= 2.90 vs. mdn non IT = 2.80, U = 1810.00; Z= -1.501, ns, r =-0.13	No
HR as part of a bundle	Hypothesis 4c: There is a difference in maturity between firms that include HR in a bundle and firms that exclude HR.	Mdn HR= 3.10 vs. mdn non HR = 2.60, U = 1333.50; Z= -3.531, p <.001, r =-0.31	Yes
Procurement as part of a bundle	Hypothesis 4d: There is a difference in maturity between firms that include Procurement in a bundle and firms that exclude Procurement.	Mdn Pro= 3.20 vs. mdn non Pro = 2.60, U = 1185.00; Z= -4.420, p <.001, r =- 0.39	Yes
Marketing as part of a bundle	Hypothesis 4e: There is a difference in maturity between firms that include Marketing in a bundle and firms that exclude Marketing.	Mdn Mar= 3.10 vs. mdn non Mar = 2.85, U = 603.00; Z= -0.473, p <.001, r = 0.04	Yes
Data Analytics as part of a bundle	Hypothesis 4f: There is a difference in maturity between firms that include Data Analytics in a bundle and firms that exclude Data Analytics.	Mdn DA= 3.20 vs. mdn non DA = 2.80, U = 541.00; Z= -2.380, p <.002, r =- 0.21	Yes

As a next step in our analysis we decoded a number of variables to dummy variables, basically because they were measured on a nominal or ordinal level. Examples include: type of sector (private or public), number of firm employees provided in classes, geographical regions, and also the services as included or excluded in a bundle. We checked for multi-collinearity, making use of the VIF function to indicate the degree of significance between independent variables [37]. Moreover, tolerance values were defined to check multi-collinearity [38]. All variables included met the required criteria for tolerance ($>.2$) and VIF (>10). We also checked the homogeneity of variance, residuals and linearity. We deleted outliers from the analyses [39]. Consequently, 104 observations could be used. As the data set is relatively small we opt to pairwise exclude cases of the sample to deal with missing values.

Our data contains five (5) firms that can be indicated as high leverage points, meaning that we have to conduct additional analyses to see if they influence the regression model. First, we measured the standardized difference between independent variables by means of a standardized DF Beta analysis to indicate if these five firms influence the model parameters. Based on the measurements we concluded that the five cases did not influence the model as a whole. Second, based on Cook's distance analyses (highest value is 0.19) we find evidence that the five cases do not affect the model. From a leverage value perspective we also tested the five cases to determine if a single case influences the model. [40] argue that if the leverage-value is higher than $(3 * (k + 1)/N)$, in which k indicates the number of predictors and N the number of the sample, an individual case influences the model significantly resulting in an additional analyses. By conducting this third step we find that the highest leverage value is 0.11 which means that no evidence was found that the model was affected. Fourth, by using Mahalanobis distance we find that based on 4 predictors and a sample of approximately 100 cases the highest value is 7, which is far below 18. The latter is seen as a critical level to conduct additional research. Finally, to measure if a single case influences the variance of regression coefficients we used the covariance ratio. Table 4 shows that all values that were found are lower than the critical value (0.85), which means that the influence of the cases are not significant.

Table 4. Results of high leverage points

Case	Standardized DF Beta constant	Standardized DF Beta (number of bundled services)	Standardized DF Beta (Private firm versus Public firm)	Standardized DF Beta (Marketing excluded versus included)
Firm 2	0.06	-0.11	0.07	0.18
Firm 6	0.61	-0.82	0.23	0.51
Firm 14	0.09	-0.09	-0.02	-0.06
Firm 17	-0.20	-0.10	0.14	0.13
Firm 87	-0.17	-0.09	0.12	0.11

Case	Standardized DF Beta (0 - 5,000 employees or 20,000 and more)	Cook's Distance	Leverage Value	Mahalanobis Distance	Covariance Ratio
Firm 2	-0.44	0.06	0.03	1.91	0.63
Firm 6	-0.48	0.19	0.11	6.82	0.68
Firm 14	0.35	0.04	0.03	1.91	0.78
Firm 17	0.26	0.04	0.01	0.88	0.64
Firm 87	0.22	0.03	0.01	0.88	0.75

As we opted to conduct an explorative study a stepwise regression was used. The results of the regression analysis is shown in Table 5. The first step of the stepwise method exists of the constant combined with the 'number of bundled business services' resulting in 26% explained variance ($R^2 = 0.26$). Next, we combined the dummy's number of bundled business services, Market characteristics, and Marketing excluded from a bundle versus included, resulting in an increase of the explained variance to 41% ($R^2 = 0.41$). Finally, in the third step the constant, the number of bundled business services, Market characteristics, Marketing excluded from a bundle versus included, and the dummy number of employees were included. The explained variance increased further to 46%.

Table 5. Stepwise regression

	Beta	Standard Error Beta	Standardized Beta
Step 1			
Constant	2.26	0.15	-
Number of Business Services	0.21	0.05	0.51***
$F = 21.76 \ (p < 0.001)$			
$R^2 = .26$			
Step 2			
Constant	2.17	0.14	-
Number of Business Services	0.29	0.05	0.69***
Market characteristsics (Private firm with Business Services versus Public firm with Business Services)	-1.18	0.33	-0.37**
Marketing excluded from a bundle versus included	-0.70	0.29	0.27*
$F = 14.37 \ (p < 0.001)$			
$R^2 = .41$			
Step 3			
Constant	2.05	0.15	-
Number of Business Services	0.29	0.05	0.69***
Market characteristsics (Private firm with Business Services versus Public firm with Business Services)	-1.12	0.41	-0.26**
Marketing excluded from a bundle versus included	-0.74	0.28	-0.28*
Number of employees (0 to 5,000 versus 20,000 employees or more)	0.32	0.15	0.21*
$F = 12.59 \ (p < 0.001)$			
$R^2 = .46$			

* $p < .05$ ** $p < 0.01$ *** $p < 0.001$

5 Discussion

5.1 Constructs

When discussing the construct *Bundle strategy* our results indicate a correlation between the strategy of firms to bundle business services and a perceived degree of maturity. This finding may assume that firms that apply this strategy may achieve a higher degree of organizational effectiveness. Sourcing literature [41] illustrate that firms that put effort in developing and shaping a sound sourcing strategy are more able to outsource operational tasks while mitigating risks. This implies that firms need some degree of maturity to deal with complex arrangements. The survey results of the firms' *experience in managing bundled services* show that the degree of experience in managing multiple business services correlate with their maturity. The interviews as well as the questionnaire data demonstrate that the vast majority of firms started with centralization of business services by means of implementing SSCs. Based on previous research [42], we argue that firms that originally set up modularized business services already gained experience in managing complex services. As such, firm experiences influenced their maturity level positively. With regard to the construct *Market characteristics* we found no difference in maturity between private and public firms. We assumed that there would be a difference as firms that act in the public sector have better process management skills to deal with organizational complexity [36], which, in turn, influence the maturity level of firms positively. An explanation might be the limited number of public firms that were part of the survey. An equal percentage of private and public firms might show other insights. Regarding the construct *Finance and Accounting* our research demonstrate that when the F&A function forms a part of a bundle this correlates with the level of firm maturity. An explanation for this finding could be that F&A was one of the first business functions that was organized by means of a shared service center [6]. We may assume that since then firms have built dedicated capabilities and have gained experience in managing complex services. Consequently, their maturity increased over time. The results show no difference in maturity when firms include or exclude the construct *IT* as part of a bundle business services. The fact that no significant differences were found could be explained by previous insights in management concerns, relating to IT. Based on an extensive survey [26] found a number of business-IT related concerns, including business-IT alignment, increase business agility and managing influential technologies (i.e. Business Intelligence, cloud computing). We may assume that if firms are able to deal with these concerns effectively, their degree of maturity will increase.

With respect to the constructs *HR, Procurement, Marketing, Data Analytics*, our research shows significant differences in correlations between these functions and firm maturity. It may be assumed that these type of services can be characterized as knowledge-intensive, which is a prerequisite to support primary business processes. Literature [43] reveal that firms that include knowledge-intensive business services as part of their strategy are more ready to apply innovation. As such, these firms should be mature enough to manage organizational complexity. Another explanation might be the influencing role of capabilities. Bundling multiple business services implies that firms have to accumulate specific capabilities that can only developed over a long period of time (i.e. path dependency). This is consistent with [44] who studied bundled services from a multisourcing perspective. They argue that the replication of client specific capabilities takes significant time and effort. As a result, the presence of firm specific capabilities assume a certain degree of maturity to manage business services effectively.

When interpreting the results of the regression analysis we focus on step 3 as we used the stepwise method in particular. Based on the standardized regression coefficients the research shows that the number of business services has the strongest impact on maturity. An increase of business services correlates with a higher degree of maturity.

In the second step the dummy Market characteristics and Marketing were included. We found a negative linear relationship between these variables and maturity. This means that the maturity of a firm acting in the public market is lower, compared to a firm in the private market. The same goes for the Marketing function, as adding this function to a bundle does not increase firm maturity. Finally, addressing the size of the firm, we find a positive linear relationship to the level of firm maturity. Based on the outcome of the regression model the R^2 measure of 0.46 indicate that 46% of the data is predicative. This fits with our aim to conduct a highly exploratory study. The final regression function can be constructed as:

Maturity of business services = 2.05 + 0.29 (number of business services) – 1.12 (public or private firm with business services) – 0.74 (marketing as part of business services) + 0.32 (>20.000 employees).

In other words the maturity of firms in managing business services correlate with the number of business services included and the size of the firm. With regard to the number of business services our interviews revealed that before the bundling process firms modularized services by means of separate entities (i.e. shared service centers). As a next step firms gradually added services to a bundle to deal with organizational complexity. This finding is related to previous research [7] in which the authors call for more research why firms gradually bundle services over time. With regard to the size of the firm we argue that specifically large private-oriented firms have the capacity to attract highly skilled personnel with the experience to deal with the complexity of managing bundled services. Moreover, we may assume that large firms are more able to develop capabilities to support bundled services compared to smaller firms. As the research objective of this paper is to study the effects of bundling business services on firm maturity we used variance tests and regression analysis. Both analyses demonstrate that private-oriented firms are more mature compared to public-oriented firms. More-over, firms with a high number of employees are more mature compared to smaller sized firms. However, our study reveals significant differences between both analyses. Variance tests show that firms that bundle business services are more mature compared to firms that manage a single type of service. The same goes for the functions Finance and Accounting, HR, Procurement, and Data Analytics that are more mature compared to firms that exclude these functions in a bundle.

These differences do not show up in the results of the regression analysis. It can be argued that these differences in analyses are due to other effects. Mann-Whitney variance tests are based on bi-variate relationships, which exclude other effects as is the case in using regression tests. Another difference between both tests lies in the Marketing function. Variance tests show that firms that include Marketing are more mature compared to firms that exclude Marketing in a bundle. This result is in contrast with the regression test that illustrates that including Marking in a bundle does not lead to a higher maturity. An explanation can be found in the way in which the variables are tested. When using regression analysis the variables under study are tested without changing other variables. This means that the other variables are seen as constant and only the partial correlation between the two variables is tested which are controlled by the other constant variables, as is not the case when conducting variance tests. We may argue that the outcome of the regression test is, therefore, more robust compared to the variance test.

5.2   Implications for Practice, Limitations and Suggestions for Further Research

Addressing the managerial implications, firms' executive management should develop a conscious bundling strategy taking the studied influencing factors into account. By gradually adding business services to a bundle, managers are able to strengthen their capabilities and redesign their organizational structure. As such, they are able to manage organizational complexity while limiting the degree of uncertainty. Importantly, firms should modularize their business services first as a prerequisite to bundle and unbundle business functions. Moreover, firms should develop processes to cater for changing circumstances when business services are added or removed of a bundle.

Our study identifies multiple issues that require further research. First, considering the managerial complexity of bundled services we recommend more detailed research to the effects of establishing relationships between business departments (demand-oriented) and delivery units (supply-oriented). Relevant topics are related to the effects of managing bundles services on existing or new type of sourcing capabilities and governance mechanisms. Second, a limitation is imposed by the unbalanced response to what extent sourcing modes are provided in-house (i.e. shared service centers) or outsourced to the market. We suggest that future research will examine this effect and their influence on firm maturity in more detail. Third, in future research, a more extensive survey among firms is helpful to develop our model further in order to generalize the results. Future empirical research is necessary to study the relationships between the variables and their effect on firm maturity. To really understand causal mechanisms a longitudinal research approach is necessary. In this paper we only try to focus on covariance and we refrained from statements implying effects or impacts, being aware that effects may also be inverse to what is proposed in the research model. In addition, scholars may create insights in how bundled services have an impact on firm effectiveness and performance. Future research could examine this effect.

6   Conclusions and Contribution

The aim of this research was to study the effects of modularization and, next, bundling services on firm maturity in the context of business services. Based on a questionnaire and in-depth face-to-face interviews we found evidence for the relevance of influencing factors. Although directed on model testing, this research is highly exploratory. The results as presented in this paper are a first attempt to interpret bundling effects on firm maturity. The findings provide evidence that the number of business services and the size of the firm correlate with the maturity of a firm.

Since empirical research on the bundling of modularized business services is scarce, our contribution of this study is threefold. First, the vast majority of research on business services studied individual sourcing modes (i.e. shared services centers or outsourcing services). We studied various influencing factors from a holistic perspective (i.e. complementary sourcing modes) and relate the outcome of bundling effects to firm maturity. This is contrary to previous research that studies bundling effects from an outsourcing perspective [7]. Secondly, as the topic of modularization of business services is under-researched, our study contributes to partially filling this gap by studying specific business services in more detail and explain bundling effects on firm maturity. Third, this study also contributes to IT sourcing practitioners by increasing the awareness of the relevance of bundling various business services and its effect on maturity. We expanded previous research of [7], who studied bundled ITO/BPO services in the period 2003 and 2008 by taking a more in-depth view on business services and provided actual insights.

Acknowledgement. The authors wish to thank Thomas d'Hooghe and Kris Goudriaan for their preliminary work and pretests of the data.

References

1. Lacity, M.C., Willcocks, L.P.: Advanced Outsourcing Practice: Rethinking ITO, BPO and Cloud services. Palgrave Macmillan, London (2012)
2. Oshri, I., Kotlarski, J., Willcocks, L.P.: The Handbook of Global Outsourcing and Offshoring, 3rd edn. Palgrave Macmillan, London (2015)
3. Wegener, A.: Kommunale Dienstleistungspartnerschaften. Mit Shared Services zu einer effektiveren Verwaltung. Bertelsmann, Gütersloh (2007)
4. McIvor, R., MacCracken, M., McHugh, M.: Creating outsourced shared services arrangements: lessons from the public sector. EMJ **29**(6), 448–461 (2011)
5. Lacity, M.C., Khan, S.A., Yan, A.: Review of the empirical business services sourcing literature: an update and future directions. J. Inf. Technol. **31**(3), 269–328 (2016)
6. Ulbrich, F., Borman, M.: Preventing the gradual decline of shared service centers. In: Proceedings of the Eighteenth Americas Conference on Information Systems, Seattle, 9–12 August 2012
7. Willcocks, L.P., Oshri, I., Hindle, J.: Best-of-breed versus bundled services. Rethinking ITO, BPO and Cloud Services. In: Lacity, M.C., Willcocks, L.P. (eds.) Advanced Outsourcing Practice. Palgrave Macmillan, London (2012)
8. Willcocks, L.P., Oshri, I., Hindle, J.: To bundle or not to bundle? Effective decision-making for business and IT service, Research paper Accenture in association with London School of Economics (2009)
9. Janssen, M., Joha, A.: Emerging shared service organisations and the service-oriented enterprise: critical management issues. Strat. Outsourcing Int. J. **1**(1), 35–49 (2008)
10. Cherbakov, L., Galambos, G., Harishankar, R., Kalyana, S., Rackham, G.: Impact of service orientation at the business level. IBM Syst. J. **44**(4), 653–668 (2005)
11. Iansiti, M., Levien, R.: The Keystone Advantage: What the New Dynamics Of Business Ecosystems Mean for Strategy, Innovation, and Sustainability. Harvard Business School Press, Boston (2004)
12. Quinn, J.B.: The intelligent enterprise a new paradigm. Acad. Manag. Exec. **19**(4), 109–121 (2005)
13. Arsanjani, A.: Developing and integrating enterprise components and services. Commun. ACM **45**(10), 30–34 (2002)
14. Baldwin, C.Y., Clark, K.B.: Design Rules: The Power of Modularity. MIT Press, Cambridge (2000)
15. Miozzo, M., Grimshaw, D.: Modularity and innovation in knowledge-intensive business services: IT outsourcing in Germany and the UK. Res. Policy **34**, 1419–1439 (2005)

16. Martin, J.A., Eisenhardt, K.M.: Cross-business synergy: recombination, modularity and the multi-business team. Acad. Manag. Proc. **1**, 1–6 (2003)
17. Goldstein, S.M., Johnston, R., Duffy, J., Rao, J.: The service concept: the missing link in service design research? J. Oper. Manag. **20**, 121–134 (2002)
18. Versteeg, G., Bouwman, W.A.G.A.: Business architecture: a new paradigm to relate business strategy to ICT. Inf. Syst. Front. **8**, 91–102 (2006)
19. Bapna, R., Barua, A., Mani, D., Mehra, A.: Cooperation, coordination, and governance in multisourcing: an agenda for analytical and empirical research. Inf. Syst. Res. **21**(4), 785–795 (2010)
20. Basole, R.C., Rouse, W.B.: Complexity of service value networks: conceptualization and empirical investigation. IBM Syst. J. **47**, 53–70 (2008)
21. Lacity, M., Khan, S., Yan, A., Willcocks, L.P.: A review of the IT outsourcing empirical literature and future research directions. J. Inf. Technol. **25**(4), 395–433 (2010)
22. Child, J.: Organization: A Guide To Problems and Practice. Harper & Row, London (1984)
23. Galbraith, J.R.: Designing Organizations: An Executive Guide to Strategy, Structure, and Process. Jossey-Bass, San Francisco (2002)
24. Lacity, M.C., Willcocks, L.P.: Global Information Technology Outsourcing: In: Search of Business Advantage. Wiley, Chichester (2001)
25. Gewald, H., Dibbern, J.: Risks and benefits of business process outsourcing: a study of transaction services in the German banking industry. Inf. Manag. **46**, 249–257 (2009)
26. Luftman, J., Zadeh, H.S., Derksen, B., Santana, M., Rigoni, E.H., Huang, Z.: Key information technology and management issues 2011–2012: an international study. J. Inf. Technol. **27**, 198–212 (2012)
27. Kim, H.J., Shin, B., Lee, H.: The mediating role of psychological contract breach in IS outsourcing: inter-firm governance perspective. Eur. J. Inf. Syst. **22**(5), 529–547 (2013)
28. Lavikka, R., Smeds, R., Jaatinen, M.: Coordinating the service process of two business units towards a joint customer. Prod. Plan. Control **20**, 135–146 (2009)
29. Plugge, A.G., Bouwman, W.A.G.A., Molina-Castillo, F.J.: Outsourcing capabilities, organizational structure and performance quality monitoring: towards a fit model. Inf. Manag. **50**(6), 275–284 (2013)
30. Bardhan, I., Mithas, S., Lin, S.: Performance impacts of strategy, information technology applications, and business process outsourcing in US manufacturing plants. Prod. Oper. Manag. **16**(6), 747–762 (2007)
31. Wiener, M., Saunders, C.: Forced coopetition in IT multi-sourcing. J. Strat. Inf. Syst. **23**(3), 210–225 (2014)
32. Kazanjian, R.K., Drazin, R.: An empirical test of a stage of growth progression model. Manag. Sci. **35**(12), 1489–1503 (1989)
33. Burn, J.M.: Information systems strategies and the management of organizational change - strategic alignment model. J. Inf. Technol. **8**(4), 205–216 (1993)
34. Cameron, K.S., Quinn, R.E.: Diagnosing and Changing Organizational Culture. Jossey-Bass, San Francisco (2006)
35. Lacity, M.C., Fox, J.: Creating global shared services: sourcing lessons from Reuters. In: Willcocks, L.P., Lacity, M.C. (eds.) The Practice of Outsourcing. Palgrave Macmillan (2009)
36. Kakabadse, A., Kakabadse, N.: Outsourcing in the public services: a comparative analysis of practices, capabilities, and impact. Pub. Adm. Dev. **21**, 401–413 (2001)
37. Myers, R.H.: Classical and Modern Regression with Applications. PWS-KENT, Boston (1990)
38. Menard, S.: Applied Logistic Regression Analysis. Thousand Oaks, SAGE (2002)

39. Chatterjee, S., Hadi, A.S.: Influential observations, high leverage points, and outliers in linear regression. Stat. Sci. **1**(3), 379–393 (1986)
40. Stevens, J.P.: Applied Multivariate Statistics for the Social Sciences, 5th edn. Routledge, New York (2012)
41. Aubert, B.A., Beaurivage, G., Croteau, A.-M., Rivard, S.: Firm strategic profile and IT outsourcing. Inf. Syst. Front. **10**(2), 129–143 (2008)
42. Borman, M.: Applying multiple perspectives to the BPO decision: a case study of call centres in Australia. J. of Inf. Tech **21**, 99–115 (2006)
43. Doloreux, D., Shearmur, R.: Innovation strategies: are knowledge-intensive business services just another source of information? Ind. Innov. **20**(8), 719–738 (2013)
44. Su, N., Levina, N.: Global multisourcing strategy: integrating learning from manufacturing into it service outsourcing. IEEE Trans. Eng. Manag. **58**(4), 717–729 (2011)

Software Bots - The Next Frontier for Shared Services and Functional Excellence

Vipin K. Suri[1], Marianne Elia[1], and Jos van Hillegersberg[2(✉)]

[1] Shared Services International Inc., Mississauga, ON, Canada
{vipinsuri,mariane.elia}@ssinsights.com
[2] Faculty of Behavioural, Management and Social Sciences, Industrial Engineering and Business Information Systems, University of Twente, Woodbridge, ON, Canada
j.vanhillegersberg@utwente.nl

Abstract. A Software Bot is a fundamental element of Robotics Process Automation (RPA). RPA can be deployed to automate repeatable, mundane, rules-based work-flowed process tasks across multiple functions in an organization, including Shared Services. While RPA holds high promise, using Software Bots for process automation is not straightforward. The purposes of this research are to (1) examine where Software Bots currently are being deployed in Shared Services organizations and (2) understand the business case, drivers and challenges. We conducted a survey involving Shared Services leaders, functional leaders and RPA experts and discuss the best practices for analysing and optimizing the business benefits of implementing Software Bots. The majority of the companies surveyed have limited application of Software Bots in automating their business processes and are finding difficulties in quantifying tangible savings and identifying cost of implementation. Based on these results we identify functional processes which are candidates for automation using Software Bots and outline implementation steps to automate processes beyond business process optimization.

Keywords: Shared Services · Functional services · Robotic Process Automation · Software Bots

1 Introduction

Robotic Process Automation (RPA) is the concept of using a software platform of "virtual robots" to manipulate existing application software in the same way that a human does to process a transaction [1]. Imagine a world in which the meaning of "work" has been redefined for millions of people. Where our service economy can actually focus on providing services, delivered by an engaged talent pool that is innovating such services. In this new world, work would no longer be a "four-letter word" associated with functioning within repeatable systems with mundane transactional processes. Instead, this other world would have workers who re-think end-to-end processes on a more holistic level with the goal of simultaneously impacting several factors: quality, efficiency, cost-effectiveness, functionality, customer satisfaction and compliance while creating remarkable delivery of business support services. 2015 was to RPA what 1994

© Springer International Publishing AG 2017
I. Oshri et al. (Eds.): Global Sourcing 2017, LNBIP 306, pp. 81–94, 2017.
https://doi.org/10.1007/978-3-319-70305-3_5

was to the Internet - an auspicious start, but we haven't seen anything yet. Thanks to RPA, we are well on our way to creating the business operations of the future. However, none of us can really predict just how revolutionary it will be [2].

Using a combination of literature study, discussions with RPA experts, survey and in-depth interviews we address the following research questions:

1. What is the value potential of process automation using Software Bots?
2. How is the business case approved and by whom?
3. Which processes have been automated using Software Bots and in what functional areas of Shared Services organizations?
4. What are the challenges with implementing Software Bots in Shared Services organizations?
5. What benefits have been achieved by using Software Bots in Shared Services organizations?

This paper is organized in following sections: Sect. 1 has just provided an introduction to Robotic Process Automation and set the stage for our study. Section 2 is a review of literature related to Software Bots and RPA. Section 3 presents data collection methods. Section 4 provides findings and analysis of data collected and Sect. 5 outlines the conclusions and future research.

2   Literature Review

There is often a tension between business operations needs and the allocation of IT resources. While the overarching mandate of an organization is to improve service and reduce costs, the resources and priorities of the two groups are often misaligned. This can result in constrained business growth and performance. Willcocks and Lacity conclude that in pursuit of reduced costs and improved services, businesses have transformed over the past few decades using the principles of Centralization, Standardization, Optimization, Relocation and Technology Enablement. The researchers conclude that the next logical step is to automate [3]. For most businesses, the best candidates for automation are often "back office" processes, where the goal is to provide faster, customer focused service to customers and to reduce high processing costs and error rates; these are processes that are mundane and require entering repetitive data into multiple systems where the systems don't talk to each other [4].

Back offices are where the operational support systems for services are created, managed, and delivered. Back offices are always under pressure to contain costs in highly competitive industries like insurance and financial services, but cost efficiency must be balanced with other performance imperatives such as service excellence, business enablement, scalability, flexibility, security, and compliance. From years of research on back offices, we have learned that low-performing back offices can be transformed to high-performing back offices through six transformation levers: centralized physical facilities and budgets, standardized processes across business units, optimized processes to reduce errors and waste, work relocation from high cost to low cost destinations, technology enablement with, for example, self-service portals, and automate services [3].

The business disruption caused by artificial intelligence and related technologies (cognitive, machine learning and RPA) is already here and more business disruption is on the way. In 1999, the big business disruption was the use of offshoring to create labor arbitrage. The new disruptor is automation arbitrage, a term Gartner is using to describe the recalibration of human labor to drive business outcomes. The initial low-hanging fruit in this arena is RPA. It is relatively low cost, quick to implement and unobtrusive; thus it starts what will likely be one of the most important conversations in the next five years regarding how automation will change the value proposition in all organizations [5].

Major business functions that offer opportunities for process improvement through RPA include supply chain management, sales, finance and accounting, and human resources. RPA is ideal for preventing error rates, reducing variability, improving cycle time, and increasing productivity in processes that follow a standard procedure with minimal deviation. Software Bots can perform repetitive, monotonous, high-volume tasks, freeing workers to focus on activities that require higher-order thinking. High-volume bulk processing functions within tools such as enterprise resource planning (ERP) systems or core databases are ideal candidates for RPA, as are desktop applications and workflows that require information gathering from multiple sources. For tasks too small and diverse for IT changes, RPA offers an alternative to outsourcing and offshoring [6].

Finance functions are under significant pressure across all industries and specifically in the financial services sector. Some of the major challenges in the financial services sector are to reduce costs and support decreasing margins, to improve speed, volumes and quality of information provided to focus on delivery of value adding insights to the business. The RPA implementation burdens (costs and timelines) are relatively insignificant, compared to major IT platform updates. Therefore, it is likely that RPA will quite quickly convert from a differentiator delivering a competitive advantage to a standard practice that needs to be followed for survival. RPA provides a competitive advantage by helping to meet today's challenges by radically improving cost efficiency under growing pressure on costs, helping to remain in control in the constantly changing environment and allowing to focus skilled resources on driving value creation for the business. RPA is quickly evolving into a new hot topic in the Finance world as significant potential has become evident. And most of large players in the financial services sector are either assessing possibilities to benefit from RPA or even proceeding with the first implementations [7].

Finance leaders obsess about transformation levers - people, process and technology. However, today's solutions save the requisite investment in an expensive ERP platform, have typically leaned heavily on the equation of people and process. Less expensive resources located offshore delivering transactions, plus added process improvement equals significant savings. Up until now the technology component has mainly been limited to communication widgets that facilitate workflow and e-invoicing.

RPA is the application of flexible tools to automate manual activity for the delivery of business processes or IT services. It is most applicable to rules driven, data-intensive processes that are repetitive in nature. They can cross multiple systems, and include multiple decision points/calculations. They require an electronic input or trigger to commence working, yet the underlying technologies are still emerging, each taking a different approach [8]. RPA is a way to automate repetitive and often rules-based processes. These transactional processes are typically located within a Shared Services centre or another part of the back office. Software, commonly known as 'Robot' or "Bot", is used to capture and interpret existing IT applications to enable transaction processing, data manipulation and communication across multiple IT systems. Multiple robots can be seen as a virtual workforce, working as a back-office processing centre but without the human resources. Software Bots undertake processes similar to human counterparts and can work on multiple processes just like a Shared Services staff member can learn to work on an accounts payable process and a travel and expenses process. The robots use a 'virtual machine' and dedicated logins to interact with different applications and systems in the same way as human teams [9].

RPA does not replace Business Process Management (BPM), but rather complements it. RPA and BPM are each suited to automating different types of processes. BPM solutions are best suited for processes requiring IT expertise on high-valued IT investments like ERP and Customer Relationship Management (CRM) systems. BPM solutions are developed by IT staff. The two distinguishing attributes of RPA software are that it is designed for non-programmers to use and it does not disturb existing systems. This means that the threshold of business processes worth automating are substantially lowered. Now, those swivel chair processes that are owned by operations and are too small to justify the use of IT development resources can be automated by business operations staff. RPA solutions are typically deployed by business operations staff with IT oversight (but not with IT developers) for processes that require business and process expertise. The significantly lower IT investment costs now makes automating these processes financially beneficial. Pat Geary, CMO for Blue Prism, said: "We are not trying to replace enterprise IT, and we are not really trying to compete with BPMS. It's really this long tail of processes that are typically deployed by humans that are most suitable for RPA. Humans can be redeployed to more intelligent decision-making tasks" [3, 10].

For many enterprises considering Robotic Process Automation, concerns around security are preventing action. While RPA is one of the most popular enablers of services, there is plenty of mistrust, and sometimes fear, around the idea of unleashing an army of robots on enterprise systems. In many cases, it is the IT department, often for right reasons, that presents the main hurdle. While an often touted 'benefit' of RPA is that the business itself can implement robotic solutions with little input required from IT, the truth of the matter is that an organization will need engagement of IT in design and deployment if it needs them to partner on a solution, especially when things go wrong. Despite these concerns, the market for RPA is undoubtedly growing. The danger is that in the current feeding frenzy, it is tempting for companies to build a 'quick and dirty' robotic capability that lacks security, scalability, and sustainability. While there may be cost benefits in the short-term, there is a good chance that the company will pay for it in risk and scale, in the long-run [11].

An example of potential reduction in Finance & Accounting (F&A) operations costs shows the impact of RPA as reported in [12]:

- Baseline cost of onshore F&A operations 100%
- Cost reduction due to offshoring (43%)
- Reduced cost of off-shored F&A operations 57%
- Cost reduction due to RPA implementation (15–22%)
- RPA implementation and running cost (2%)
- Reduced cost of optimized F&A operations 33–40%

Gartner estimates that by 2017, autonomics and Robotic Process Automation (RPA) will drive a 60% reduction in the cost of many IT services, primarily through automating repetitive tasks currently performed by humans. Potential applications of RPA solutions include traditionally labour intensive areas such as service desks and customer care centres, as well as a broader range of functions in IT operations, such as network, storage, server and application management, database administration, virtual machine provisioning, process orchestration and teleconferencing. Service delivery model options include partnering directly with a software provider such as Arago, BluePrism or IPsoft; working with a service provider that licenses smart software; or working with a provider that offers a home-grown solution [13].

The stewardship responsibilities of CFOs often make them, understandably, quite conservative. Though there is some evidence of uptick in embracing newer concepts such as cloud and mobile in the finance organization, is untested robotics software a stretch too far for finance leaders? What assurances does the CFO need to move forward? Does the controls environment change? What are the implications of RPA upon the organization? Proponents of robots in the finance functions must be prepared to answer these questions [8].

Robotic Process Automation (RPA) is being deployed in shared service organizations as the next transformation lever beyond centralization, standardization, optimization, relocation to low cost areas, and use of enabling technologies. Although shared service organizations have long-deployed enabling technologies like standard Enterprise Resource Planning (ERP) packages, self-service portals, and low-level automation tools like scripting and screen scraping, RPA is a new breed of software that allows enterprise-safe automation of processes [14].

In industries ranging from banking and insurance to healthcare and the life sciences, robotics offer companies benefits that include [6]:

- Fast ROI: Robotics tools are fast, easy and relatively inexpensive to implement - development in six to eight weeks is typical for faster realization of return on investment. Outsourcing consultancy Everest Group reports that RPA can reduce costs by up to 65%. And RPA's ability to log data at the transactional level enables ongoing decision-making that is fast, accurate and predictive.
- Flexibility: Depending on project requirements, robotic tools can be developed either in "batch mode" to complete end-to-end processes or when human intervention is indispensable, in "assisted mode."
- Security: RPA can be integrated with multiple applications at the presentation layer, ensuring that clients' applications are not modified or enhanced by the robot. It also carries no risk of unauthorized data access: Since the business function leverages the

already-available underlying application, access authorization concepts are automatically inherited.

Robotic Process Automation is not a temporary trend and it is an evolution of technology in support of automating processes. One of the great potential advantages of robotics is that it offers an affordable, relatively easy to implement and a cost-effective solution.

3   Data Collection Methods

Despite the huge potential for RPA and software bots in shared services, little is known of their application and business value in this area. In this study, we address the five research questions stated in the introduction by conducting a survey of RPA Professionals, Shared Services Leaders and Functional Leaders in USA, Europe, Canada, China, Singapore and India. The survey was sent to over 150 leaders and 42 respondents from companies in nine industries participated in the survey. To gain additional insights, indepth interviews were conducted with 12 respondents who have implemented Software Bots. Figures 1 and 2 show the distribution of respondents by industry and by revenue.

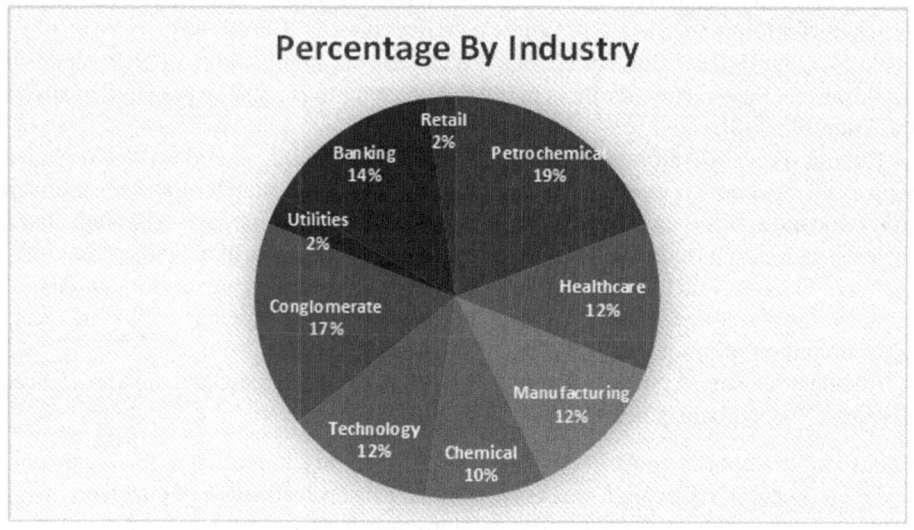

Fig. 1. Distribution of respondents by industry

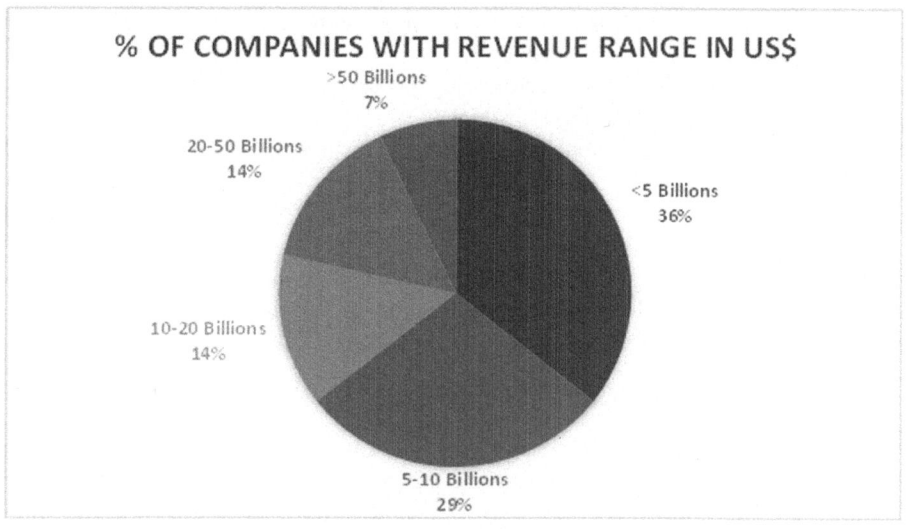

Fig. 2. Distribution of respondents by revenue

In addition to the demographic questions asked in the survey, the survey participants were asked 21 questions. The questions asked were:

1. Have you heard about RPA?
2. Have you heard about Software Bots?
3. How can RPA be defined and classified?
4. Do Software Bots have the potential for automating processes within your shared services organization?
5. Have Software Bots been implemented within your company?
6. If Software Bots have been implemented within your company, who developed the software for you?
7. What is the current status of implementing Software Bots in your shared services and functions within your company (please check all applicable answers)?
8. Have you received tangible or intangible savings through implementation of Software Bots (please check all applicable answers)?
9. When were Software Bots adopted within your company (please check all applicable answers)?
10. Did you create a business case for Software Bots?
11. What was the basis of your business case?
12. Who approved the business case for adopting Software Bots?
13. What were the difficulties in developing the business case for adopting Software Bots anywhere within your company (please check all applicable answers)?
14. What non-financial factors were considered critically important in the development of the business case for Software Bots?
15. Which functional processes do you think are candidates for automation using Software Robots (please check all applicable answers)?

16. What processes should not be considered for automation using Software Bots (please check all applicable answers)?
17. What are the challenges for automating processes using Software Bots (please check all applicable answers)?
18. What are the perceived/actual benefits of Software Bots (please check all applicable answers)?
19. What are the key shortcomings of Software Bots (please check all applicable answers)?
20. If you were to further automate your processes, what methodology will you use?
21. Which one of the following outcomes is most important in automating processes in your functions and shared services within your company?

Survey responses were summarized in an Excel spreadsheet for analysis purposes.

4 Results

4.1 What Is the Value Potential of Process Automation Using Software Bots?

All of the respondents indicated that they have heard about RPA and Software Bots. They were divided in their views about the value potential of Software Bots for automating processes within their Shared Services organizations. 28.5% indicated that the Software Bots have vast potential whereas 43% and 28.5% indicated Software Bots have large and small potential respectively within their organizations. These results indicate the diversity in organizational operations and organizational maturity levels. In response to the question regarding how RPA can be defined and classified, the following answers were provided. Definitions provided were used to assess the degree to which respondants were familiar with RPA. This was used for analysis purposes including the assessment of the validity of participants' responses to the other questions contained in the survey:

- As Peter Moller from Deloitte often says "these are macros on steroids". They enable to automate and speed up the data processing across systems.
- Software that performs faster, error free, devoid of human challenges of time/age/ health
- Replicating human activities through the use of a computer based system
- RPA is the application of technology that allows employees in a company to configure computer software or a "robot" to capture and interpret existing applications for processing a transaction, manipulating data, triggering responses and communicating with other digital systems.
- Semi-automatic, run book automaton
- Robot Process Automation or a software to let a robot mimic what a human is operating from a computer

4.2 How Is the Business Case Approved and by Whom?

70% of the respondents mentioned that a business case for Software Bots was created within their organizations and the primary basis of their business case was reduced operational costs (33%), FTE reduction (33%), improved customer service (17%) and improved quality (17%). The business case for adopting Software Bots was approved by the CEO in 28% of the cases and in other cases it was approved by the COO or the Shared Services Leader. Based on responses received, the common primary difficulties in developing the business case for adopting Software Bots anywhere within their companies can be summarized as:

- Difficulty in quantifying tangible savings (57%)
- Difficulty in estimating FTE reductions (29%)
- Difficulty in identifying cost of implementation (14%)
- Lack of co-operation from IT group (29%)

These findings are similar to those cited in the literature: Finance directors are unclear about the hard benefits of RPA. They see the numbers in other processes such as claims management, but can only imagine the business case for the Finance function [8].

Similarly, the most common non-financial factors considered as critically important in the development of the business case for Software Bots can be summarized as;

- Existence of controls environment (71%)
- Governance Structure (29%)
- Approval of external auditors (29%)
- Disruption in operations (14%)
- Motivation of employees (71%)

4.3 Which Processes Have Been Automated Using Software Bots and in What Functional Areas of Shared Services Organizations?

The respondents thought that the following functional processes are candidates for automation using "Software Robots" (see Table 1):

Table 1. Functional processes are candidates for automation using "Software Robots"

Finance function	HR function	IT function
Accounts Payable	Payroll	Ticket Management
Order-to-Cash	Hire-to-Retire	Database
Procure-to-Pay		Management
General Ledger		
Financial Analysis		
Financial Reporting		

57% of respondents also mentioned that processes requiring intelligence in the first phase of roll out, all processes requiring judgement (except parts of these which can be automated) and recruitment processes should not be considered for automation using Software Bots.

4.4   What Are the Challenges with Implementing Software Bots in Shared Services Organizations?

The respondents identified the following challenges for automating processes using Software Bots:

- Lack of resources (29%)
- Fear of job loss by employees (43%)
- Unclear division of responsibilities between IT and Functional organizations (29%)
- Lack of standard processes (43%)
- Budget constraints (29%)
- Lack of management support (14%)
- No viable business case (14%)
- The fear to automate a messy process instead of streamlining it - and the potential issues with future changes and regression testing (14%)
- RPA solutions are very expensive and pricing policy very obscure (14%)
- Weak change management process across the organisation and most precisely in IT operations (14%)
- Lack of understanding of what RPA means and where it can be applied (14%)

The key challenges identified for automating processes using Software Bots are fear of job loss by employees, lack of standard processes, unclear division of responsibilities between IT and functional organizations, lack of resources and budget constraints. These implementation challenges are similar to those cited in the literature: the biggest challenge is the kind of cultural change that you need for automation. The challenge is that bridge between RPA being an IT tool and the business side of it (Lacity and Willcocks 2016).

4.5   What Benefits Have Been Achieved by Using Software Bots in Shared Services Organizations?

The respondents identified the perceived/actual benefits of Software Bots as follows:

- Reduction in FTEs (71%)
- Elimination of errors (86%)
- Increased speed of operations (100%)
- Utilization of FTEs on more value-added activities (86%)
- Improved customer service (57%)
- Improved agility (14%)
- Improved capacity management (14%)
- Increased customer satisfaction (71%)
- Increased agility to handle more work during peak periods (57%)
- Increased Quality (57%)
- Well-being of Operators as they are off-loaded of non-rewarding tasks (14%)
- Better auditing of all transactions (14%)
- Reduced fraud (14%)

Key shortcomings of Software Bots were identified as follows:

- Business disruption (43%)
- Employee anxiety (43%)
- No tangible benefits (29%)
- Difficult to implement (29%)
- By reducing the processing costs even further than offshoring, RPA will reduce the incentive to further optimize processes, creating the risk of complexity and reducing the implementation speed of future changes (14%)
- Capacity of existing systems to handle increased volumes (14%)

In summary, responses received identified, the key benefits associated with Software Bots as increased speed of operations, elimination of errors, utilization of FTEs on more value-added activities, increased customer satisfaction, reduction in FTEs, improved customer service, increased quality and increased agility to handle more work during peak periods whereas the key associated shortcoming were identified as business disruption, employee anxiety, no tangible benefits and difficult to implement. The benefits cited in literature are similar: RPA software programs are faster and more accurate than humans. They have super-human stamina, offering 24/7 productivity with no processing handoffs due to shift changes. They can be scaled up quickly to handle seasonal or unanticipated spikes in work volume. And if they need to be shut down temporarily, they can simply "go to sleep" [6].

Our survey and in-depth interviews reveal that there needs to be a business case for the implementation of Software Bots in Shared Services. Forward-looking organizations seeking to drive long-term value are finding many advantages to implementing Software Bots in Shared Services. In 47% of the companies, external solution providers in conjunction with internal IT organizations were used to develop the software necessary for implementing Software Bots within their shared services organizations.

In one of the respondent company's canteen there is a poster which says "Drink coffee and make stupid things faster and with more energy". The concern is that they see RPA a bit like that. That does not mean RPA cannot be useful, and it may prove an interesting temporary solution to lots of problems. However, they are also concerned about the risk of complexity it will create and the added dependency on external software providers. Process standardization, improvement in service quality and cost reduction are the most important outcomes in automating processes in Shared Services. Some organizations still feel that if they were to further automate their processes, they will use ERP and/or other enterprise management systems instead of Software Bots. They think that RPA is not the solution to all needs as ERP and BPM can be alternate ways to automate processes.

The results clearly show that Software Bots are a very new phenomenon. The bots were adopted in Shared Services organizations about 6–12 months ago in 30% of the companies whereas 30% of the companies have not implemented any Software Bots in their Shared Services organizations. The adoption rate for Software Bots in European Shared Services organizations is much higher than those in North American organizations whereas it is much smaller in Asian organizations. Also, the adoption rate in larger companies (annual revenue greater than US$10 Billions) is higher than those in smaller companies. Based on the results, there was no differentiation by industry. The implementation in other companies is at various stages with most of them conducting pilot tests or developing business cases. Governance is a key and so is a stable IT infrastructure. New type of skills (Change Managers, RPA Developers, and Robot Farm Managers etc.) are emerging.

In this paper, we have indicated both possibilities and limitations of what Software Bots can do in the arena of Shared Services. What this means is that in future years, we will see much more transformation in the nature of Shared Services work. It is difficult to assess the impact of Software Bots on jobs but as automation of low-level jobs continues, fewer people will be needed in these job categories. A backlash from employees is expected due to increased adoption of Software Bots but as the new job categories emerge, the employees will begin understanding the economics of service delivery and the opportunities to work in higher decision-making environments.

5   Conclusions and Future Research

In this research paper we have focused on understanding the use and experiences of RPA and Software Bots in automating processes within Shared Service organizations. The results indicate that currently Software Bots have been implemented to a limited extent in Shared Services organizations although the value potential is being increasingly recognized by these organizations.

Economic growth will result in faster adoption of Software Bots but will have limits to their applicability due to greater demand for specific skills required to oversee the work done by Software Bots. Companies will need to deal with inevitable growth in data in future and Software Bots will provide only a partial solution. Our prediction is that some of the work being outsourced today will be brought in-house as the adoption of Software Bots increases in companies.

The key benefits of Software Bots that have been identified by the service organizations participating in this research, including increased speed of operations, elimination of errors, utilization of FTEs on more value-added activities, increased customer satisfaction, reduction in FTEs, improved customer service, increased quality and increased agility to handle more work during peak periods are similar to those benefits cited in the literature by non-Shared Services organizations. The key implementation challenges identified through this research are unclear division of responsibilities between IT and functional organizations, lack of understanding of what RPA means and where it can be applied, lack of management support and weak change management process across the organisation. These identified key implementation challenges are the same as those cited in the literature by non-service organizations.

For many processes, RPA can take the human touch point out of the equation and eliminates subjective errors. The RPA experts conclude that rather than cutting back on FTEs, staff can be redeployed into roles where, free of the routine, transactional work, they can leverage their know-how and expertise to deliver far greater value. While RPA can drive down errors, duplications, or high processing costs, the additional benefit of refocusing staff in Shared Services organizations on analytics means that all-important business insights and intelligence can be leveraged for improved decision-making. This means improving end-to-end process efficiency and effectiveness. Software Bots provide an alternative career path that retains the best talent by offering the opportunity to develop new, in-demand skillsets within a Center of Excellence (CoE).

In order to maximize benefits from the implementation of Software Bots an organization should start where there is volume and not where there are problems, and then centralize, standardize repeatable processes, run a pilot, optimize for immediate value and optimize for future value. A responsibility relationship chart should be developed to clarify the roles and responsibilities of business groups and IT groups during implementation of Software Bots so that the business processes are owned by the process owners and technical issues are addressed by IT. A RACI (Responsible, Accountable, Consult and Inform) chart is a good tool to document the division of responsibilities.

Research is known to yield insights that are ripe for further research. While there are many questions that could be raised, we suggest three future research areas namely: (1) Role of IT in implementing Software Bots in Shared Services organizations, (2) Components of a compelling business case for implementing Software Bots in Shared Services organizations and (3) As Software Bots alter the "social dynamics" of organizations, exploration of the theoretical underpinning of Sociomateriality Theory to better understand how Software Bots alter the human-technology relationship [15].

References

1. Alsbridge: Introduction to Robotic Process Automation (2016). www.alsbridge.com
2. Institute for Robotic Process Automatio: Introduction to Robotic Process Automation: A Primer. Institute for Robotic Process Automation in association with Carnegie Mellon University (2015)
3. Willcocks, L.P., Lacity, M., Craig, A.: The IT Function and Robotic Process Automation. LSE (2015)
4. BluePrism: Blue Prism Software Robots - Introducing the Virtual Workforce (2012)
5. Gartner: Robotic Process Automation (RPA): From Hype to Reality. http://www.gartner.com/webinar/3461417?srcId=1-4411694165
6. Smith, M.: A Refresher on Robotic Process Automation (2016). https://medium.com/@_MatthewJSmith/a-refresher-on-robotic-process-automation-97001f1f2025
7. E&Y: Robotic process automation in the finance function of the future (2016)
8. The robots are coming? Implications for financial shared services. ACCA Global. http://www.accaglobal.com/us/en/technical-activities/technical-resources-search/2015/september/robots-and-the-future-of-finance.html
9. Deloitte: The robots are coming Moving beyond traditional methods of automation (2015)
10. Willcocks, L.P., Lacity, M., Craig, A.: Robotic Process Automation at Xchanging. LSE (2015)
11. Hodge, B.: How to Manage Risk and Ensure Control – What to Look Out for in Robotic Process Implementation (2017)
12. Munter, S.: Robotic Process Automation. ANZ Banking Group (2016)
13. Fausti, M.: Old Dogs Learn New Tricks - Disruptive Technologies and Evolving Sourcing Tools. ISG (2017)

14. Lacity, M., Willcocks, L.P.: Robotic Process Automation: The Next Transformation Lever for Shared Services (2016)
15. Parmiggiani, E., Mikalsen, M.: The facets of sociomateriality: a systematic mapping of emerging concepts and definitions. In: Aanestad, M., Bratteteig, T. (eds.) SCIS 2013. LNBIP, vol. 156, pp. 87–103. Springer, Heidelberg (2013). doi:10.1007/978-3-642-39832-2_6

Capturing Stakeholder Engagement: CSR and Gender Equality in Global In-House Centres

Fay Davidson[✉], John Wreford, Kevan Penter, and Brian Perrin

School of Accounting, Curtin University, U1987, Bentley, WA, Australia
{fay.davidson,john.wreford,kevan.penter}@postgrad.curtin.edu.au,
brian.perrin@curtin.edu.au

Abstract. Understanding the strategic relevance or significance of Corporate Social Responsibility (CSR) in the international offshore business process outsourcing (OBPO) context requires examination of the complexity of conflicting interests of competing stakeholders, philosophical and theoretical perspectives within the frameworks of different cultures, legal systems and attitudes. This research makes an original contribution to the study of CSR activities of organisations involved in OBPO. The findings could be useful for other researchers in the areas of CSR and compliance, for evaluating or comparing other programs, or used to assist businesses involved in OBPO to target their CSR strategies. This chapter investigates how CSR, particularly the contribution of CSR to gender equity in the workforce, as it is applied and implemented by organisations that engage in OBPO. It contributes to a stream of research that addresses critical success factors for OBPO relating to relationships and end-user customers.

Keywords: Corporate Social Responsibility · Global in-house centres · Gender

1 Introduction

Offshore business process outsourcing (OBPO) is the delegation of one or more business processes to an offshore captive centre or a third party service provider [1–3]. The aim of this paper is to investigate CSR (in terms of its application of gender reporting and gender equity objectives) and implementation in OBPO organisations with Global In-house Centres (GICs). In this international OBPO context, different cultures, legal systems and attitudes impact on the implementation of CSR. This research examines how gender equity as a factor of CSR can be applied to understand how CSR and OBPO combine strategically (or otherwise) in business models designed to strive for efficiencies and appeal to investors.

The research at hand varies from earlier research in that it seeks to explore a specific area of corporate behaviour that is contested and contentious. CSR creates tension between the costs to shareholders and profits, of delivering CSR strategies versus benefits from improving the image of corporate citizenship and building positive

© Springer International Publishing AG 2017
I. Oshri et al. (Eds.): Global Sourcing 2017, LNBIP 306, pp. 95–110, 2017.
https://doi.org/10.1007/978-3-319-70305-3_6

relationships with stakeholders off or onshore. This research will examine the intersection of CSR and an area of OBPO not previously investigated.

1.1 Contribution of this Research

This paper investigates how CSR, particularly the contribution of CSR to gender equality in the workforce, is applied and implemented by organisations that engage in OBPO. Addressing gender equity within the OBPO industry may provide a tool for managing high rates of staff attrition (i.e. turnover), which has been recognised as a major problem for the whole industry [4]. Our research finds that female staff frequently make up at least 50% of staff working in operational roles in OBPO GICs located in India and the Philippines, but women are under-represented in senior management roles. As a consequence, female workers in OBPO tend to be paid less, employed at lower levels and consequently may show lower levels of organisational engagement. Thus, a commitment to gender equality as part of CSR initiatives is highly likely to increase staff engagement, and reduce turnover, with consequent overall improvement in OBPO industry performance.

Other researchers in the areas of CSR and compliance may find the results of the research useful for evaluating or comparing other programs, or to target their CSR strategies.

2 Literature Review

2.1 OBPO

The value of the global Offshore BPO (OBPO) market total revenues are estimated to be

> *"$140,316.1m in 2016, representing a compound annual growth rate (CAGR) of 4.4% between 2012 and 2016… - The performance of the market is forecast to decelerate, with an anticipated CAGR of 3.1% for the five-year period 2016–2021, which is expected to drive the market to a value of $163,764.0m by the end of 2021"* [5].

With such a large modern market it is instructive to have our attention drawn to the similarities of the early colonial mercantilist ventures into new world markets for resources and cheap labour [6] and the beginnings of modern OBPO business practices that still source global resources and labour.

> *"The current high level of interest in offshoring is a logical extension of the large-scale outsourcing phenomenon that occurred in the 20th and early 21st centuries (Weber, 2004) although offshoring has existed as an organisational and societal issue since the dawn of the Industrial Revolution…"* [7].

Metters and Verma [8] argue that "Information technology (IT) outsourcing most likely began in 1949 with ADP performing payroll processing for other firms", and that offshore service work started in the U.S. in the 1970s before modern telecommunications. Metters and Verma [8] explain that "At that time, a few firms sent large batches of paperwork that was not time sensitive to the Caribbean by ship…large scale IT outsourcing is generally traced to the 1990 decision by Eastman-Kodak, a Fortune 200 firm, to outsource virtually all its IT functions" [8].

Previous OBPO research investigating has focused on managing offshore relationships [9], "developing ways to measure success (Aubert et al. 2004; Lacity et al. 2010; Lee et al. 2004), or critiquing implications for managing personnel and labour metrics (Capron, 2009; Ho 2003)" [9]. An earlier literature review of BPO academic articles reviewed 87 research articles published between 1996 and 2011 in 67 journals. Most of all the BPO research papers were published in the period since 2008. 58% of the published papers have addressed Offshore BPO (OBPO). Lacity et al. [10] identify three themes in OBPO research: BPO decisions, BPO outcomes, and miscellaneous BPO research themes. It is noteworthy that none of the 87 OBPO papers reviewed covered the links between CSR and OBPO; nor do Lacity et al. identify any research about the links between stakeholders and offshoring decisions [10].

Strasser and Westner [11] review 95 articles published between 2010 and 2013 dealing with IS Offshoring. They identified Wreford et al. [12] as the only research approaching customer satisfaction and BPO success. There was no published research addressing the issues of CSR specifically as an element of the OBPO captive business model located. Lacity and Willcocks [13] point to the strain between competing interests in offshoring relationships;

"The provider's centralised culture is looking to generate growth, while the globally dispersed delivery teams want to please both their supervisors and customers, which can leave them caught between conflicting cultures" [13].

Neither Gonzalez et al. [14] or Oshri and van Uhm [15], identify any researched links between OBPO staff and shareholder stakeholders and corporate offshoring decisions. This gap in the research means that there has been no academic investigation of the importance or effect of consumer satisfaction, domestic political responses, or labour relations on organisational decisions to embark in OBPO involving a captive model.

Offshoring may occur through outsourcing to offshore service providers that hire, train, supervise, and manage their own personnel, and the organisation becomes the vender in the OBPO relationship. Alternatively, an organisation may set up service operations in another country, but the management of staff and processes are handled by the organisation rather than by an external contractor or vendor [16]. Formally called captive centres these offshore operations are increasingly demanding recognition as Global In-house Centres (GICs).

Oshri and van Uhm [15] observe that GICs have developed their own development trajectory of four phases since decisions to move into India in 1985. The fourth phase, since 2010, is marked by a reduction in captive start-ups, and a pattern of re-shoring/back-shoring or near-shoring [15, 17]. Despite some estimates that the growth in the global value of OBPO has decreased in the last three years [4], future decisions about reaching into the global labour marketplace, engaging in OBPO or back-shoring, will rely more than ever before on the ability to answer questions about strategy, stakeholder engagement and impact. Oshri poses two questions that challenge OPBO.

- *"...how should a parent company strategically perceive its captive centre in view of its allocation and use of resources?*

- *Secondly, what sets of capabilities should companies develop offshore to support the evolution of a captive centre?"* [17].

An organisation's decision to locate some part of its operations where it will be better positioned to leverage lower cost resources, particularly human resources, can awaken consumer criticism based on perceptions of the organisation valuing profit over customer satisfaction. Consumers and public sentiment may question support for the workers in the home country, or raise challenges to the acceptance of cultural and racial diversity when sourcing a global workforce. In the home country, there is hostility to offshoring particularly offshoring services that are first connection services - customer call centres. There is also cognizance of other manufacturing and production jobs being moved offshore and an equivalence being drawn between offshoring and some kind of racial and cultural blame that can be placed on the shoulders of the 'other'. In this worldview, there is a simple understanding that jobs that could and should be done 'at home' are going offshore and given to foreign workers.

Multinational corporations are routinely critiqued for social and environmental harm occurring in their supply chains. These examinations and expectations call into their legitimacy and their responsibilities as corporate services. The organization needs the support of its customers and other stakeholders in order to reach its business objectives. This support is manifested through recurrent transactions and trust in the brand and social behaviours of the organisation.

> *"Some corporations react by attempting to influence public opinion in general and the perception of their key stakeholders in particular by counter-communication…and the fact that multinational corporations operate within numerous and sometimes contradictory legal and moral contexts, makes a simple adaption to external expectations difficult. It is a social contract that reflects the unique challenges of this century"… "business firms are often required to establish the third form of legitimacy: moral legitimacy"* [18].

Wreford et al. [12] discuss the connections between demonstrating corporate social responsibility and the social or moral license to operate. The social license to operate is an element contributing to consumer support, and balancing the expectations of stakeholders. The need to capture the approval of customers and stakeholders is crucial to the sustainability of organisations seeking to obtain the efficiencies of off-shoring business processes to locations with lower operational inputs. CSR is one of the capabilities that contribute to the set of resources required to develop offshore capabilities.

2.2   CSR

> *"The Corporate Social Responsibility (CSR) field presents not only a landscape of theories but also a proliferation of approaches, which are controversial, complex and unclear"* [19].

Generally, the literature acknowledges that since the 1800s there has been some notion of the interaction between the corporate world and civil society. Determining the origins or oldest existing model of CSR largely depends on how CSR is defined by historians, analysts or researchers. For example, the loosest definitions recognise any act by a business that imitates a kindness or concern for civil society. Within that framework, any business organisation that considered the health or safety of workers or their families could be construed as engaging in acts of corporate social responsibility.

Crane [20] argues that some of the first acts of corporations acknowledging their role as corporate citizens were linked to the American Civil War (1861–1865). However, in Britain at about the same time the Cadbury family were beginning production in Birmingham and were soon to establish the Bourneville Trust as a way to offer their employees cheap, healthy housing.

By the turn of the century, there was growing interest in incorporations in Europe and America maintaining societal trust [20]. Endicott-Johnson was making housing and health schemes available to (often) migrant workers in New York. However, the real links came with the First World War, and support by business of the YMCA. During this period in Germany the Waldorf–Astoria cigar factory established an on-site kindergarten for the children of factory workers. Crane argues that the depression opened the door for corporations to look after market share and Labour, and it is in this period that in the USA, Kellogg implemented a 30-hour week for staff.

There is general acknowledgement in the literature that since the 1800s there has been some notion of the interaction between the corporate world and civil society. The long history of corporate responsibility suggests that in the early decades of the 21st century, a new social contract between business, government, and society is taking shape.

Despite the ragged and contested origins of understandings of corporations as participants in the civilian society, there is some convergence in the literature about the emergence of the self-awareness of the corporate citizen appearing in the second half of the 20th century [20]. A.B. Carroll, one of the leading researchers in the field "traces the evolution of the CSR construct beginning in the 1950s, which marks the modern era of CSR. Definitions expanded during the 1960s and proliferated during the 1970s. In the 1980s, there were fewer new definitions, more empirical research, and alternative themes began to mature" [21].

The long history of corporate responsibility suggests that in the early decades of the 21st century, a new social contract between business, government, and society was evolving. Answers to the question when is it right for business to become involved in the community, not merely the market, invites analysis from many disciplines and political dispositions. The questions of business and business scholars alike tend to centre on when is it right, not merely appropriate, for business to become involved in the community beyond just the market. Answers to that question invite analysis from many different fields including politics, business, and economics, and the attendant theories and sub-disciplines.

CSR literature can be divided into three areas or themes.

- The academic endeavour or "problematizing". This area engages with theories of business, regulation, defining CSR, and political economy.
- "Doing CSR" is literature that tells about CSR initiatives, how they worked, where they worked, whether or not certain organisations are practising CSR or in fact guilty of the opposite.

- "Working CSR", some researchers investigate how organisations include CSR as an operational matter; how CSR is measured, why firms choose the CSR programs they do and how much organisations spend [22–24].

Practising and publicly reporting CSR, presents an organisation as ethical and worthy of trust, and in doing so, captures the goodwill, empathy and trust of stakeholders especially clients, customers and labour, in home countries. The development and maintenance of trust has been identified as a factor of off-shoring success [12]. This move toward overt and targeted CSR responses and public reporting is prompting the strategic alignment of CSR with core business.

"[CSR] is becoming established in many corporations as a critical element of strategic direction, and one of the main drivers of business development, as well as an essential component of risk management...rapidly moving from the margins to the mainstream of corporate activity..." [25].

CSR initiatives and practice help demonstrate the moral authority of the corporate citizen. It is a part of the social contract that reflects the unique "challenges of this century. As the social and economic landscape continues to shift, business faces a dynamic reality: Legitimacy is never guaranteed—it must be earned every day." [21] There is little research at hand that looks specifically at CSR in the OBPO context of captive or global in-house centres.

Carroll argues that for modern businesses the reality is that CSR is an essential element of the social contract between operations and the community. Galbreath [26] accommodates both formal and informal social contracts:

"...the "formal" social contract defines a firm's explicit responsibilities, including generating returns for shareholders, obeying laws and regulations, creating jobs, paying taxes, and honouring private contracts...the "semiformal" social contract reflects society's implicit expectations...such as adherence to global labour and environmental standards (e.g. SA 8000, AA 1000, ISO 14031) that are not required by law, industry norms and codes of conduct, fulfilling brand promises and contributing philanthropically to the community" [26].

Moon [27] argues CSR is a concept with its meaning always subject to political bias, evaluation, and semantic assumptions. Matten and Moon [28] position CSR as a cluster concept that overlaps many fields of research and always subject to differing interpretations. Crane et al. continue this theme by arguing CSR cannot be defined except as a field of study that has at its core "the subject of social obligations and impacts of corporations in society" [20]. Crane et al. find that "despite the homage to many disciplines, CSR as an academic endeavour fits firmly in the field of business and management" [20] and summarise the existing research as dealing with

"...broad questions about the changing relationship between business, society and government, environmental issues, corporate governance, the social and ethical dimensions of management, globalisation, stakeholder debates, shareholder and consumer activism, changing political systems and values, and the ways in which corporations can respond to new social imperatives" [20].

Although the scope and application of CSR are "essentially contested and difficult to measure", [28], and the definition of corporate social responsibility can be 'fluid' [29]. CSR is widely understood as activity that recognises the social imperatives of business success and addresses the social externalities beyond transactional relationships.

"CSR can be applied in many ways to mean ethical business practice, ethical businesses, commitment to environment alongside profit, and corporate social performance (McWilliams et al., 2006, p. 8; Secchi, 2007; Windsor, 2006) and social accounting or corporate accountability" [30].

It combines technical processes of measuring and reporting social performance with political processes of redefining rights and responsibilities, particularly through different forms of stakeholder engagement.

"CSR's significance for wider societies is signalled by the growing social imprint of business, particularly multinational corporations (Hertz, 2001; Monbiot, 2000), and by the encouragement given to business by governments to assume greater responsibility for public policy issues (Matten et al., 2003; Moon, 2002)" [31].

The trend toward customer awareness of CSR and increased demands for public reporting to government agencies is contributing to the strategic alignment of CSR with core business. CSR is often incorporated into business models as a self-regulatory measure to encourage a positive impact on the environment, sustainability, the community, consumers and employees. Often the requirements of CSR have been determined by the objectives of the companies themselves to appeal to consumer or shareholder sentiment.

"Practising and publicly reporting CSR, presents an organisation as ethical and worthy of trust, and in doing so, captures the goodwill, empathy and trust of stakeholders especially clients, customers and labour, in home countries. The development and maintenance of trust are integral to off-shoring success" [9].

Kelly and Noonan [32] draw on Giddens' perspective of the changing nature of risk, and the notion of trust as an emotional commitment. Emotional commitment is the glue that keeps customers loyal to brands and businesses and is especially important in maintaining a customer base despite unpopular offshoring activities.

"[CSR] is becoming established in many corporations as a critical element of strategic direction, and one of the main drivers of business development, as well as an essential component of risk management...rapidly moving from the margins to the mainstream of corporate activity..." [33].

CSR is growing in importance to companies because there is an increase in expectations of corporate operations about corporate social responsibilities [33]. Increasingly Australian companies are required by Australian law to comply with international standards for investment in foreign countries, and, formal international requirements are increasing particularly in the arena of global multinationals. While it may not be correct to refer to these guidelines and expectations as international regulations, these include: The OECD Guidelines for Multinationals, The Global Reporting Initiative, ISO 26000 and the United Nations Norms on the Responsibilities of Transnational Corporations and Other Business Enterprises, among others. This Global monitoring and other drivers, have brought increasing pressure on the multi-national companies to embed (CSR) in day-to-day operations and is prompting the strategic alignment of CSR initiatives.

"Some think of CSR as "business ethics or philanthropy or environmental policy", "corporate social performance and corporate citizenship" (McWilliams et al., 2006:8; also Secchi, 2007; Windsor, 2006), or social accounting or corporate accountability" [34].

Neither Oshri and van Uhm [15], Pisani and Rickert [35], or Wiener et al. [36] identify any research about the importance or effect of consumer satisfaction, domestic political responses, or labour relations on organisational decisions to involve a captive model of offshoring. Kelly and Noonan [32] argue that while risk has been investigated as an element in establishing and maintaining offshoring relationships, the more emotional perspectives of anxiety, and the notion of trust as an emotional commitment in the context of the contemporary globalisation of social relations, have been overlooked.

2.3   How CSR is Measured

There is contention in the literature about the costs and benefits of CSR to the organisation. Some companies use a variety of benchmarking strategies to track their performance. However, the value of CSR strategies to shareholders, customers and the organisation is largely unknown and under-theorised. Orlitzky et al. [37] argue that CSR is not cost neutral while many others theorise or attempt to quantify the value of CSR behaviour. Recent Australian Government Treasury research concluded that there is "…the need to develop better measures of corporate social responsibility within Australia" [38].

Some companies recognise that participating in voluntary initiatives on CSR can help manage risks, create new business opportunities and improve the prospects for sustainability of the company [9], and enhance moral legitimacy. Moral legitimacy refers to moral judgments about the corporation's output, procedures, structures, and leaders. "It [moral legitimacy] is socially and argumentatively constructed by means of considering reasons to justify certain actions, practices, or institutions and is thus present in discourses between the corporation and its relevant publics" [39].

Moir also prompts us to consider for those businesses that do undertake what might be termed "Corporate Social Responsibility", what is actually socially responsible behaviour as opposed to corporate image management or other activities aimed predominantly at business benefits? [40]. Moir is suggesting that CSR could be construed as merely window dressing without much substance and that different stakeholders have competing needs and tensions in relation to CSR implementation. Despite the increased focus on CSR, Schleimer and Rice [41] and the Australian Centre for Corporate Social Responsibility (ACCSR) [42], believe that the progress toward real change in corporate attitude toward CSR reporting in annual reports has been only modest. Further, Schleimer and Rice [41] claim that some CSR reports are only carefully tailored statements that promote the company's image rather than real gains in social good.

A measure or indicator could be used as a comparator to determine the substance of CSR initiatives. Various stakeholders can have competing needs and tensions in relation to CSR implementation. Interestingly, CSR literature indicates that staff are one of the primary targets for the publications and promotion of an organisation's CSR activities. The literature also identifies these OBPO success factors.

- Trust
- Relationship management
- Contract

- Location
- Intercultural capabilities
- Client and OBPO supplier expectation match

Gender was nominated as one of the most challenging, but also the most likely to have set targets of the 17 United Nations sustainable Development Goals addressed by respondents to the 2017 ACCSR State of CSR Annual Review [42]. In this study 'gender' is used as a comparator for CSR initiatives and 'staff' as the primary stakeholder group.

3   Case Study Method

Using publicly available material and interview data, model how CSR is managed in parent organisations by reviewing strategies, stakeholders and impact of a single indicator. The CSR indicator is diversity and inclusion with particular reference to gender equity. The single stakeholder, in this case, is staff because the literature tells us this is one of the key target groups. An objective is as far as possible to test the alignment of parent CSR practices with global in-house centres.

3.1   Strategies

Examining the strategic motivations and implementation began by examining publicly available quantitative and qualitative data. Some reporting is compulsory for large Australian organisations, and some reporting is pursued the purpose of keeping pace with other competitor organisations in the field. This mimetic behaviour has been investigated through an institutions theory by Penter et al. [43].

- Workplace Gender Equality Agency (WGEA) requires organisations to report on the composition of the workforce by gender, part-time and full-time employment role, etc. WGEA uses this data to calculate a 'like-for-like' gender pay gap across sectors and for national and state comparisons.
- Male Champions of Change/CEOs for Gender Equity is a group of concerned CEOs who have agreed to leadership behaviours and actions to improve gender equity. For example not speaking or going to conferences that do not demonstrate gender balance.
- The Australian Institute of Company Directors (AICD) has placed expectations on boards of public companies to achieve 30% female representation on Australian Securities Exchange (ASX) top 200 boards by the end of 2018.
- Australian Workplace Equity Index (Pride in Diversity) AWEI is about the demonstration of support for LGBTI inclusion in the workplace.
- Equal Employment Opportunity Commission/Disability inclusion.
- Reconciliation Action Plans = Indigenous inclusion - closing the gap between indigenous health and education outcomes.

- Australian Stock Exchange (ASX) Corporate Governance Principles and Recommendations (3rd edition, 2014) require listed companies to publish details of their gender diversity policy, objectives and annual achievements.

These reporting mechanisms indicate that there is already a wealth of public reporting in this space just in relation to staff, and some of this reporting relates to customers. The reporting of this high-level data is reflective of the United Nations Gender Mainstreaming. "Mainstreaming involves ensuring that gender perspectives and attention to the goal of gender equality are central to all activities" [31]. The reported data is also rich because it requires disclosure about policies and activities.

3.2 Stakeholders

OBPO stakeholders include labour, consumers, legislators and regulators, and shareholders and others. How can the competing stakeholder positions be best explained and accommodated? There is evidence that boards with higher proportions of female members tend to have greater investments in CSR [44], and that gender has a significant influence on trust and CSR satisfaction, with male employees generally more trustful than female workers [45]. Telstra, ANZ and Westpac all seek to produce recruitment materials for staff working offshore that rounds off their commitment to staff and draws attention to supportive workplace cultures.

3.3 Case Study Data

The Australian New Zealand (ANZ) Banking group is a selected case study. The ANZ is one of Australia's Big Four Banks and demonstrates its commitment to CSR through its CSR strategy, checking its supply chain and public reporting. The ANZ has a corporate responsibility framework,

> "...Reports publicly every six months, reported nine independent audits of major suppliers in 2011. Toby Kent, ANZ's head of corporate responsibility (CR) in 2011, observed that in some organisations CR is just PR. Yet there are many organisations which are moving to act in more sustainable ways, Kent says. Those doing it best are companies that closely tie their corporate responsibility activities to the core business" [46, 47].

ANZ India acknowledges CSR activities through activities focussed on staff, for example, diversity, inclusion, [44] and, strategic alignment of core business of the bank with the education of the community as future consumers, leadership for women, and disability employment. ANZ also tell us that they provide the same staff development and training to staff in India and Australia, with the objective of there being no difference between the retail ANZ Bangalore and ANZ Brisbane.

ANZ under the slogan 'ANZ in Bangalore' developed an integrated captive that was fully assimilated into the parent company and has now expanded that centre (known as ANZ Operations, Technology and Shared Services) to more than 7,000 staff. Staff members in Bangalore were given the same corporate, and organisational training as staff in the parent company, and HR and corporate policies and controls were the same as in other parts of the ANZ bank [48]. The then Managing Director of ANZ OTSS summarised the culture of ANZ's Bangalore captive centre, "We revere the culture here [in Bangalore], but we remember who we are. We are not here as apologists. We make sure that all staff know about our standards and our values" [42]. ANZ was selective in the business processes transferred offshore, with a former CEO noting.

"ANZ understands customers want to be able to talk to staff in Australia about their banking and financial services needs. As a result, we have a clear policy that all call centres for Australian customers will remain in Australia" [49].

This statement by a former CEO appears to be an example of the end customers as a major stakeholder in the organisational field exerting a strong influence over the choice of business processes to be performed in the offshore captive centre. Questions remain though about the equivalence of the boundaries around diversity, inclusion and leadership that are necessarily cultural and therefore differ between Australia and India.

In 2016 the ANZ reported to the Australian Workplace Gender Equality Agency about its gender equality performance in Australia. The publicly available results 2014–2015 show staff of 12161 non-managers, of which 30% were males and 70% females, and 10526 managers of which 60% are male and 40% female. The board consisted of 2 females and five males [50].

The ANZ Bank was in the Australian workplace equality index top 10, and the top Australian employer for LGBTI inclusion in 2017.

These reported results show that while the majority of ANZ staff is female only a small number of female staff is placed in management positions. The ANZ was silent on public disclosure about female GIC staff and the gender pay gap offshore, but did report disability inclusion in India, "In India for example, we employed 15 people with a self-disclosed disability in 2012, and a further 18 have been recruited over the last six months" [47].

Driving gender equity in the workplace can be included in CSR activities but as Strachan reminds us

"The examination of gender inequalities presents a picture of differences ... national and regional labour markets vary; national legislative frameworks are different; the type of employing organisation and employment contract differs, and women themselves are a heterogeneous group" [51].

But she goes on to draw similarities:

"Women are more likely than men to experience insecure employment; a gender pay gap is widespread; horizontal segregation by gender abounds with women occupying a narrower range of occupations than men which frequently reflect women's accepted social roles of nurturer; and vertical gender segregation is an international issue as women remain a very low proportion of senior managers, CEOs and company board members" [51].

In 2016 the new CEO of ANZ Bank Shane Elliot published a statement

"I acknowledge and am personally deeply disappointed that our own bank has not met the standards that our customers, shareholders and employees expect. We know that it is going to take a lot of hard work and meaningful action to regain trust, and we are committed to creating sustainable changes" [52].

The ANZ apology was in response to information gathered from customers and stakeholders in Australia, and acknowledged performance could be improved in expectations in the offshore procurement CSR, but no explicit acknowledgement of outcomes in GICs. Balancing the expectations of shareholders, complying with applicable laws, managing the implementation of CSR programs, and evaluating the efficacy of CSR goals, are some of the issues confronting companies.

4 Conclusion

That it is the responsibility of business to be profitable is shared as a basic premise by both Carroll and Friedman, but the questions of business and business scholars alike tend to centre on when is it right, not merely appropriate, for business to become involved in the community, not just the market.

This research explored a specific area of corporate behaviour that is contested and contentious. The inherent tensions in CSR are the immediate costs as non-core business, versus, improving the image of the corporate citizen; and the benefits, if any, to the relationships with stakeholders where CSR is being delivered off or onshore. Support for CSR implementation in captive or GICs is supported by the strength of organisational commitment to, or the style and willingness to implement and of CSR implemented in the captive. Utilising CSR as a management tool to assist in attracting and retaining staff in GICs may provide leverage in containing and possibly reducing high rates of staff turnover (sometimes referred to as staff attrition or churn). Improving the outcomes for women employed in the organization, implementing structural and systemic change that supports the career development of women is vital to establishing employee engagement and retention of female staff and potential leaders.

If Corporate Social Responsibility is to be more than "corporate spin", client companies must focus detailed attention on the CSR outcomes they are achieving at their OBPO captive operations or Global In-house Centres. Our research into GIC in India and the Philippines has found that these operations are making a positive contribution to the communities in which they are sited, a point frequently mentioned by staff employed in these GIC.

With respect to gender equity issues, GIC are clearly providing significant opportunities for well-qualified females to gain paid employment in roles that are seen as high status in their local communities. There is some evidence that the OBPO industry is gradually reducing barriers to gender equity (such as those of culture, status and cast identified by Levina and Vaast [1].

In our research, we have observed GIC where women made up at least 50% of the workforce, but also observed that in some of these GIC, females were under-represented in senior management roles [50].

Thus, there is both a CSR requirement and opportunity for the parent companies of GIC to apply the same gender equity principles to their captive operations as they do in their home countries. Notwithstanding some of the traditional cultural barriers that may exist, our research has also enabled us to observe some outstanding female leaders of large captive operations, noting that ANZ Bank's very large and successful captive operation (ANZ Operations, Technology and Shared Services) in Bangalore is now headed by a female executive, Pankajam Sridevi, who also has overall responsibility for ANZ's OBPO hubs in Chengdu and Manila.

However, this focus on the advancement of women in management does not bind us to the usual exclusion of women at other levels, or, as Grosser describes to the "taking a 'how to succeed' perspective, of liberal feminism that tends to be "uncritical of the gendered (male) nature of organisations". Instead, we argue that a continuing focus on CSR, and research focussing on "missing voices" [31] over the next decade, may see significant positive gains in gender equity through the OBPO industry.

Matten and Moon [28] remind us that defining CSR is not just a technical exercise but also a normative and ideological exercise that varies across nations. So simple evaluations of CSR copied from home country to host must be cognizant of how moral understandings and cultural understandings translate across shores.

4.1 Limitations

A limitation on the capacity to generalise from this research is its focus on client (i.e. outsourcing) companies that operate primarily from Australia with captive operations located in India or the Philippines. Investigation of the depth and breadth of the types and style of CSR practised by organisations, particularly those operating in languages other than English would enrich the knowledge base.

There is evidence in the literature that contracts and well-developed business plans alone do not stand as indicators of success [50, 51] and that managing relationships between stakeholders, cultural difference and cross-cultural management is capturing more scholarly attention across the globe.

4.2 Further Research

Questions for further analyses and research could investigate:

Is there any difference in the strength of each variable that contributes to the types of CSR exercised in captives?

How do stakeholder's (in particular labour, consumers' and management's) values influence organisational commitment to CSR?

What are the influence of cultural difference on the depth to which CSR practices are embedded within an organisation and the alignment of CSR practices within global in-house centres?

How important is CSR in OBPO success?

References

1. Levina, N., Vaast, E.: Innovating or doing as told? Status differences and overlapping boundaries in offshore collaboration. MIS Q. 32(2), 307–332 (2008)
2. Whitaker, J., Mithas, S., Krishnan, M.: Organizational learning and capabilities in onshore and offshore business process outsourcing. J. Manage. Inform Syst. 27(3), 11–42 (2011)

3. Wreford, J., Penter, K., Pervan, G., Davidson, F.: Seeking opaque indifference in offshore BPO? In: Kotlarsky, J., Oshri, I., Willcocks, L.P. (eds.) Global Sourcing (2012), pp. 175–193. Springer, Heidelberg (2012). doi:10.1007/978-3-642-33920-2_11
4. Lacity, M.C., Iyer, V., Rudramuniyaiah, P.S.: Turnover intentions of Indian IS professionals. Inform. Syst. Front. **10**(2), 225–241 (2008)
5. SPi Global Market Reports.: List of figures, charts and diagrams in BPO services global industry guide 2017., Global Data: http://www.spi-reports.com/product/591369, 3 (2017)
6. Stern, P.J., Wennerlind, C. (eds.): Mercantilism Reimagined: Political Economy in Early Modern Britain and Its Empire. Oxford University Press, New York (2013)
7. Davis, G., King, W., Ein-Dor, P., Torkzadeh, R.: IT offshoring: history, prospects and challenges. J. Assoc. Inf. Syst. **7**(1), 32 (2006)
8. Metters, R., Verma, R.: History of offshoring knowledge services. JOM **26**(2), 141–147 (2008)
9. Davidson, F., Wreford, J., Pervan, G., Penter, K.: Capturing CSR: doing good offshore. In: Kotlarsky, J., Oshri, I., Willcocks, L.P. (eds.) Global Sourcing 2014. LNBIP, vol. 195, pp. 98–113. Springer, Cham (2014). doi:10.1007/978-3-319-11367-8_7
10. Lacity, M.C., Solomon, S., Yan, A., Willcocks, L.P.: Business process outsourcing studies: a critical review and research directions. JIT **26**(4), 221–258 (2011)
11. Strasser, A., Westner, M.: Information systems offshoring: results of a systematic literature review. J. Inform. Tech. Manage. **26**(2), 70–142 (2015)
12. Wreford, J., Davidson, F., Pervan, G., Penter, K.: Opaque indifference and corporate social responsibility: a moral license for offshore BPO? In: Oshri, I., Kotlarsky, J., Willcocks, L.P. (eds.) Global Sourcing 2013. LNBIP, vol. 163, pp. 192–209. Springer, Heidelberg (2013). doi:10.1007/978-3-642-40951-6_12
13. Lacity, M.C., Willcocks, L.P.: Outsourcing business processes for innovation. MIT Sloan Manage. Rev. **54**(3), 63 (2013)
14. Gonzalez, R., Llopis, J., Gasco, J.: Information systems offshore outsourcing: managerial conclusions from academic research. Int. Entrep. Manage. J. **9**(2), 229–259 (2013)
15. Oshri, I., Van Uhm, B.: A historical review of the information technology and business process captive centre sector. JIT **27**(4), 270–284 (2012)
16. Oshri, I., Kotlarsky, J., Willcocks, L.P.: The Handbook of Global Outsourcing and Offshoring, 3rd edn. Springer, Heidelberg (2015). doi:10.1007/978-1-137-43744-0
17. Oshri, I.: Offshoring Strategies: Evolving Captive Center Models. The MIT Press, Boston (2011)
18. Suchman, M.C.: Managing legitimacy: strategic and institutional approaches. Acad. Manage. Rev. **20**(3), 571–610 (1995)
19. Garriga, E., Melé, D.: Corporate social responsibility theories: mapping the territory. J. Bus. Ethics **53**(1), 51–71 (2004)
20. Crane, A., Matten, D., Moon, J.: The emergence of corporate citizenship: historical development and alternative perspectives. In: Handbook of Research on Global Corporate Citizenship, pp. 25–49 (2013)
21. Carroll, A.B.: Corporate social responsibility: evolution of definitional construct. Bus. Soc. **38**(3), 268–295 (1999)
22. Costa, R., Menichini, T.: A multidimensional approach for CSR assessment: the importance of the stakeholder perception. Expert Syst. Appl. **40**(1), 150–161 (2013)
23. Pérez, A., Del Bosque, I.R.: Measuring CSR image: three studies to develop and to validate a reliable measurement tool. J. Bus. Ethics **118**(2), 265–286 (2013)
24. Chaudhary, R.: Corporate social responsibility and employee engagement: can CSR help in redressing the engagement gap? SRJ **13**(2), 323–338 (2017)

25. Clarke, T., Branson, D.M.: The SAGE Handbook of Corporate Governance. Sage Publications, London (2012)
26. Galbreath, J.: Building corporate social responsibility into strategy. Euro. Bus. Rev. **21**(2), 109–127 (2009)
27. Moon, J.: The social responsibility of business and new governance. Gov. Oppos. **37**(3), 385–408 (2002)
28. Matten, D., Moon, J.: "Implicit" and "explicit" CSR: a conceptual framework for a comparative understanding of corporate social responsibility. Acad. Manag. Rev. **33**(2), 404–424 (2008)
29. Thomas, G., Nowak, M.: Corporate Social Responsibility: A definition, Graduate School of Business Working Paper Number 62. Graduate School of Business, Curtin University of Technology, Perth (2006)
30. Young, S., Thyil, V.: Corporate social responsibility and corporate governance: role of context in international settings. J. Bus. Ethics **122**(1), 1–24 (2014)
31. Grosser, K., Moon, J.: Gender mainstreaming and corporate social responsibility: reporting workplace issues. J. Bus. Ethics **62**(4), 327–340 (2005)
32. Kelly, S., Noonan, C.: Anxiety and psychological security in offshoring relationships: the role and development of trust as emotional commitment. JIT **23**(4), 232–248 (2008)
33. Klettner, A., Clarke, T., Boersma, M.: The governance of corporate sustainability: empirical insights into the development, leadership and implementation of responsible business strategy. J. Bus. Ethics **122**(1), 145–165 (2014)
34. Secchi, D., Bui, H.T.M: Group effects on individual attitudes toward social responsibility. J. Bus. Ethics, 1–22 (2016)
35. Pisani, N., Ricart, J.E.: Offshoring of services: a review of the literature and organizing framework. Manag. Int. Rev. **56**(3), 385–424 (2016)
36. Wiener, M., Vogel, B., Amberg, M.: Information systems offshoring-a literature review and analysis. Inform. Syst. **27**, 455–492 (2010)
37. Orlitzky, M., Schmidt, F.L., Rynes, S.L.: Corporate social and financial performance: a meta-analysis. Org. Stud. **24**(30), 403–441 (2003)
38. Brine, M., Brown, R., Hackett, G.: Corporate social responsibility and financial performance in the Australian context. Econ. Round Up Autumn **47** (2007)
39. Scherer, A.G., Palazzo, G.: The new political role of business in a globalized world: a review of a new perspective on CSR and its implications for the firm, governance, and democracy. J. Manage. Stud. **48**(4), 899–931 (2011)
40. Moir, L.: What do we mean by corporate social responsibility? Corp. Govern. **1**(2), 16–22 (2001)
41. Schleimer, S., Rice, J.: Australian corporate social responsibility reports are little better than window dressing. The Conversation (2017). http://theconversation.com/australian-corporate-social-responsibility-reports-are-little-better-than-window-dressing-66037
42. Australian Centre for Corporate Social Responsibility.: The 10th year – progress and prospects for CSR in Australia and New Zealand: The state of CSR in Australia and New Zealand annual review (2014); The longest running study of CSR practises down under. ACCSR Docklands Victoria (2017)
43. Penter, K., Wreford, J., Pervan, G., Davidson, F.: Offshore BPO decisions and institutional influence on senior managers. In: Oshri, I., Kotlarsky, J., Willcocks, L.P. (eds.) Global Sourcing 2013. LNBIP, vol. 163, pp. 93–116. Springer, Heidelberg (2013). doi: 10.1007/978-3-642-40951-6_6
44. Brammer, S., Millington, A., Rayton, B.: The contribution of corporate social responsibility to organizational commitment. Int. J. Hum. Resour. Manage. **18**(10), 1701–1719 (2007)

45. Rosati, F., Calabrese, A., Costa, R., Pedersen, E.R.G.: The impact of gender, education and age on employee attitudes towards corporate social responsibility. In: Global Cleaner Production & Sustainable Consumption Conference (2016)
46. UNSW Business School.: Corporate social responsibility: A fig leaf for capitalism or path to a better world (2012). https://www.businessthink.unsw.edu.au/Pages/Corporate-Social-Responsibility-A-Fig-Leaf-for-Capitalism-or-Path-to-a-Better-World.aspx
47. ANZ Bank: ANZ Corporate Responsibility Report: interim Report (2013). http://www.anz.com/resources/2/8/287acb004f90e250a33cff5fd4649a8e/ANZ_CRInterim_(2013).pdf
48. ANZ Bank: ANZ in India (2016). https://www.anz.com/india/en/about-us/our-company/anz-india/
49. ANZ Bank: Notice of meeting for 2006 ANZ General Meeting (2006). https://www.anz.com/documents/au/investor/agm/2006/271006.pdf
50. Workplace Gender Equality Agency (2016). https://www.wgea.gov.au/sites/default/files/public_reports/tempPublicReport_g4f5ndg2f4.pdf
51. Strachan, G., Adikaram, A., Kailasapathy, P.: Gender (in) equality in South Asia: problems, prospects and pathways. S. Asian J. Hum. Resour. Manag.2(1), 1–11 (2016)
52. ANZ Bank 2016: 2016 Half year Corporate Sustainability Update (2016). http://www.shareholder.anz.com/sites/default/files/anz_2016_half_year_corporate_sustainability_report_-_030516_final_9.45am.pdf

Cloud Readiness as an Enabler for Application Rationalization: A Survey in the Netherlands

Erik Beulen[✉]

TIAS School for Business and Society, Warandelaan 2,
PO Box 90153, 5000 LE, Tilburg, The Netherlands
e.beulen@tias.edu

Abstract. For over a decade both cloud computing and application rationalization are IT-strategy priorities in most organizations. Cloud computing has grown in the last decade and will continue to grow steadily. Most organizations struggle with reducing the number of applications. There remains a strong resistance from the business, to consolidate and standardize the legacy application platforms. Potentially migrating legacy applications to Software-as-a-Service applications resolves the business migration concerns. As the Software-as-a-Service functionality is a ready to use functionality which can be assessed prior to phasing out legacy applications. This is a distinct difference from a scenario where legacy applications will be replaced by to-be-(custom)-build applications. Also the implementation roadmap of Software-as-a-Services applications is much shorter and most of the Software-as-a-Services applications have data migration tools to import the data from the legacy applications into the new environment. A survey of 124 organizations indicated weak negative linear relationship between the estimated percentage Software as a Service applications and the envisioned number of applications for organizations with +500 applications for the period 2017–2022 (three two year intervals).

Keywords: Application rationalization · Cloud computing · Cloud migration · IT-strategy · Legacy applications and Software-as-a-Service

1 Introduction

For over a decade organizations prioritizing cloud computing and the cloud computing spend increased and is expected to increase in the next decade [1, 2]. The 2016 projected growth for the worldwide public cloud services market is 17.2% ($208.6 billion). Software as a Service is expected to grow 21.7% in 2016 to reach $38.9 billion [3]. The advantages of cloud computing include cost savings, cost flexibility, replacing CAPEX by OPEX, faster deployment, improved quality, reduction of risks, enabling standardization and reduce vendor lock-in [4–7]. Still there are a large number of concerns that have to be addressed prior to transforming legacy applications into cloud solutions. The risks of cloud computing include cloud computing market maturity, the application portfolio readiness for cloud computing, ability to measure and meet service levels, security, data privacy and compliancy risks, business case risks including cost overrun

© Springer International Publishing AG 2017
I. Oshri et al. (Eds.): Global Sourcing 2017, LNBIP 306, pp. 111–123, 2017.
https://doi.org/10.1007/978-3-319-70305-3_7

of a cloud migration and availability of knowledge in the retained organization to manage cloud computing service providers [8, 9].

Also application rationalization is an integral part of the IT-strategy of many organizations [10–12]. There is no rule of thumb for the number of applications organizations needed. This is dependent on diversity of the business operations of an organization and the size of an organization. However organizations with a 500+ application portfolio need to consider application rationalization. Market indications for the target number of applications are below 250 applications and if possible below 100 applications. Reduction of the number of applications and standardizing the software is reducing the maintenance costs and risk profile [13–15]. However for IT-departments to convince business representatives of the need for applications rationalization is not straightforward as in most organization the IT budget is with the business representatives [16]. An often heard argument is concerns about the ability to capture specific business requirements in the consolidated application [17, 18]. Also service continuity throughout the migration is often a concern of business representatives [19–21]. Software-as-a-Service addresses these concerns, as the cloud functionality is a ready to use functionality which can be assessed prior to phase out legacy applications. This is a distinct difference from a scenario where legacy application will be replaced by to-be-(custom)-build applications. Also the implementation roadmap of Software-as-a-Services applications is much shorter [22–25]. Furthermore most of the Software-as-a-Services applications have sophisticated data migration tools to import the data from the legacy applications into the new environment [26, 27].

This application rationalization strategy is also different from strategies we have observed in the market where legacy applications were upgraded to be ready for hosting on an Infrastructure-as-a-Service platform [28, 29]. The hosting on an Infrastructure-as-a-Service platform is improving the application performance and reducing the infrastructure maintenance costs, but not necessary resulting in application rationalization [30, 31]. The application migration roadmap of applications on Infrastructure-as-a-Service platforms will not be faster than the roadmap for an application migration roadmap for traditional datacenters.

Also this strategy is different from replacing legacy applications by applications developed on a Platform-as-a-Service environment. A Platform-as-a-Service will reduce the implementation roadmap significantly [32–34] but the assessment of the functionality of the new applications cannot be performed prior to phasing out legacy applications.

By leveraging Service-as-a-Service to achieve application rationalization, organizations can achieve two elements of their IT-strategy, increasing cloud computing and application rationalization, resulting in a simplified and more cost effective information technology service provisioning.

2   Hypotheses

Applications need to be hosted. In this research includes four hosting options. In additional to the traditional data center, the cloud services Infrastructure-as-a-Service, Platform-as-a-Service and Software-as-a-service are considered in this research. The focus in this research is on Software-as-a-Service, as this is best addressing the business application rationalization concerns related to the ability to assess the functionality prior to phasing out the legacy applications and migration risks related to the service continuity and timelines. This research explores the correlation between the percentage Software-as-a-Service applications versus the total number of applications (Pearson correlation – [35–38]). The hypotheses test if the percentage of Software-as-a-Service applications is a predictor for the total number of applications for organizations with +500 applications. For organizations with <500 applications the impact of Software-as-a-Service on application rationalization is expected to be less as there is not a high number of applications. In this research we expect that a higher percentage of Software-as-a-Service applications is linked to a lower total number of applications for organizations with >=500 applications (downhill correlation). The hypotheses are tested for three two-year periods: 2017–2018, 2019–2020 and 2021–2022. The 95% critical values of the correlation coefficients decide if r is significant or not. This will provide insides in the expected impact of the adoption of Software-as-a-Service on application rationalization.

ρ = percentage SaaS applications versus total # applications for organizations with >=500 applications

$H_{0\,(2017\text{-}2018)} : \rho = 0$
$H_{A(2017\text{-}2018)} : \rho < 0$

$H_{0\,(2019\text{-}2020)} : \rho = 0$
$H_{A(2019\text{-}2020)} : \rho < 0$

$H_{0\,(2021\text{-}2022)} : \rho = 0$
$H_{A(2021\text{-}2022)} : \rho < 0$

3   Data Collection

The data for this research is collected by a survey. The survey was submitted to ICT Media, a Dutch organization that facilities IT decision makers in the Netherlands. The members of this community are Chief Information Officers and their direct reports. The response rate was 3.5% (124 responses to 3,500 invitations). However a large number of respondents provide responses which included inconsistencies such as high spend percentages for cloud computing and no allocation to any of the cloud computing categories. Other respondents didn't complete the survey. The number of responses that has been taken into account is 58, which reduced the response rate from 3.5% to 1.7%. In the analyses only the 58 respondents are taken into account. The survey was an anonymous survey; therefore, it is not possible to conclude the representativeness of the sample (58 responses versus total community of 3,500 members). However, the spread over the different sectors and spread of the size of the organizations the respondents represent do not indicate that the respondents are not representative for the community, which was also confirmed by ICT Media.

The survey was conducted in Dutch. An English translation of the survey in include in the appendix. The participants completed their response via a portal. The responses were collected from 24 October to 15 November 2016. The potential participants received one friendly reminder the second week the survey was introduced.

4   Survey Population Characteristics

The participating organizations include national and international organizations. Over 25% of the participating organizations generate over 25% of their revenues outside the Netherlands (see Fig. 1). As expected the larger organization are predominantly the international organization. Over half of the international organizations operate in manufacturing. The sectors government, education and healthcare are the dominant sector in the participating national organizations, with respectively 7, 5 and 5 organizations.

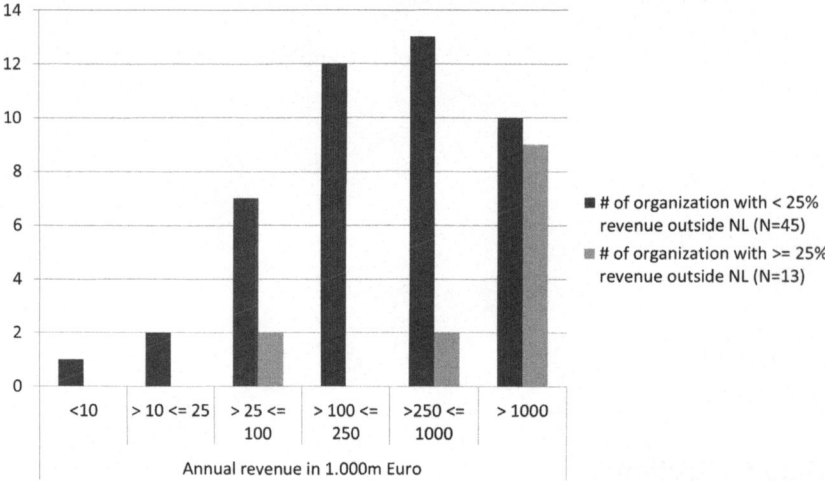

Fig. 1. Participating organizations by annual revenue in 1.000m Euro – split in national and international organizations – N = 58.

The cloud computing usage related to application hosting is increasing in the years to come (December 2016 follow by three two year intervals: 2017–2018, 2019–2020 and 2021–2022). The cloud computing usage is differentiated into Infrastructure-as-a-Service, Platform-as-a-Service and Software-as-a-Service. The contribution to application rationalization these different types of cloud computing is different. The adoption of Software-as-a-Service has the highest contribution to application rationalization where Infrastructure-as-a-Service has the lowest contribution. The envisioned number of applications hosted by Software-as-a-Service will growth from 14% of the number of the total number application in December 2016 to 35% in December 2022. The contribution of the traditional datacenters will decrease. The importance of Infrastructure-as-a-Service and Platform-as-a-Service will increase over time but the growth rate is lower than the growth rate of Software-as-a-Service platforms (see Fig. 2).

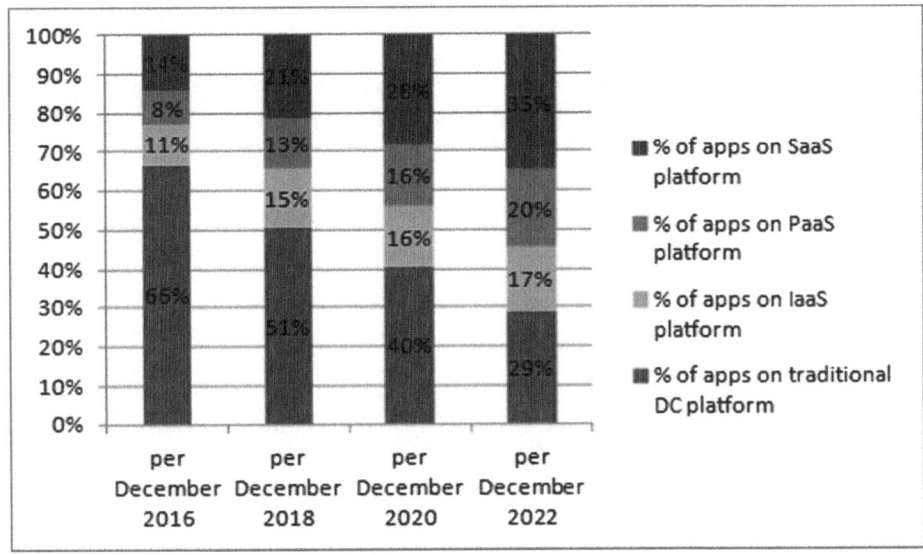

Fig. 2. Percentage of the application hosted by traditional DC platforms, Infrastructure-as-a-Service, Platform-as-a-Service and Software-as-a-Service per December 2016–2022 (N = 49).

However the cloud spend of the total IT spend is relatively low, 41% of the participating organizations have spent in 2016 less than 5% on cloud computing and 84% of the participating organizations have spent in 2016 25% or less on cloud computing (see Fig. 3).

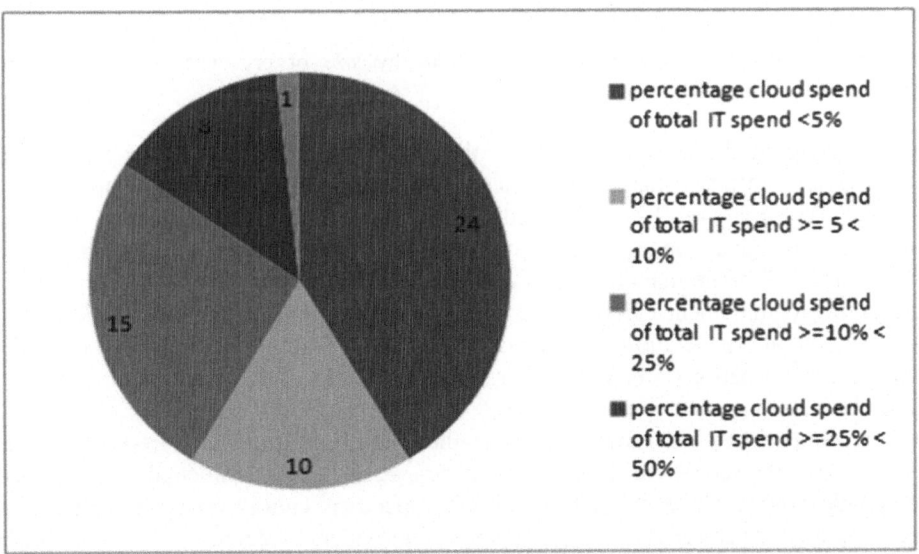

Fig. 3. Number of organizations per category percentage cloud spend of the total IT spend (<5%, >=5% < 10%, >=10% < 25% and >=25% < 50%) (N = 58).

The envisioned number of applications of the participating organizations is reducing in the years to come (three two year intervals: 2017–2018, 2019–2020 and 2021–2022). The large organizations (annual revenue >=250m Euro, N = 34) on average have three times the number of applications of small organizations (annual revenue < 250m Euro, N = 24) (see Fig. 4). However if in the group of large organizations the three organizations with the largest number of applications are removed the remaining large organization only have twice the number of applications of the small organizations.

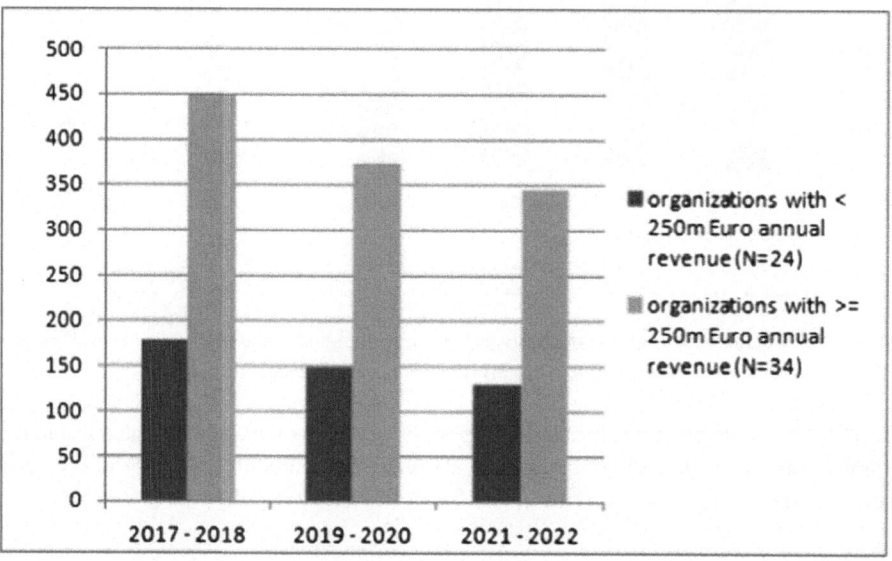

Fig. 4. Envisioned average number applications by size of organization (<250m Euro and >=250m Euro annual revenue).

In the survey the respondents ranked the advantage and risks of cloud computing, detailed for Infrastructure-as-a-Service, Platform-as-a-Service and Software-as-Service. The survey results are detailed in Figs. 5 and 6. The standardization of applications is the highest ranked advantage for Software-as-as-Services (3.72 score on 1–5 Likert scale). A large manufacturing organization (respondent 104) is levering cloud computing to implement a global standard to enable the connection of local back offices. An agricultural organization (respondent 58) leverage Software-as-a-Service to facilitate the transformation of the retained organization from a IT delivery organization into an orchestrator organization.

The data privacy and security risks are the highest risks for Software-as-a-Service (3.92 and 3.90 scores on 1–5 Likert scale). A large governmental organization (respondent 69) added reaching the maximum capacity of cloud solutions as a risk. This risk is limited to private clouds as cloud service providers by default will increase their capacity if there is an additional demand from their clients. This organization also flagged the delivery risks of an integration (cloud services and legacy services) as part of the migration as severe risk.

The number of participants was too small to analyze the ranking of the advantages and risks by sector and/or by size of the organization.

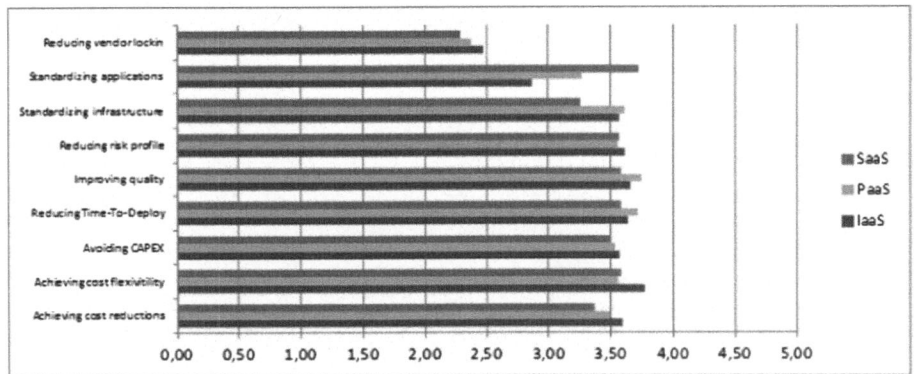

Fig. 5. Advantage of cloud computing (IaaS, PaaS and SaaS) – Likert scale 1–5 – N = 58.

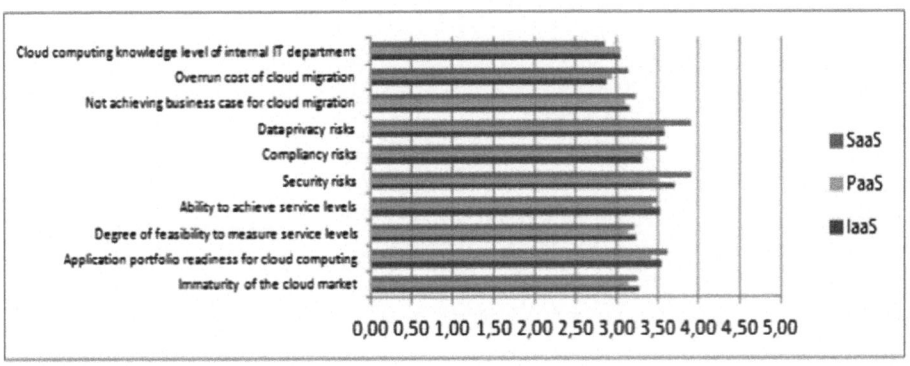

Fig. 6. Risks of cloud computing (IaaS, PaaS and SaaS) – Likert scale 1–5 – N = 58.

5 Data Analyses

The impact of Software-as-a-Service on application rationalization was tested for the responding organizations with >=500 applications. The hypotheses are tested for three two-year periods: 2017–2018, 2019–2020 and 2021–2022. The 95% critical values of the correlation coefficients decide if r is significant or not.

The number of responding organizations with >=500 applications was limited to 16 organizations (N = 16). The preferred minimal number of responses is 25 (David, 1938). The low number of responses will impact the reliability of the tests.

ρ = percentage SaaS applications versus total # applications for organizations with >=500 applications

$H_{0\ (2017\text{-}2018)}$: $\rho = 0$
$H_{A(2017\text{-}2018)}$: $\rho < 0$

$R^2 = 0{,}0858$ and $r = 0{,}29291637$

The calculated r indicates a weak downhill (negative) linear relationship (see Fig. 7).

df=n−2=16−2=14

The critical values associated with df=14 are ±0,497. If r is r is greater than the positive critical value, then r is significant. Since r=0,29291637 and 0,29291637<0,497, r is not significant and the line cannot be used for prediction.

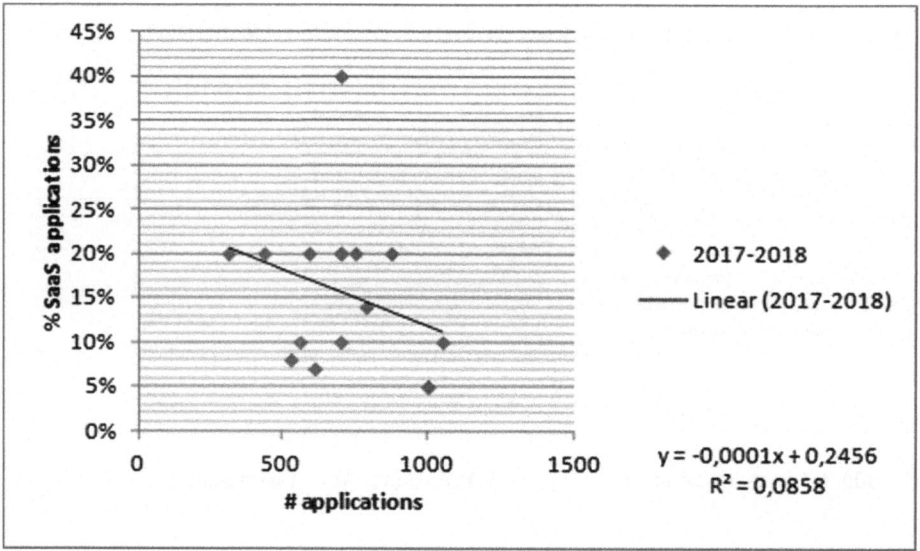

Fig. 7. Correlation of envisioned % of Software-as-a-Service applications and total number of applications in 2017–2018 (N = 16).

ρ = percentage SaaS applications versus total # applications for organizations with >=500 applications

$H_{0\ (2019\text{-}2020)} : \rho = 0$
$H_{A(2019\text{-}2020)} : \rho < 0$

$R^2 = 0{,}1183$ and $r = 0{,}34394767$

The calculated r indicates a weak downhill (negative) linear relationship (see Fig. 8).

df=n−2=16−2=14

The critical values associated with df=14 are ±0,497. If r is r is greater than the positive critical value, then r is significant. Since r=0,34394767 and 0,34394767<0,497, r is not significant and the line cannot be used for prediction.

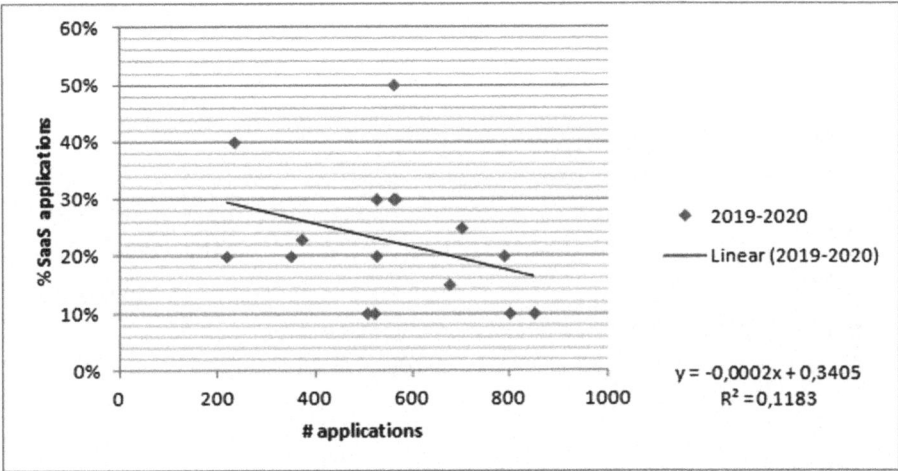

Fig. 8. Correlation of envisioned % of Software-as-a-Service applications and total number of applications in 2018–2019 (N = 16).

ρ = percentage SaaS applications versus total # applications for organizations with >=500 applications

$H_{0\ (2021-2022)}: \rho = 0$
$H_{A(2021-2022)}: \rho < 0$

R^2=0,1617 and r=0,402119385

The calculated r indicates a weak downhill (negative) linear relationship (see Fig. 9).

df=n−2=16−2=14

The critical values associated with df=14 are ±0,497. If r is r is greater than the positive critical value, then r is significant. Since r=0,402119385 and 0,402119385<0,497, r is not significant and the line cannot be used for prediction.

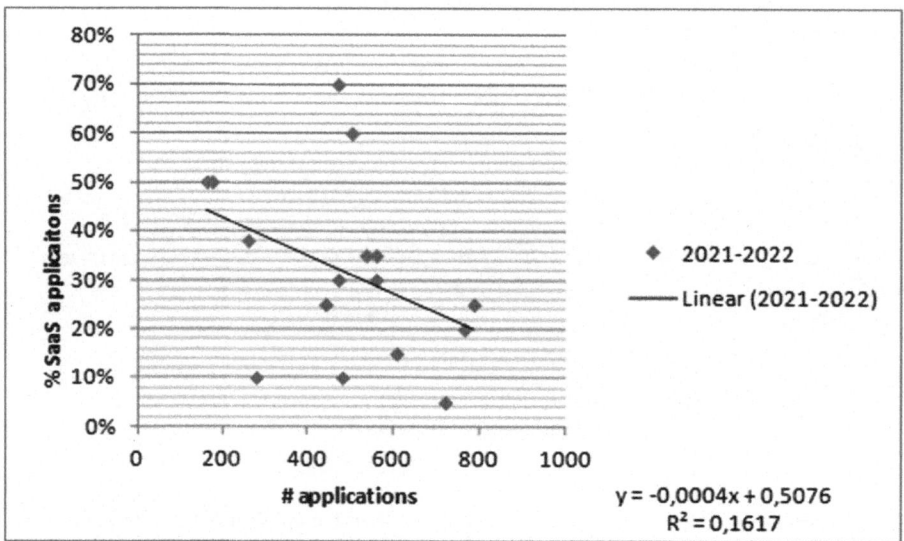

Fig. 9. Correlation of envisioned % of Software-as-a-Service applications and total number of applications in 2021–2022 (N = 16).

6   Conclusions

All three H_0 hypotheses were accepted however the data showed a weak negative linear relationship between the estimated percentage Software as a Service applications and the envisioned number of applications for organizations 500+ applications for the period 2017–2022 (three two-year intervals). The weak negative linear relationship became stronger over time (2017–2018 versus 2019–2020 and 2021–2022, and 2019–2020 versus 2021–2022). This indicates that leveraging Software-as-a-Service applications in application rationalization programs has to be considered.

To understand the correlation between Software-as-a-Service applications and application rationalization better additional research is required. The survey can be conducted in other countries. An increased number of data point will give additional insides. Also expert interviews with Chief Information Officers and their direct report can be conducted to understand cloud adoption and application rationalization in the context of the IT strategy better.

7 Acknowledgements

The author would like to thank Rob Beijleveld, Jennifer Roos and Arnoud van Gemeren from ICT Media (www.ictmedia.nl) for inviting the members of the ICT Media community to participate in the survey and for facilitating the execution of the survey.

References

1. Anderson, E., Warrilow, M.: Market Insight: Cloud Shift — The Transition of IT Spending From Traditional Systems to Cloud. Gartner research report, ID: G00301664, 18 May (2016)
2. McGrath, B.: CloudView 2016: Customer Budgets Shift to the Cloud. IDC research report, doc # US40852416, June 2016 (2016)
3. Gartner: Gartner Says Worldwide Public Cloud Services Market to Grow 17 Percent in 2016. Press release, September 15 (2016). www.gartner.com/newsroom/id/3443517
4. Avram, M.: Advantages and challenges of adopting cloud computing from an enterprise perspective. Procedia Technol. **12**, 529–534 (2014)
5. Beulen, E., Koolen S.: Cloud computing. In: Willcocks, L., Oshri, I., Kotlarsky, J. (eds.) Proceedings Sixth Global Sourcing Conference, March 12–15 (2012)
6. Gangwar, H., Date, H., Ramaswamy, R.: Understanding determinants of cloud computing adoption using an integrated TAM-TOE model. J. Enterp. Inf. Manage. **28**(1), 107–130 (2015)
7. Oliveira, T., Thomas, M., Espadanal, M.: Assessing the determinants of cloud computing adoption: an analysis of the manufacturing and services sectors. Inf. Manage. **51**(5), 497–510 (2014)
8. Moreno-Vozmediano, R., Montero, R., Llorente, I.: Key challenges in cloud computing: enabling the future internet of services. IEEE Internet Comput. **17**(4), 18–25 (2013)
9. Rittinghouse, J., Ransome, J.: Cloud Computing: Implementation, Management, and Security. CRC Press, London (2016)
10. Galliers, R., Leidner, D.: Strategic Information Management: Challenges and Strategies in Managing Information Systems. Routledge, London (2014)
11. Sun, L., et al.: Evaluating business value of IT towards optimisation of the application portfolio. Enterp. Inf. Syst. **10**(4), 378–399 (2016)
12. Ward, J., Peppard, J.: The Strategic Management of Information Systems: Building a Digital Strategy. Wiley, London (2016)
13. Fenton, N., Bieman, J.: Software Metrics: A Rigorous and Practical Approach. CRC Press, London (2014)
14. McKeen, J., Smith, H.: Developments in practice XXXIV: application portfolio management. Commun. Assoc. Inf. Syst. **26**(1), 9 (2010)

15. Sjøberg, D., et al.: Quantifying the effect of code smells on maintenance effort. IEEE Trans. Softw. Eng. **39**(8), 1144–1156 (2013)
16. McAfee, A.: What every CEO needs to know about the cloud. Harv. Bus. Rev. **89**(11), 124–132 (2011)
17. O'Driscoll, K.: The agile data modelling & design thinking approach to information system requirements analysis. J. Decis. Syst. **25**(sup1), 632–638 (2016)
18. Wiegers, K., Beatty, J.: Software Requirements. Pearson Education, London (2013)
19. Carroll, N., Helfert, M., Lynn, T.: Towards the development of a cloud service capability assessment framework. In: Mahmood, Z. (ed.) Continued Rise of the Cloud. Computer Communications and Networks, pp. 289–336. Springer, London. doi:10.1007/978-1-4471-6452-4_12
20. Ganesan, A., Chithralekha, T.: A survey on survey of migration of legacy systems. In: Proceedings of the International Conference on Informatics and Analytics, August, p. 72 (2016)
21. Ravindran, K., Adiththan, A., Iannelli, M.: Benchmarks to compare cloud service providers for seamless customer migration. In: 2016 8th International Conference on Communication Systems and Networks (COMSNETS), January, pp. 1–8 (2016)
22. Chaisiri, S., Lee, B., Niyato, D.: Optimization of resource provisioning cost in cloud computing. IEEE Trans. Serv. Comput. **5**(2), 164–177 (2012)
23. Gao, J., Bai, X., Tsai, W., Uehara, T.: Saas testing on clouds-issues, challenges and needs. In: 2013 IEEE 7th International Symposium on Service Oriented System Engineering (SOSE), March, pp. 409–415. IEEE (2013)
24. Huang, K., Shen, B.: Service deployment strategies for efficient execution of composite SaaS applications on cloud platform. J. Syst. Softw. **107**, 127–141 (2015)
25. Kim, M., et al.: Building scalable, secure, multi-tenant cloud services on IBM Bluemix. IBM J. Res. Dev. **60**(2–3), 8–10 (2016)
26. Beyer, M., Thoo, E., Zaidi, E., Greenwald, R.: Magic quadrant for data integration tools. Gartner research report. ID: G00303221, 8 August (2016)
27. Rao, R., Prakash, P.: Improving security for data migration in cloud computing using randomized encryption technique. IOSR J. Comput. Eng. **11**(6), 39–42 (2013)
28. Nabi, M., Khendek, F., Toeroe, M.: Upgrade of the IaaS cloud: issues and potential solutions in the context of high-availability. In: 2015 IEEE International Symposium Software Reliability Engineering Workshops (ISSREW), November, pp. 21–24 (2015)
29. Teixeira, M.: Migrating legacy web apps to cloud computing environments: an architectural and economic perspective. In: Proceedings of the 22nd Brazilian Symposium on Multimedia and the Web, November, pp. 3–4 (2016)
30. Kuhlenkamp, J., Rudolph, K., Bermbach, D.: AISLE: assessment of provisioned service levels in public IaaS-based database systems. In: Barros, A., Grigori, D., Narendra, N.C., Dam, H.K. (eds.) ICSOC 2015. LNCS, vol. 9435, pp. 154–168. Springer, Heidelberg (2015). https://doi.org/10.1007/978-3-662-48616-0_10
31. Wu, L., et al.: SLA-based resource provisioning for hosted software-as-a-service applications in cloud computing environments. IEEE Trans. Serv. Comput. **7**(3), 465–485 (2014)
32. Garrison, G., Kim, S., Wakefield, R.: Success factors for deploying cloud computing. Commun. ACM **55**(9), 62–68 (2012)
33. Pahl, C.: Containerisation and the PaaS cloud. IEEE Cloud Comput. **2**(3), 24–31 (2015)
34. Sandikkaya, M., Harmanci, A.: Security problems of platform-as-a-service (PaaS) clouds and practical solutions to the problems. In: 2012 IEEE 31st Symposium Reliable Distributed Systems (SRDS), pp. 463–468 (2012)
35. Cohen, J., Cohen, P., West, S., Aiken, L.: Applied Multiple Regression/Correlation Analysis for the Behavioral Sciences. Routledge, London (2013)

36. David, F.: Tables of the Ordinates and Probability Integral of the Distribution of the Correlation Coefficient in Small Samples. Cambridge University Press, Cambridge (1938)
37. Hayes, A.: Introduction to Mediation, Moderation, and Conditional Process Analysis: A Regression-Based Approach. Guilford Press, Guilford (2013)
38. Hedges, L., Olkin, I.: Statistical Methods for Meta-Analysis. Academic Press, Amsterdam (2014)

Management of Multi-cloud Computing

Paul Alpar[1]([⊠]) and Ariana Polyviou[2]

[1] University at Marburg, Universitätsstr. 24, 35037 Marburg, Germany
alpar@wiwi.uni-marburg.de
[2] University of Cyprus, University Avenue, 2109 Nicosia, Cyprus
polyviou.ariana@ucy.ac.cy

Abstract. Cloud computing can be considered a form of information technology outsourcing (ITO). However, it is more flexible than traditional ITO because no service volumes and no long contract periods need to be fixed. Companies that employ cloud computing may use several cloud service suppliers at the same time. Similarly, many companies that employ traditional ITO have contracts with several vendors. If the rendered services need to be coordinated, additional efforts are needed to manage this multi-sourcing environment. We find that the coordination arrangements known in multi-sourcing also occur in multi-cloud computing, but that significant differences exist in the actual coordination implementation. Based on the technology applied in cloud computing, new software has been developed to automate the integration tasks. In addition, many new players who offer coordination of multiple clouds as a service have entered the market.

Keywords: Cloud computing · Private cloud · Hybrid cloud · Multi-cloud · SaaS · PaaS · IaaS

1 Introduction

Cloud computing has become an important way of providing computing services. It originates from technologies like virtualization, service-oriented architectures, grid computing, and principles like on-demand computing [1]. We adopt the definition of cloud computing given by the U.S. National Institute of Standards and Technology (NIST): "Cloud computing is a model for enabling ubiquitous, convenient, on-demand network access to a shared pool of configurable computing resources (e.g., networks, servers, storage, applications, and services) that can be rapidly provisioned and released with minimal management effort or service provider interaction" [2]. We define multi-cloud computing as an organization's use of two or more cloud services that are owned by independent organizations.

Most of the individuals and organizations, which use the Internet, are likely to use some applications built on public clouds (e.g., internet search, maps, navigation, encyclopedia, calendars). However, these applications are usually not integrated with other applications. Such use of individual applications in the public cloud without integration with internal or other external applications, does not require much coordination effort by companies and is not the subject of this paper. We investigate multi-cloud computing where some interdependence between the services exists.

© Springer International Publishing AG 2017
I. Oshri et al. (Eds.): Global Sourcing 2017, LNBIP 306, pp. 124–137, 2017.
https://doi.org/10.1007/978-3-319-70305-3_8

Two cloud services may be closely related to each other. For example, if a company employs a cloud application for ERP from one provider and a CRM application from another, then their integration is needed and could be supported by the two service providers. Even if the two service providers do not collaborate, the client needs to coordinate the two services (e.g., to format the output of one application so it can be input into the other application and to decide when the data exchange should take place). The interdependence of the services might also impose that the providers offer the same type of service and compete for the business of the client. In this case, the client has to coordinate when and how much service to acquire from each service provider, but they will not be willing to collaborate much.

Recent studies underline that the phenomenon of multi-cloud computing is becoming more widespread. For example, a survey of German companies between 20 and 2500 employees in 2015 revealed that their favorite use of cloud computing is shifting from the exclusive usage of the private (or only one public cloud) to the deployment of hybrid and multi-clouds [3]. Another world-wide survey among 1060 professionals conducted in 2016 by RightScale revealed that companies employ on average 1.7 private clouds and 1.5 public clouds (while experimenting with another 1.3 private and 1.5 public clouds) [4]. The need for coordination of cloud services from different providers generates challenges (see below) that are not encountered when the service is provisioned only by one provider or by several providers with independent services. Despite the growing use of multi-cloud computing, the problem of coordination and management in the environment of multi-cloud computing has not been conceptually addressed by existing literature. To this end, this paper aims to analyze the approaches to coordination of multiple clouds from different cloud service providers and to assess the possible advantages and disadvantages of these arrangements.

The paper is structured as follows: in the next section, we briefly recapitulate the characteristics of cloud computing and its different forms. In the third section, we analyze the coordination modes in multi-sourcing of IT services as a possible reference for multi-cloud computing. This is followed by a closer look into multi-cloud computing. Then, we apply the coordination modes identified in the third section to multi-cloud computing and discuss tools that are already available for this purpose. In the sixth section, we analyze the differences of the coordination modes incl. the potential problem of lock-in. The paper is wrapped up by short conclusions.

2 Cloud Computing

The use of cloud computing brings numerous benefits to organizations. Cloud computing provides computing services which can autonomously scale up or down the capacity of IT resources so as to adapt to the demands of the organization at any time [5–7]. It eases the remote access to the organization's IT resources from anywhere and at anytime regardless of the terminal device or the geographical location [8, 9]. Additionally, cloud computing reduces the needs of the organization in terms of maintenance and IT management overheads, as a large amount of IT resource maintenance shifts from the organization to the cloud provider [10, 11]. Also from a financial perspective, cloud computing minimizes the IT investment and maintenance costs and contributes in moving the IT expenses from capital expenditure (CAPEX) to operation expenditure (OPEX) [12].

Cloud computing can be decomposed into different service models determined by the level of abstraction. Table 1 describes the basic characteristics of each of the layers and provides examples of related cloud services. NIST identifies three basic service models for cloud computing: Software as a Service (SaaS), Platform as a Service (PaaS) and Infrastructure as a Service (IaaS) [2]. IaaS refers to the provisioning of "processing, storage, networks, and other fundamental computing resources". PaaS denotes the "capability provided to the consumer to deploy onto the cloud infrastructure consumer-created or acquired applications created using programming languages, libraries, services, and tools". SaaS relates to "applications running on a cloud infrastructure which are accessible from various client devices through either a thin client interface, such as a web browser or a program interface" [2].

Table 1. Summary of cloud computing services as illustrated in [5].

Service	Description	Product type	Examples of vendors & services
SaaS	Applications and software accessed virtually via the Internet	Web applications	Salesforce.com (CRM)
PaaS	Platform of services which assist the application development process and accessed virtually via the Internet	Platform fostering the programming APIs and frameworks	Google App Engine & Microsoft Azure
IaaS	Virtualized hardware and storage onto which infrastructure can be built form scratch	Virtual machines infrastructure, storage management	Amazon EC2

These services are mostly presented as layers or a stack where the client interacts with a SaaS (perhaps via a web browser), which sits on top of a PaaS, which sits on an IaaS. However, other use patterns of cloud services are also possible. For example, a client application or a SaaS can use IaaS directly without any PaaS; a platform service (PaaS) can be provided on physical devices without an IaaS architecture. In addition to these generic services, suppliers offer meanwhile a number of more specific services, usually named "something" as a service. For example, Disaster Recovery-as-a-Service (DRaaS) replicates data and applications of a client so he can continue business the moment a disaster occurs (e.g., destruction of his data center due to an earthquake).

Cloud computing can also be classified based on its deployment level into public, private, and hybrid cloud. Public cloud is the most commercial form of cloud offered on a shared basis by a third party entity. This entity is usually a designated service provider who manages and hosts the resources. The resources are accessed by the general public on an on-demand basis by more than one tenant [13]. Private cloud is a "fully functional cloud that is owned, operated and presumably restricted to a particular organization" [13, p. 37]. Private clouds are characterized by isolated and secured resources and are used by organizations that do not desire to share VMs or servers with others, mainly due to the sensitivity of the data stored (e.g., healthcare or financial data) [12]. A hybrid cloud combines both, public and private cloud computing resources. Third-party vendors provide public clouds while private clouds are the private computing resources hosted or rented by the user organization.

In multi-cloud environments one or more cloud layers, deployment levels and cloud providers are combined in order for organizations to maximize the benefits acquired by the use of cloud services. Section 4 of this paper provides a thorough analysis of multi-cloud computing literatures.

3   Multi-sourcing

Cloud-computing is a form of IT outsourcing as a provider is contracted for a limited time to deliver a service. Many organizations use more than one IT outsourcing provider, what is referred to as multiple supplier sourcing [14] or simply multi-sourcing. Since this arrangement is older than multi-cloud computing, it can serve as a basis for development of concepts for coordination in multi-cloud computing. Therefore, in this section we analyze the characteristics of multi-sourcing and the approaches to coordinate relationships with multiple IT outsourcing providers. Multi-sourcing itself is often compared to single sourcing (e.g., [14, 15]) to derive its potential advantages and disadvantages.

The use of multi-sourcing entails a number of advantages including:

- Lower price. There is an expectation that clients who employ multi-sourcing ITO can achieve better prices compared to single-sourcing [16–18]. The expectation is based on the assumption that the client is at a better position to negotiate favorable prices than when facing only one vendor, but also on evidence from practice [16, 18].
- Better service quality. The client can improve the quality of outsourced services by selecting suppliers who specialize on certain services (best of breed approach), rather than "shopping everything in one place" [18, 19].
- More flexibility. Contracts can be better adjusted to the actual needs due to the modularization, in terms of the number of providers, contract lengths, and contract volumes [17, 18].
- Lower financial risk. Financial troubles of a vendor, an unfavorable change in the vendor's strategy, or an acquisition of the vendor by another vendor who services a competitor are all possible changes that are not controllable by the client but could harm the relationship and quality of service. They are easier to cope with if the client maintains other outsourcing relationships so that not all services are at risk at the same time.
- Less lock-in. Users try to avoid becoming too dependent on one supplier because he may act opportunistically otherwise. High dependence on one supplier is referred to as lock-in. It means that switching to another supplier will incur high costs. This potential problem can be reduced with multi-sourcing because the client does not rely on one supplier only [16, 20].

- Quicker access to new technology. Some of the vendors can be chosen because they use new, perhaps not yet proven technologies [19].

On the negative side, multi-sourcing can lead to additional cost and new risk:

- Additional cost. It obviously takes more time and effort to search for and select more than one supplier and to close several contracts. After the contracts become operational, the performance of several vendors needs to be monitored [18, 21] individually and in total.
- The blame game. When problems arise, it may be difficult to determine which of the suppliers is/are responsible for the problem and need to fix it [14]. Often, a vendor points to other vendors as culprits.
- Poor attention to contract. When outsourcing volume is split into several smaller contracts, the volume of some contracts may become too small to attract vendors to bid for them or to make them pay much attention to an existing relationship [20].
- No relationship-specific investments. Suppliers do not invest into the relationship with the client because they do not consider the contract worth it. But clients may also invest too little [20].

As with multi-cloud computing, the need for coordination only arises if there is interdependence between the outsourced services [15]. Literature mainly proposes two modes of coordination (see Table 2): the mediated model and the direct model [22]. In the first model, one of the vendors is chosen by the client to coordinate all vendors and he guards the client from potential problems of multi-sourcing as much as possible (therefore, also referred to as the vendor guardian model in [15]). In the direct model, the client handles the effort of coordination by himself. This effort can be quite considerable. In one case, it meant the creation of a service management layer, redesign of business processes, documentation of processes and vendor interfaces [18]. In another case, a bank established a project management office that first only took care of contracts but later increased its services to units initiating ITO relationships [16].

Table 2. Coordination modes in IT multi-sourcing

Coordination mode	Coordination agent
Direct	Client
Mediated	Vendor

The collaboration of vendors is difficult to mandate per contract independently of the coordination mode. This is partly because common service output is not easily attributable to the individual performance of service providers. Stated differently, individual service providers may fulfill their SLAs, but the output needed by the client may still be unsatisfactorily. Two approaches can be used to improve the situation [15]. In one approach, integrated SLAs are envisioned which accomplishment requires an integrated effort by two or more suppliers. Another approach suggests the development of operating level agreements (OLAs). Such agreements describe how the providers plan to work with each other on a daily basis but they are not enforceable like SLAs.

This section discussed the concept of multi-sourcing as a predecessor of multi-cloud computing. Section 4 analyzes multi-cloud computing in detail.

4   Multi-cloud Computing

Multi-cloud computing regards a "serial or simultaneous use of services from diverse providers to execute an application" [23]. It provides the organization with the ability to decide for its provisioning of cloud computing resources from multiple providers or the combination of public and private cloud services, so as to reach maximum benefit [24].

The use of multi-cloud computing provides numerous advantages to organizations as widely discussed in [5, 23–25]:

- Combination of service features. Multi-cloud computing enables organizations to combine different features and services offered by different cloud services in order to reach organizational goals.
- Cost optimization. Organizations are able to combine cloud services from multiple providers such that they can reduce the cost associated with the purchase of cloud services.
- Risk of failure and reliability. If applications are duplicated at different cloud providers, which may span across different geographical regions, then the risk of interruption due to infrastructure failure could be minimized.
- Lock-in. Applications, which are able to run on different cloud infrastructures, can be easily migrated from one provider to the other and hence the organization is more flexible in discontinuing the collaboration with a specific provider.

Despite its benefits, the use of multi-cloud computing may involve several challenges such as:

- Access and authorization. As the use of multi-cloud computing fosters the easier transfer of services from one service to the other, the organization needs to be additionally careful on providing authorization and access of staff members in doing so as well as on the process for revoking such rights, e.g., when staff members leave the company.
- Security. In a multi-cloud environment where services from different providers are employed, the organization holds more responsibility for the secure communication and exchange of data between the services.
- Integration of services. The combination of more than one cloud provider might impose additional overheads in terms of building the data exchange mechanism and integrating the services.
- Performance. Performance outcomes from different providers need to be combined in order to be able to optimize the resource allocation according to the client's requirements. The same is true for accounting data. All cloud providers deliver such data but they need to be integrated and made comparable because the price structures usually differ. Then, the client can exchange services where possible, ideally in an automated fashion following pre-set rules. It is also important to terminate

resources that are not needed anymore to save cost. Manual analyses of performance should only be needed when the client's requirement change so that service selection rules need to be changed.

- Support. Support for clients' users (perhaps even self-service features) should be designed in such a way that the users do not need to care which cloud provider is actually delivering a service.

Multi-cloud computing allows organizations to search for the right combination of services in terms of features, functionality, flexibility, cost etc. [24]. However, each cloud service has its own characteristics and therefore differs from other cloud services on the market that offer similar services. As a result, coordination services are needed when two or more cloud providers are involved. For example, the provided images of the same operating system (e.g., Linux) may vary slightly, but significantly. The prices may be set in different units and sizes, which does not allow an automatic comparison without suitable calculations. Specific offerings often include additional features, which although nice to have, make switching providers even more difficult.

When two (or more) cloud services are integrated, their combination can be undertaken at different service levels. Figure 1 shows all possible combinations of services provided by two providers in terms of the three service models. Alternatively, the integration of cloud services is classified into bilateral and hub-based integration [26]. In the first case, the exchange of data and use of functions between two services work via specifically developed or already available public APIs. In the second case, a connection to a hub affords integration with all other applications that are already connected to the hub.

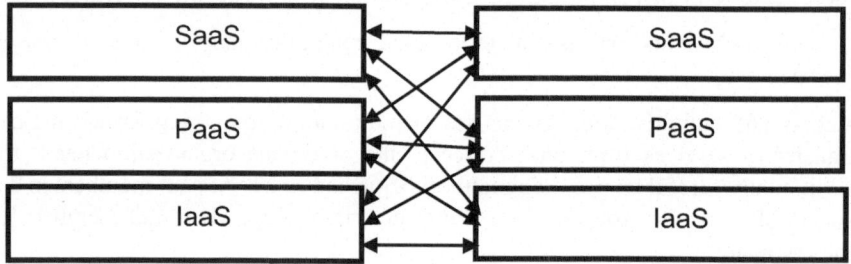

Fig. 1. Possible combinations of cloud services from two providers

5   Multi-cloud Coordination

5.1   Coordination Modes

Similarly to multi-sourcing, the coordination of the services in multi-cloud environments may occur either directly or through a mediator.

In the direct model, organizations are in charge of directly coordinating the cloud services used. In such cases, organizations usually make use of off-the-shelf tools that provide coordination assistance. For example, off-the-shelf software are able to provide a unified interface to different cloud storage offerings, making them in this way, easily interchangeable, and increasing the flexibility and reliability of this infrastructure service [27]. Additionally, organizations may make use of more sophisticated software (e.g., from Rightscale [28]) that are able to control the use of different operating system images (like images from Linux or Windows) and "understand" the different stack standards used by different cloud computing suppliers. Such software interface and combine services that these suppliers offer through SaaS, PaaS, or IaaS. The software can also start or terminate a cloud service as necessary. Providers of these software often advertise that such software can be used by business users without help from IT specialists as a self-service. This may be especially the case when clients use popular cloud applications because already programmed interfaces, called connectors, may exist for these service combinations. For example, this could be a connector between a CRM and an ERP application, both provided by different suppliers through a cloud service. Such tools can run on premises, at the software supplier, or somewhere else in the cloud (see Subsect. 5.2 for more information on tools). However, there are exceptions to this off-the-shelve tool dominating approach. For example, Common-wealth Bank of Australia developed its own standards and got cloud providers to adhere to them [29]. However, the implementation of the layer that manages the use of several cloud services by their IT department relied on a purchased software tool (ServiceMesh). In any case, direct coordination requires IT staff with advanced skills because of high complexity. It may afford the firm more control and perhaps save some coordination cost.

The mediated model also exists in multi-cloud computing, but it differs from the model in multi-sourcing. The mediator is often a company that does not offer a cloud service itself, but it combines different cloud offerings for the client by making them compatible. In addition, the company monitors the operation of all involved services and may accomplish other necessary tasks for the client. Some suppliers of such services call themselves Managed Public Cloud Provider (however, their service may also relate to a hybrid cloud). They use specific off-the-shelf tools for the integration of cloud services or develop some software for the task by themselves. If such services are contracted on a time basis, they represent classical ITO. In other words, coordination of clouds is outsourced in the "old" way while the actual services are rendered via cloud computing. Often, the mediator does not only help in operating a multi-cloud but also in planning for it. This saves time and cost in deploying a suitable cloud environment. In some cases, the mediator may also offer some cloud computing at SaaS, PaaS, or IaaS level getting closer to the mediated multi-sourcing model. In general, the mediated model is quick to implement, but it often comes with high costs. Some of these costs can be saved if the mediator helps the client to make better use of the multiple clouds.

As mentioned above, integration of cloud services can also be accomplished with a hub (similar to EAI). If the hub itself is offered via cloud, then this can be called integration-platform-as-a-service (iPaaS). Several such services are available in the market such as for example AtomSphere from Dell Boomi (Fig. 2) [30]. Figure 2 shows how integration of Salesforce and Netsuite can be implemented on this platform.

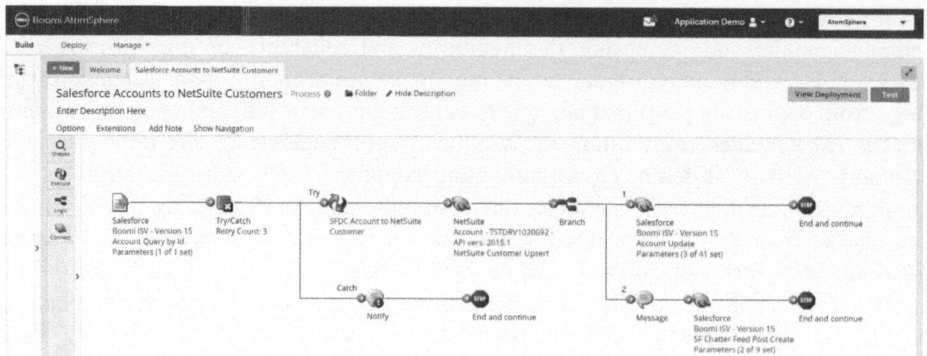

Fig. 2. Example of AtomSphere from Dell Boomi [30]

If users can even create complex processes on the platform, then this can be referred to as Business-Process-Management-Platform-as-a-Service (see, for example Fujitsu RunMyProcess, 2017 [31]). In these cases, a client may use the hub directly, but the integration of cloud services is actually accomplished by a mediator offering and maintaining the hub.

Table 3 presents the common coordination modes in multi-cloud computing.

Table 3. Coordination modes in multi-cloud computing

Coordination mode	Coordination agent
Direct	Client (mostly tool-based)
Mediated	Third party (mostly tool-based)

In practice, mixed coordination modes also occur. For example, a client can accomplish some integration tasks while other tasks are outsourced to the mediator. This is the mode, we usually encountered in interviews with big companies. These companies already hire or have people on board who can develop code for controlling clouds. Small and medium-sized firms in Germany mostly (85%) use services of a provider for cloud management [3].

Although there are similarities between the benefits and the challenges in multi-cloud computing and multi-sourcing solutions, changes of providers in a multi-cloud may occur much more often and at a faster pace. For this reason, automated coordination tools and technologies are needed for the management of the multi-cloud provisioning of services. Therefore, we briefly touch upon some of them in the next sub-section, beyond those that have already been mentioned.

5.2 Tools and Technologies

There are several tools and approaches for increasing interoperability in multi-cloud environments. One way to increase interoperability among components of different cloud providers is to use standardized open source software. Standardization bodies might not formally recognize such standards, but the support by important industry players and their wide use can contribute to making them a de facto standard. For example, Openstack [32] is supported by AT&T, IBM, HP, Intel, Rackspace, Red Hat, and many other organizations. Openstack can also be used with serverless technology where assignment of workloads to physical servers is automated by the technology and hidden from higher levels.

A number of open source tools exist that support integration of services at different levels. For example, Cloud Foundry [33] can be used to establish integration at the PaaS level. If applications are encapsulated in so called containers then they can be easily moved at the IaaS level. A container includes an application with its binaries, system libraries, and other components necessary to run it but they share the operating system kernel as opposed to virtual machines. Such a container can be executed on almost any Linux or Windows operating system and the infrastructure where they run (see for example Docker, 2016 [34]).

Another approach is to make use of specific application programming interfaces (APIs) provided by each provider and integrate the access to and use of the clouds in one application as it is done, for example, by above mentioned RightScale (RightScale, 2016 [28]). The new application, however, is a proprietary solution.

Cloud service integration can be very simple if specific connectors for specific software combinations exist. Such connectors are already available for widely used software. At the application level, a connector is available from Celigo, for example, that integrates the CRM application from SalesForce with the ERP application NetSuite OneWorld [35]. The integration of these packages at the SaaS level is easy, therefore. If a connector does not exist, it needs to be custom developed.

6   Comparison of Arrangements and Their Coordination

Multi-sourcing and multi-cloud-computing hold basic differences as illustrated in Tables 2 and 3. First, the coordination agent in the mediated model in multi-cloud-computing is a third party rather than one of the vendors providing IT services. Second, in the direct mode, the client remains the coordinator, but in multi-cloud computing the client will usually rely more on ready-made tools.

Except for these differences, a number of other differences also exist:

Prices. Clients can achieve better prices in multi-sourcing than single-sourcing (e.g., [16, 18]) because of a stronger competition between providers. The market in cloud computing is competitive so providers need to offer competitive prices in most regions and prices do not change for individual clients. Clients can achieve savings through multi-clouds mainly by buying at the best prices available (everything else considered constant) and less through negotiation or threats of using another provider. Therefore, multi-clouds also can lead to cost savings but through a different mechanism than multi-sourcing. Another way to achieve better prices is by committing to certain volumes (e.g., AWS Reserved Instances), although the client gives up some flexibility this way.

Service quality. Service quality improvement can be achieved in both cases by choosing providers who specialize in the outsourced service. For example, a client can use the best ERP and SCM available in the cloud without worrying about their installation and maintenance while still paying for them on demand.

Flexibility. The increase in flexibility is much higher through multi-cloud computing than multi-sourcing because long-term contracts are not needed and switching of suppliers is usually easier.

Financial risk. In cloud computing, there are no long-term contracts and switching of assets or employees do not occur. The financial risks for clients are, therefore, lower than in multi-sourcing. For example, if an ITO provider goes bankrupt, the client may still be responsible for the employees who were transferred to the provider.

Lock-in. The danger of lock-in can be reduced with multi-cloud computing like with multi-sourcing but new dangers also arise as will be explained next. Lock-in can occur at three levels in the context of cloud computing:

- Clients may lock-in into an application run in the cloud. This is really not different than dependence on an application run on own hardware and system software.
- Clients may become dependent on a provider of cloud services who uses a proprietary solution to offer his service. If a provider sticks to open software standards, a move to another provider should not be too difficult. Clients are mostly warned of this type of lock-in.
- Clients may become dependent on a provider of managed services who created a proprietary solution for integration of cloud services. This threat also exists but it is seldom mentioned. The safest strategy for clients is to demand from the coordination provider to use open source tools or at least those tools that are widely used in the market, as much as possible. This way switching to another managed cloud service provider should be less painful.

Access to new technology. Multi-cloud computing is characterized by rapid innovation and entrance of many new software producers and service providers. Therefore, it is fairly easy for a client to try new technologies by using providers who invented new products or adopted new technologies. This trial is also not very risky (unless it leads to data leaks or other serious problems) because the decision can be easily reversed.

Coordination cost. These additional costs should not be disregarded in either of the computing models. The above cited survey of small and medium-sized firms in Germany revealed that about 55.5% of overall costs for cloud computing were costs for infrastructure usage while about 45.5% were spent for coordination [3].

"Finger-pointing". Like in multi-sourcing [14], the likelihood that it becomes more difficult to identify the culprit when a problem occurs rises with the number of providers. Unfortunately, this may especially occur when severe security breaches happen, as shared responsibility with respect to security (see above) is sometimes not properly executed.

Small contracts and relationship-specific investments. Fear has been expressed that splitting the outsourcing volume to several providers may lead to contracts that are too small to attract vendors or make them pay much attention to the relationship [20]. However, providers in cloud computing usually do not invest into relationship-specific assets. Of course, big client volumes (and client numbers) enter indirectly into their planning of locations for equipment but not with a specific client in mind. Since there are no long-term contracts, relationship-specific investments would weaken their position against such clients. They also set up their services in such a way that handling of small volumes does not create significant overhead. Therefore, they can and will take any volume of business. Reduced contract sizes do not create any problems.

Integrated SLAs and OLAs. It has been suggested that integrated SLAs or OLAs can be set up to improve the collaboration of vendors in multi-sourcing ITO [15, 18]. This will usually not work in cloud computing as providers make their contracts and deliver services independently of each other. They are only willing to make guarantees for their service.

7 Conclusion

This paper has analyzed coordination modes in multi-sourcing and multi-cloud computing environments. Our analysis shows that the coordination modes for ITO and cloud computing are only same on the surface. First, the mediator assumes a different role. In ITO, it is usually one of the outsourcing vendors, while in cloud computing it is a firm specializing in (multi-)cloud management. The main reason for this situation is that coordination of different cloud services is an ongoing and complex task, if best results from a cloud environment are sought. Another difference is that in both modes, direct or mediated, many tools for coordination in cloud computing exist meanwhile. This, again, is necessary for the flexible and cost-effective use of clouds.

However, the coordination necessity also creates significant costs. This is especially obvious in the mediated coordination mode. The costs reduced by the optimal use of multiple clouds are partly offset by the coordination costs. Therefore, clients must consider all the costs in their decisions on cloud computing.

References

1. Hamdaqa, M., Tahvildari, L.: Cloud computing uncovered: a research landscape. Adv. Comput. **86**, 41–84 (2012)
2. Mell, P., Grance, T.: The NIST definition of cloud computing (Technical report). National Institute of Standards and Technology, U.S. Department of Commerce. Special Publication. Technical report (2011)
3. Büst, R., Hille, M.: Multi-Cloud-Management im deutschen Mittelstand. Hybrid- und Multi-Cloud-Konzepte als Basis der digitalen Transformation. Crisp Research AG (2015)
4. RightScale: State of the Cloud Report. Technical report (2016). http://www.rightscale.com/
5. Buyya, R., Yeo, C.L., Venugopal, S., Broberg, J., Brandic, I.: Cloud computing and emerging IT platforms: vision, hype, and reality for delivering computing as the 5th utility. Future Gener. Comput. Syst. **25**(6), 599–616 (2009)
6. Durkee, D.: Why cloud computing will never be free. Commun. ACM **53**(5), 62–69 (2010)
7. Vaquero, L., Rodero-Merino, L., Caceres, J., Lindner, M.: A break in the clouds: towards a cloud definition. ACM SIGCOMM Comput. Commun. Rev. **39**, 50–55 (2009)

8. Hsu, P., Ray, S., Li-Hsieh, Y.: Examining cloud computing adoption intention, pricing mechanism, and deployment model. Int. J. Inf. Manag. **34**(4), 474–488 (2014)
9. Miller, M.: Cloud Computing: Web-Based Applications That Change the Way You Work and Collaborate Online. Que Publishing Company, Indianapolis (2009)
10. Jennings, R.: 5 Financial Benefits of Moving to the Cloud in WEBROOT Inc. http://www. webroot.com/ie/en/business/resources/articles/cloud-computing/five-financial-benefits-of-moving-to-the-cloud
11. Marston, S., Li, Z., Bandyopadhyay, S., Zhang, J., Ghalsasi, A.: Cloud computing — the business perspective. Decis. Support Syst. **51**(1), 176–189 (2011)
12. Armbrust, M., Fox, A., Griffith, R., Joseph, A.D.: Above the Clouds: A View of Cloud Computing, University of California at Berkley. https://www.eecs.berkeley.edu/Pubs/TechRpts/2009/EECS-2009-28.pdf
13. Marks, E.A., Lozano, B.: Executive's Guide to Cloud Computing. Wiley, Hoboken (2010)
14. Currie, W.L.: Using multiple suppliers to mitigate the risk of IT outsourcing at ICI and Wessex water. J. Inf. Technol. **13**, 169–180 (1998)
15. Bapna, R., Barua, A., Mani, D., Mehra, A.: Cooperation, coordination, and governance in multisourcing: an agenda for analytical and empirical research. Inf. Syst. Res. **21**(4), 785–795 (2010)
16. Levina, N., Su, N.: Global multisourcing strategy: the emergence of a supplier portfolio in services offshoring. Decis. Sci. **39**(3), 541–570 (2008)
17. Poston, R.S., Kettinger, W.J., Simon, J.C.: Managing the vendor set: achieving best pricing and quality service in IT outsourcing. MIS Q. Exec. **8**(2), 45–58 (2009)
18. Barboza, M., Myers, M., Gardner, L.: Information technology multisourcing at fonterra: a case study of the world's largest exporter of dairy ingredients. In: European Conference on Information Systems (2011)
19. McLellan, K., Marcolin, B.L., Beamish, P.W.: Financial and strategic motivations behind IS outsourcing. J. Inf. Technol. **10**, 299–321 (1995)
20. Lacity, M.C., Willcocks, L.P., Rottman, J.W.: Global outsourcing of back office services: lessons, trends, and enduring challenges. Strateg. Outsourcing: Int. J. **1**(1), 13–34 (2008)
21. Barthélemy, J.: The hidden cost of IT outsourcing. MIT Sloan Manag. Rev. **42**, 60–69 (2001). Massachusetts Institute of Technology
22. Wiener, M., Saunders, C.: Forced coopetition in IT multi-sourcing. J. Strateg. Inf. Syst. **23**, 210–225 (2014)
23. Petcu, D.: Multi-cloud: expectations and current approaches. In: Proceedings of the 2013 International Workshop on Multi-cloud Applications and Federated Clouds (MultiCloud 2013), New York, p. 1 (2013)
24. Buyya, R., Barreto, D.: Multi-cloud resource provisioning with Aneka: a unified and integrated utilisation of microsoft azure and amazon EC2 instances. In: International Conference on Computing and Network Communications (CoCoNet) (2015)
25. Moreno-Vozmediano, R., Montero, R.S., Llorente, I.M.: Multicloud deployment of computing clusters for loosely coupled MTC applications. IEEE Trans. Parallel Distrib. Syst. **22**(6), 924–930 (2011). IEEE Computer Society
26. Ebert, N., Schlatter, U.: Cloud-basierte integration. Inform. Spektrum **40**(3), 278–282 (2017)
27. MultCloud. https://www.multcloud.com/tutorials/multiple-cloud-storage-manager.html
28. RightScale. http://www.rightscale.com
29. Schlagwein, D., Thorogood, A., Willcocks, L.P.: How commonwealth bank of Australia gained benefits using a standards-based, multi-provider cloud model. MIS Q. Exec. **13**(4), 209–222 (2014)
30. Dell Boomi. https://boomi.com/
31. Fujitsu RunMyProcess. https://www.runmyprocess.com/

32. OpenStack. https://www.openstack.org/software/
33. Cloud Foundry. https://www.cloudfoundry.org/
34. Docker. https://www.docker.com/
35. Celigo. https://www.celigo.com

The Digitisation Gestalt: A Case Study

Michelle Hurdle[✉]

Perth, WA, Australia
Mahurdle20@gmail.com

Abstract. Organisations are increasingly impacted, directly and indirectly, by digital disruption. This continuing single case study examines an Australian statutory authority's response to digital disruption as an electronic marketplace emerges. A public-private subsidiary is established, reshaping the organisation form. A guardian model of supplier management is introduced, a revised multi-sourcing strategy is implemented and challenges are experienced managing capability and competences, client and supplier, during transition. The organisation's response is examined though the lens of both collaboration and sourcing theories to assist in the development of practical strategies for both the public and private sector.

Keywords: Sourcing decision making and configuration · Multi-sourcing · Guardian model · Supplier and client capability and competence · Digitisation and digital disruption · Collaboration theory

1 Introduction

As digital disruption displaces unlikely markets and industries, organisational form, sourcing decisions, procurement processes and internal IT structures must evolve in response. When confronted with digital disruption, how does an organisation respond? What form does the emerging organisation take? How does the organisation refresh its business model to an international service platform? What if the organisation is a statutory government authority, and is prevented from acting as a commercial entity, due to the additional layers of bureaucracy and the limitations of legislation and government policy.

This paper seeks to explore the next phase of a longitudinal case study that examines changes to an organisation responding to multiple challenges including digital disruption, implementing cloud technology, government asset disposal and ageing technology. Sourcing decision making, configuration and governance are symbiotic as the organisation attempts to monitor and manage the multiple suppliers, relationships and changes. The results achieved by this organisation are being reviewed with increasing interest by the Western Australian public sector, other Australian and international jurisdictions, competitors, partners and investors.

After the application of an agreed Sourcing Strategy, the organization's strategic response was the bespoke redevelopment of the core enterprise system. The new land

© Springer International Publishing AG 2017
I. Oshri et al. (Eds.): Global Sourcing 2017, LNBIP 306, pp. 138–149, 2017.
https://doi.org/10.1007/978-3-319-70305-3_9

registration system was built multi-tenanted on a cloud infrastructure to seize commercial opportunities in other markets and jurisdictions with end of life land registry systems.

"Cloud signals significant changes in functions and roles for internal IT" [1]. Although market attributes of cloud services have similar characteristics to commodities such as water and power, Brynjolfsson et al. point out that organisations "don't need a "Chief Electricity Officer" and a staff of highly trained professionals to manage and integrate electricity into their businesses" [2]. The transformation of the internal IT function, and determining capabilities to be retained, and change management of the legacy organisation can be a painful process if not managed well.

Capabilities, competencies and capacity required from new and existing suppliers and the current and emerging organisation are in transition and evolving. Retained capabilities may be influenced by perceptions of trust, assumptions regarding tacit knowledge and specificity. "If in-house is not seen as more trustworthy than external personnel, then transaction costs are not necessarily lower in-house in spite of high knowledge specificity" [3]. To test the hypotheses, data on tacit knowledge and knowledge specificity may be examined and correlated to findings in relation to the perceptions of trust.

2   Research Approach

The single organisation case study has access to empirical performance data and semi-structured interviews gathered during the longitudinal case study observing client and supplier organisations as the client adopts a large scale cloud technology platform. Changes in sourcing strategy have led to corresponding change to the organisation's form.

When the organisation was first examined in 2014/15, the focus was on the adoption and implementation of cloud technology, which was considered innovative and cutting edge such a short time ago. The velocity of the digital disruption is such that in the space of months, cloud infrastructure is now accepted technology and organisations ponder the value of their onsite data centre investments or long term data centre storage contracts.

The research question posed is: "what are the contributing factors to the successful digitisation of a business?" and if the digitisation is successful, the concept of "gestalt", or each factor within the newly digitised business creating a new organisation of which the value far exceeds the sum of each part.

Case study was considered the appropriate method of research given the substantial change being experienced by the organisation, to the internal and external environment. Both Eisenhardt [4] and Yin [5] confirm the process of theory building through case study research.

The case study data and access to semi structured interviews with a consistent group of interviewees can provide evidence to examine a single organisation as it responds to digital disruption. Supplier and client capabilities and competencies change in response to a revised sourcing strategy and the transition towards more increasingly sophisticated contractual and governance frameworks.

3   The Case Study Example

The subject of the longitudinal case study is a statutory monopoly of an Australian State responsible for the registration of real property transactions for approximately 2 M citizens. The State boundary is geographically large and diverse and the capital city where the majority of citizens reside is geographically isolated. The accuracy of the registry is guaranteed by the State.

The platform and systems which underpin the Registry was ageing and at end of life and extensive market research indicated that there was no acceptable off the shelf solution. Furthermore, other jurisdictions nationally and abroad also had systems that were nearing end of life.

The legacy IT function of the case study was a domestic outsourcing arrangement with multiple suppliers based on site managed by a large in-house team, managed by a Chief Information Officer (CIO). The in-house team was structured as Plan/Build/Run with a sub optimal onsite data centre.

An external factor driving change was a national push to introduce electronic settlement of property transactions. This change was similar in nature to the introduction of electronic share trading. To assist the organisation synthesise the impact of this change, a reference model for electronic markets was applied [6].

In applying this model, the organisation was able to understand its role in the emerging electronic market for real property, as a trusted information service provider that could underpin the market, subject to providing the information at the speed and accuracy that an electronic market would demand.

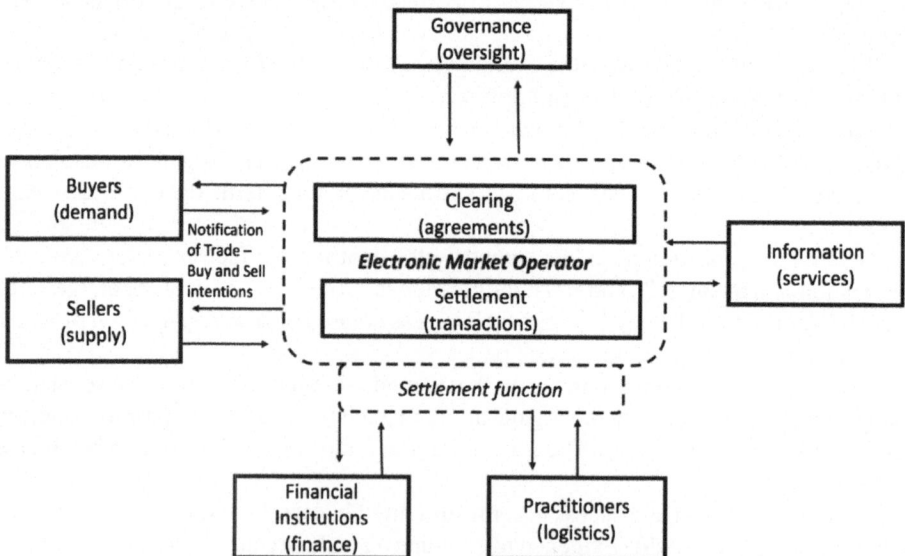

Fig. 1. Elements of a reference model for electronic markets [6].

In response to both the potential threat and opportunity, the organisation commenced a revision of its Business strategy and Information Technology strategy. A Sourcing Strategy was prepared and approved, defining key principles and providing decision making models to assist with sourcing decisions, enabling the organisations executive to prioritise the platform rebuild to both capture value and create value [7].

The organisation assessed that its provider of application development services, who also provided existing application support services, had the capability to build a new platform, and could do so under the existing contract which was due to expire in a just over eighteen months. Government contestability rules would require that the organisation go out to tender for a replacement contract. The rebuild of the platform under traditional contracting arrangements would be both time and cost prohibitive, and usual governance arrangements for projects of a similar nature would exacerbate the situation. The race to complete a viable replacement platform could only be successful in a highly collaborative arrangement with strong trust.

The organisation deemed, after careful consideration and robust debate, to enter into a joint venture type arrangement with the parent company of the application development supplier. The form of this joint venture was to stand up a subsidiary, "NewCo". This initially had multiple benefits for all parties, including but not limited to:

- Shared risk;
- A common goal;
- Reward for performance in future commercial opportunities;
- Characteristics of a public/private partnership;
- Positive behaviour changes – related to shirking and monitoring;
- Superior performance and project ahead of schedule and under budget.

Conversely, both the JV partner and the organisation have experienced some negative aspects in setting up the subsidiary and the project, including but not limited to the following:

- Long delays in contractual arrangements being established which can be attributed to legal representatives struggling with the concepts of Incomplete Contract theory;
- Organisational concerns related to conflicts of interest, perceived and real;
- Insufficient resourcing to enable adequate project management, change management, transition planning and communication.
- Establishing a subsidiary between parties from different sectors and industries has challenges, however, if successful, significant rewards.

4   Digital Disruption, Digitisation, and Digitalisation

The terms digital disruption, disruptive technology and disruptive innovation are often used interchangeably. Christensen developed the theory of disruptive innovation [8]. Large successful organisations risked failure by focussing on sustained innovation, creating opportunity for unknown competitors to develop niche products or services for niche market that disrupts the existing business model, usually at speed before market leaders are able to respond, and displaces the known market. Digital disruption may be defined as the change that occurs when new digital technologies and business models affect the value proposition of existing goods and services [9].

Land registries underpin financial and banking systems in many developed countries and there is demand to enable property transactions to occur at similar speed to other asset transactions, like share trading. Blocks chain and cryptocurrency technology is an emerging threat to this market.

Digitising, or conversion of into digital form, of hard copy land registry records resulted from the response to electronic conveyancing. The client organisation commenced scanning and electronic processing the paper records associated with land property transaction, of which there were approximately 300 K per annum.

The digitalisation resulting from both digitisation, e-conveyancing and the building of a new multi-tenanted platform on cloud technology is the catalysts for the change to the business model and the organisation, with significant impact on the internal IT structure.

5   Theory and Discussion

Successful joint ventures are collaborative efforts. Significant academic research has been undertaken reviewing collaboration and collaborative arrangements, and factors that may contribute to their success, or failure. Establishing the joint venture was integral to the case study organisation's strategic response to the emerging electronic market-place. It may be possible to look to the elements in collaboration theories, to identify success factors in the joint venture, resulting in a positive response to digital disruption.

5.1   Interorganisational Collaboration (IOC)

Interorganizational collaboration (IOC) can be defined as a cooperative, interorganizational relationship [10]. Majchrzak et al. [11] examined the dynamics of IOCs after the initial contracts have been established and found that IOCs are exceedingly unstable, dynamics defined as any change in the form or state of the IOC over time [12]. Their review identified six multifaceted dynamics characteristics of IOCs that change after the initiation or formation including:

- Goals – changes to the explicit mission or goals for the collaboration, such as adding a new goal or dropping or replacing the original goal;
- Contract frame – referring to the changes in emphasis of the formal (transactional) and informal (relational) elements in the interorganizational agreements including knowledge transfer methods, intellectual property provisions, shared risks and mutual benefits;
- Interaction style – changes in emphasis relating to interactions between partner firms, whether competitive or cooperative behaviours;
- Decision making control – is the decision making control at the top level or lower level of the partner firms;

- Organizational structure – referring to the degree of formalisation and standardisation of roles and processes of IOCs, specifically the shifts towards and away from increased structure; and
- Actor composition – membership and changes relating to key individuals in the IOC.

Majchrzak et al. [11] specify three categories of causes: between-partner differences; external sources and within IOC sources. Six patterns of dynamics are also observed. This review found that despite variability across the cases examined there were three clear distinctions in IOCs in which successful outcomes were documented:

- Changes in more characteristics;
- Changes were proactively initiated due to differences in partner interests; and
- Dynamic patterns with more complex feedback loops having a subsequent effect on other characteristics.

5.2 Collaborative Innovation Framework

The collaborative innovation framework [13] identifies four elements, all present in the case study example, contributing to collaborative innovation with key insights from each element:

Leading – dealing with adaptive challenges, situations where problems and solutions are unclear, a multi-function team is needed, learning is vital, innovation is usually necessary, and a general business goal rather than precise metrics point the way.

Contracting – the greater the innovation ambition, the more likely to have a risk-reward component in the contracting arrangement. This may take the form of a joint venture. Transformation outsourcing is not technical and will involve behavioural, organisational, social and political issues.

Organizing – teaming across organisational boundaries and functional silos is vital for adaptive and innovative work;

Behaving – lasting collaborative innovation is shaped in the context of prior work on leadership, contracting, and organising, which creates rising levels of trust, teaming and performance.

Collaboration is identified as a key point facilitating the step change in sourcing maturity beyond strategic relationship, partnering and innovation. Collaborative behaviours, demonstrated by "high trust, flexibility, risk sharing and investment of resources and time" are essential if "high performance on shared goals are to be achieved" [14].

5.3 Sourcing Decision Making and Configuration

Sourcing Strategy. The organisation developed a Sourcing Strategy, underpinned by two decision making models, Willcocks, Petheridge and Olson's "Decision making matrix on outsourcing" [15] and the "Strategic sourcing by market comparison" and a small number of key principles that would guide sourcing decisions.

Contractual Framework. A joint venture in the form of a subsidiary (NewCO) was agreed between the client and the supplier of application development services, responsible for the development of the new platform. When a client and service provider form a joint venture, it is usually to pursue the following goals [16]:

- Establishing a new venture to develop new and innovative solution and services for the clients vertical markets to keep both parties engaged and motivated and maximise profits; and/or
- The transformation of large scale (in the context of the client) complex business functions and processes of the client firms, sharing the risk for the client who is dealing with uncertainty and complexity of the changes and motivation for the supplier.

In this particular case study, both goals are present. The framework for the revised sourcing relationship between the client and the supplier and the JV/subsidiary was proposed as a strategic Master Services Agreement (MSA), 'approximately 20 pages' based on incomplete contract theory. "In the case of customized IT service outsourcing, Contracts play a minor role in the governance of the relationship" [13].

The resulting contractual framework was a 200 page MSA, with multiple schedules and a 60 page Glossary. In practice, legal counsellors from both parties have struggled with the concept of a contract being "incomplete". The formal contracts were finalised in late 2016 and the transition process to the new framework and models is in the very early stages. A summary diagram was prepared to assist all parties understand how key elements of the MSA work together (Fig. 2).

Governance, Performance, Price and Contractual Frameworks

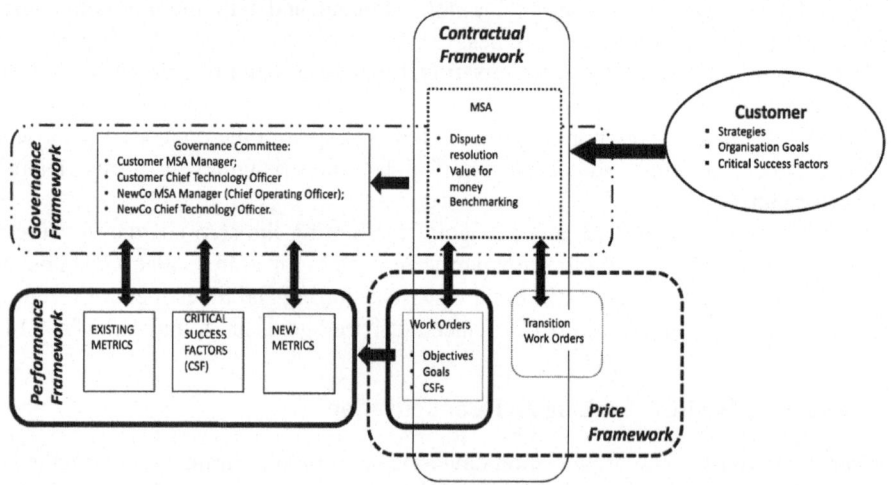

Fig. 2. Governance, performance, price and contractual framework

Performance measurement and monitoring. To evolve measurement of successful contract performance beyond the expected service level agreements, key performance indicators, reporting and meetings to critical success factors and real time performance data. Comparisons between the different performance measurement regimes can be made over time (Fig. 2).

5.4 Supplier and Client Capabilities and Competencies

Feeny and Willcocks [17] have identified nine client capabilities and four core tasks demonstrated in a retained capabilities model that is applicable to both outsourcing and cloud adoption and are critical to the client organisation. Adoption of cloud technology shifts the emphasis of the retained capability model, highlighting four crucial capabilities or attributes [18]; business savvy, architect, sourcing specialist and business innovator. This case study raises the question: are these attributes within the retained organisation, and which retained organisation, the client or the subsidiary?

Performance measurement and monitoring. To evolve measurement of successful contract performance beyond the expected service level agreements, key performance indicators, reporting and meetings to critical success factors and real time performance data. Comparisons between the different performance measurement regimes can be made over time.

5.5 Supplier and Client Capabilities and Competencies

Feeny and Willcocks [17] have identified nine client capabilities and four core tasks demonstrated in a retained capabilities model that is applicable to both outsourcing and cloud adoption and are critical to the client organisation. Adoption of cloud technology shifts the emphasis of the retained capability model, highlighting four crucial capabilities or attributes [18]; business savvy, architect, sourcing specialist and business innovator. This case study raises the question: are these attributes within the retained organisation, and which retained organisation, the client or the subsidiary?

Prior to appointing the subsidiary as the sole supplier for all its application and infrastructure services, the client directly engaged three suppliers across four contracts to provide the equivalent services, managed by an internal IT team of 60 in a build/plan/run configuration, further supported by a procurement and contract management unit. The interim IT team has been halved and is expected to be reduced further as the platform development project nears completion.

Su and Levina [19] describe the different breadth and depth of supply relationships as supply base as a set of contractual supplier relationship directly managed by the sourcing firm. Before introducing the subsidiary, the client's supply base was low breadth and high depth with the resulting disadvantages of high switching costs and the risk of supplier tacit knowledge of the client organisation (Fig. 3). The supply base is moving to the hybrid mixed type supply base, which should mitigate the disadvantages of an increased breath of supply base, limited economies of scale, higher production and supplier management costs.

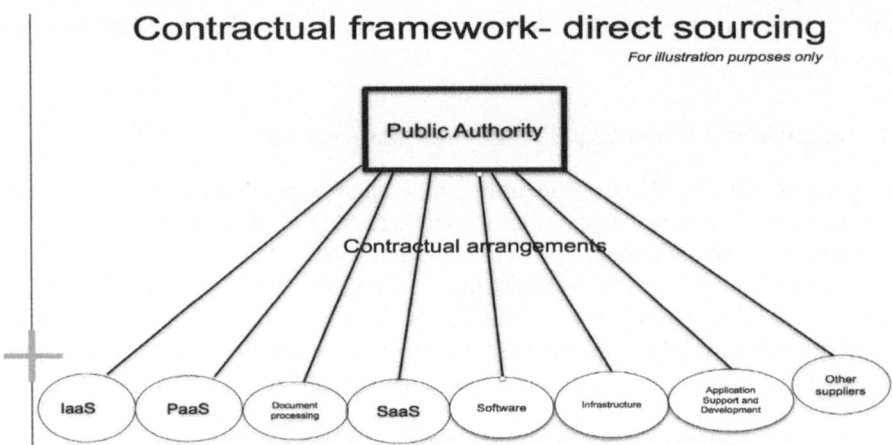

Fig. 3. Direct sourcing contractual framework, pre Guardian model

5.6   Multisourcing and Lead Provider as a Guardian

In addition to moving its supply base, the client is altering its multisourcing configuration [16], from the client as the service integrator in Fig. 3, to an interim guardian model arrangement (Fig. 4). The service integrator is a lead provider [16] and is the currently contracted application developer and a subsidiary of the joint venture partner.

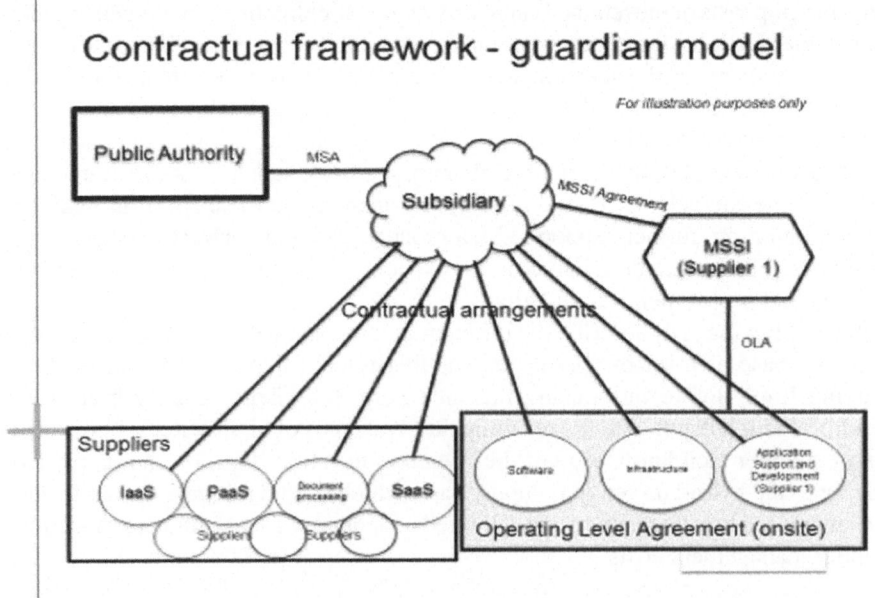

Fig. 4. Contractual framework post introduction of a Guardian model

Figure 4 demonstrates how the major contracts are novated to the subsidiary, and the MSA becomes the single contractual arrangement between the client and the subsidiary. The major contractors based onsite commit to an operating level agreement (OLA). The transition is in the early stages, however, the challenges relating to information asymmetry, managing interdependencies and supplier relationship management are emerging [16].

Trust has influenced and impacted the development of the MSA, the transition arrangements and perceptions of the value delivered by supply base, supplier configuration and the retained organisation. Trust is a key component in partnering [20], however, Willcocks and Lacity observe that "there is no such thing as instant trust in outsourcing. It is built over time through demonstrable performance" [21].

The three-pronged model of trust [14] reflected the complexities of the outsourcing environment: personal, competence-based and motivational. In this case study example, the client seeks to demonstrate value and performance that is not directly linked to a highly prescriptive and heavily monitored service level agreement.

Dibbern et al. assert "to comparatively assess the cost of outsourcing and in-house provision, managers should evaluate the required client-specific knowledge and the trustworthiness of vendor staff and own employees" [3]. Additionally, "in house transaction costs advantages resulting from high knowledge specificity disappear if vendor staff is trusted as much as or even more than in-house personnel" and "asset specificity remains an important antecedent of sourcing efficiency and outsourcing decisions".

The understanding the role of trust and the early assessment of it along with knowledge and asset specificity, may be a contributing factor to the successful response to digital disruption.

5.7 Success Factors Contributing to the Threat and Opportunity of Digital Disruption

The case study example has continuing themes of collaboration, trust, capabilities and competence from both the supplier and client. In examining the case study and considering the existing theories on collaboration, client and supplier capability and competence, theoretical principles may be identified to assist organisations better respond to continuing digital disruption.

As the organisation continues with its transition, each of these factors can be examined to identify its contribution towards the strategic response to digital disruption.

Fig. 5. Potential Digital Disruption response success factors

6   Conclusion and Further Research

Understanding how to respond to digital disruption and identifying implications for organisations is increasingly important. The case study example faces complex challenges, a public-sector authority forming a joint venture as a strategic response to an emerging electronic marketplace, and a change to the management of the organisations multisourcing configuration through the introduction of a guardian model.

The organisation's experiences may also be applied to potentially reframe the outsourcing lifecycle model to apply to 'as a Service' (XaaS) or consumption offerings that are increasingly available [22]. Can this case study contribute to a theory on responding to digital disruption? Are there elements of collaboration theory that can apply? Will the introduction of a guardian model help or hinder the management of changing and emerging capabilities?

A clear sourcing strategy, business process change, optimised organisational structure supported by supplier configurations, contractual frameworks and governance arrangements conducive to outcome over compliance, create value beyond the benefit of applying change to each of these factors in isolation. The emerging organisation, responding to the threat of digital disruption, but identifying a new markets and opportunities, is then an exemplar of the digitisation gestalt, a new 'whole' with a value that may now significantly exceed the sum of its parts.

Acknowledgements. The author would like to thank the reviewers, two who were anonymous, for their invaluable suggestions which assisted significantly in the development of this paper.

References

1. Willcocks, L.P., Venters, W., Whitley, E.A.: Moving to the Cloud Corporation: How to Face the Challenges and Harness the Potential of Cloud Computing. Palgrave McMillan (2013)
2. Brynjolfsson, E., Hofman, P., Jordon, J.: Cloud computing and electricity: beyond the utility model. Com. ACM. **53**(5), 32–34 (2010)
3. Dibbern, J., Chin, W.W., Kude, T.: The sourcing of software services: knowledge specificity and the role of trust. DataBase Adv. Inf. Sys. **47**(2), 36–57 (2016)
4. Eisenhardt, K.M.: Building theories from case study research. Acad. Manage. Rev. **14**, 532–550 (1989)
5. Yin, R.K.: Case Study Research, 2nd edn. Sage, London (1994)
6. Schmid, B., Lindemann, M.: Elements of a reference model for electronic markets. In: Proceedings of the Thirty-First Annual Hawaii International Conference on System Sciences, vol. 4. IEEE Computer Society (1998)
7. Aron, R., Singh, J.V.: Getting offshoring right. Harvard Bus. Rev. **83**(12), 135–143 (2005)
8. Christensen, C.M.: When New Technologies Cause Great Firms to Fail, 1st edn. Harvard Business Review Press (1997)
9. http://searchcio.techtarget.com/definition/digital-disruption
10. Hardy, C., Phillips, N., Lawrence, T.B.: Resources, knowledge and influence: The organizational effects of interorganizational collaboration. J. Manage. Stud. **40**, 321–347 (2003)
11. Majchrzak, A., Jarvenpaa, S.L., Bagherzadeh, M.: A review of interorganizational collaboration dynamics. J. Manage. **41**(5). (2014)
12. Van de Ven, A.H., Poole, M.S.: Explaining development and change in organizations. Aca. Manage Rev. **20**, 510–540 (1995)
13. Willcocks, L., Craig, A.: The outsourcing enterprise: Step-change: collaborating to innovate. Logica, London (2009)
14. Whiteley, E., Willcocks, L.: Achieving step-change in outsourcing maturity: Toward collaborative innovation. MISQ Exec. **10**(3), 95–109 (2011)
15. Willcocks, L., Petherbridge, P., Olson, N.: Making IT Count: Strategy, Delivery and Infrastructure. Butterworth, Oxford (2003)
16. Oshri, I., Kotlarsky, J., Willcocks, L.: The Handbook of Global Outsourcing and Offshoring, 3rd edn. Palgrave McMillan (2015)
17. Feeny, D., Willcocks, L.: Core IS capabilities for exploiting information technology. Sloan Manag. Rev. 9–21 (1998)
18. Weeks, M., Feeny, D.: Outsourcing: from cost management to innovation and business value. Cal. Manage. Rev. **50**(4), 127–147 (2008)
19. Su, N., Levina, N.: Global multisourcing strategy: integrating learning from manufacturing into IT service outsourcing. IEEE Trans. Eng. Manag. (2011)
20. Oshri, I., Kotlarsky, J., Willcocks, L.: The handbook of global outsourcing and offshoring, 2nd edn. Palgrave McMillan (2011)
21. Willcocks, L., Lacity, M.: The Practice of Outsourcing: From IT to BPO and Offshoring. Palgrave, London (2009)
22. Cullen, S., Seddon, P.B., Willcocks, L.P.: Managing outsourcing: the lifecycle imperative. MISQ Exec. **4**(1), 229–246 (2005)

Formal Control, Social Control and Guanxi in IT Outsourcing: A Study in Chinese Firms

Wen Jiang[✉]

AMBS, The University of Manchester, Oxford Road, Manchester M13 9PL, UK
w-jiang@263.net

Abstract. Despite the fast growing trend, it is reported that IT outsourcing in China is fraught with high rates of failure. The buyers of IT outsourcing services in China face difficulties in selecting service providers, negotiating managing contracts, and maintain good relationship due to a lack of systematic guidelines on which governance mechanism to deploy to manage outsourcing contracts. This research endeavors to study whether the governance mechanisms (i.e. formal control and social control) adopted in Western countries are prevalent in China, but to critique such governance mechanisms in light of the unique cultural context in China where 'guanxi' is seen to be a key enabler of outsourcing. A significant contribution study to theory is to look into IT outsourcing phenomenon with a balanced view and through an integrated theoretical lens.

Keywords: IT outsourcing · Formal control · Social control · Guanxi · China · Governance mechanism

1 Introduction

IT outsourcing (ITO) refers to outsourcing all or part of IT functions to an external party in order to achieve competence advantages from external expertise. It has grown in popularity rapidly since Kodak outsourced its IT services state the date. According to Gartner Inc. [1], the worldwide IT outsourcing market had reached $288 billion in 2013. The Asia-Pacific region is one of the growth leaders compared to other regions. Gartner Inc. [1] published that ITO markets in emerging Asia/Pacific, Latin America and Greater China all grew more than 13% in 2013 (versus 2.8% in the US).

Despite the fast growing trend, it is reported that IT outsourcing is fraught with high rates of failure. Computerworld conducted a research and reported a low successful percentage of IT outsourcing and even 50% of IT outsourcing contract were terminated in advance. In China, the buyers of IT outsourcing encounter difficulties in selecting providers, negotiating and managing contracts, and then in ensuring effective relationships with vendors.

In order to address these difficulties in the implementation of IT outsourcing, this research focuses on two perspectives: contractual governance (i.e. formal control mechanism) and relational governance (i.e. informal control mechanism) in IT outsourcing [2]. That is to say, it is very critical to a successful IT outsourcing project that the buyer manages the project formal and informally to protect the benefit and maintain the

I. Oshri et al. (Eds.): Global Sourcing 2017, LNBIP 306, pp. 150–161, 2017.
https://doi.org/10.1007/978-3-319-70305-3_10

relationship. At this juncture, it is worthwhile considering what might be different about outsourcing in China versus Western-based arrangements.

The author endeavors to study the phenomena of IT outsourcing in China to test the hypotheses that both contractual governance and relational governance are also essential in the success of IT outsourcing in China. However, given the unique Chinese cultural context, the research also tests whether relational guanxi-enabled governance arrangements are significant enablers of IT outsourcing.

To achieve both these objectives, the paper is structured as follows. In Sect. 2, we provide critical perspectives on transaction cost theory as a theoretical framework guiding the paper, control theory and guanxi theory. Section 3 proposes the research questions and the conceptual framework. While Sect. 4 outlines the added contribution of guanxi-relationships (if any) to the development of IT outsourcing in china.

2   Theoretical Framework

2.1   Transaction Cost Economics: Contractual Governance

Transaction Cost Economics (TCE) addresses the contractual, structural and governance aspects of inter-organizational transactions. TCE originates from the field of Economics and addresses the importance of contracts. TCE maintains that economic efficiency can be achieved through comparative analysis of production costs and transaction costs. Transaction costs depend on a combination of certain characteristics of the transaction taking place (i.e. asset specificity, uncertainty and frequency) and certain characteristics of human nature (i.e. bounded rationality and opportunism). When the buyer chooses the outsourcing provider, the relationship between the buyer and the provider is considered as the special asset which has little alternative use. Hence, the appropriation concern is highlighted. The buyer endeavors to make sure that the investment can't be appropriated due to the potential opportunism. When the buyer considers the future is the situation of uncertainty, he is concerned about the adaptation problem because the unexpected contingencies maybe arise. Hence, TCE proposes that the contract is important to solve the adaptation problem, and what kind of contract should be used in a certain relationship. When asset specificity increases, contracts need to be increasingly complex to mitigate the possible opportunistic behaviors by the provider. Uncertainty challenges an exchange by requiring the parties to adapt to problems raised from unforeseeable changes. It affects people's rational decision, and increases opportunism. At this time, contract needs to be as specific and detailed as possible to protect possible and inevitable changes in the exchange. Infrequent transactions also increase the likelihood of opportunistic behavior in later periods by reducing the threat of retribution. In sum, TCE sees the IT outsourcing decision as a rational decision made by a careful evaluation of transaction related factors, when transaction costs are high, outsourcing contracts need to be highly specific and complex to offset the risk of opportunism.

However, it is very difficult for the buyer to initiate the detailed contract to cover all the possible issues in the future due to bounded rationality. Hence, they have to execute the incomplete contracts with the risks of adaptation problems and the opportunistic behavior. These incomplete contracts need to be managed by alternative governance mechanisms of which hierarchical mechanisms are conceived to be particularly effective by aligning incentives, providing monitoring and realizing control by fiat [3]. Williamson [4] proposes three mechanisms (i.e. market, hierarchy or hybrid) to explain the governance over the transaction. When the buyer endeavors to choose the governance mechanism, they evaluate the transaction cost related to initiating, monitoring, modifying and executing the outsourcing contract. The mechanism whose transaction cost is the lowest will be chosen finally. According to TCE, the hybrid mechanism is considered as an intermediate form since it involves all alternative mechanisms between the extreme market and hierarchy mechanism. Obviously, both market and hierarchical governance are mixed in the hybrid mechanism, "as it sacrifices some of the high powered incentives of the market in favor of superior coordination and some cooperativeness of the hierarchy in favor of superior market incentives" [4, 5]. The extent of appropriation concern will lead the hybrid to resemble either the market or hierarchical mechanism. The more appropriation concerns lead to the more hierarchical governance.

Generally TCE is adopted as its underlying paradigm in the current literature [6]. The main reason is that the make-or-buy decision is the main topic which TCE focuses on and it is critical in the relationship between the buyer and the supplier [7, 8]. Hence, Poppo and Zenger [9] points out that the buyers endeavor to adopt different governance mechanisms in the exchanges to minimize the transaction cost. Thus, several transaction cost factors have been identified as antecedents of governance mechanisms, including asset specificity, environmental uncertainty, and behavioral uncertainty [9].

Williamson claimed that a hybrid organizational form is considered as a homogeneous category between 'market' and 'hierarchies'. However, Osborn and Baughn [10] criticized the inter-organization relationship actually consists of a heterogeneous phenomenon. They point out that the inter-organization relationships may take a wide range of forms and can serve a great variety of functions, of which economizing on transactions may only be a part [11]. Because of this heterogeneous property of hybrids, it is proposed that they should be considered a unique and separate entity. Although Williamson [12] recognizes that it is not the unique function for the governance mechanisms to minimize the transaction cost, he argues it is still the main function. However, Osborn and Hagedoorn [11] also supported this view and argued that "some alliances may be designed to reduce transaction costs, but this is not their only function" (p. 274). Furthermore, "focusing exclusively on transaction costs [.. .] may hide more than it reveals" (p. 274). As a result, research suggests that TCE alone is insufficient to study the governance underpinning outsourcing [13, 14].

TCE is also criticized for the lack of the recognition of social control. As such, an increasing body of research is pointing out that the transaction is therefore viewed out of the context, as some form of 'independent event', and TCE itself ignoring the effects of the previous and repeated transactions [3, 15]. The very nature of the 'inter-organization relationship' can be impacted by repeated transaction embedded in a wider social context. Such social contexts "which can result in informal coordination and monitoring and high trust between partners, touches upon some of the key assumptions of TCE" [16]. For example, with the increase of asset specificity in the relationship the partners tend to adopt less hierarchical mechanisms to control their relationships. Many alternative control mechanisms exist, such as "reciprocity norms, reputations, trust, personal relationships and the embeddedness of relationships in a social network of current and prior ties" [3]. These social control mechanisms are different from control by prices in the market and the administrative authority in the hierarchy. The perspective of social control offers the opportunity to broaden the recognition of control mechanisms in outsourcing relations.

2.2   Control Theory: Formal vs. Informal Control

A useful classification of control forms that complies with the previous critiques of TCE is the distinction between formal and informal control mechanisms [14]. Anderson [17] defined 'control' as a behavioral attempt to ensure individuals or teams act in a manner consistent with achieving desired goals. Jaworski *et al.* [18] divided control into formal and informal control. Formal control is delivered via a written contract stipulating performance evaluation and rewards. In contrast, informal controls, such as social norms, peer pressure, shared beliefs and experiences [19], complements contracts with social strategies designed to decrease the gap between principal and agent.

The adoption of either formal control or social control may depend on various contexts. Generally, some researchers propose the Western corporations prefer formal control to govern inter-organization relationship in the outsourcing, while the Eastern corporations prefer social control to govern the inter-organization relationship [20]. The logic depends on the assumption that the formal contract can only be adopted in the context with the complete legal system [21].

Besides this, the adoption of control mechanisms can be impacted by the cultural background of the corporations. Some researchers point out that the Eastern corporations especially Chinese corporations prefer social control since they pay attention the social ties in Chinese culture [22, 23]. However, in the recent years, there are some changes of the adoption of control mechanisms in the world. Some researchers point out the Western managers increase the adoption of social control to govern inter-organization relationship in the outsourcing [24]. On the other hand, the Eastern managers increasingly emphasize the formal control [25, 26].

Formal control rests on the contracts and social control emphasizes the importance of trust. Each control mechanism has its own strengths and weaknesses. Formal control prefers the detailed contracts in which the partners' behaviors and outcomes are defined clearly as much as possible to safeguard the opportunism. Social control can be adopted to deal with the unexpected issues since it allows the flexibility to react the issues not defined in the contracts. It is obvious that the strength of one control mechanism is the weakness of the other. Some researchers propose the complementary view that formal control and social control complement each other [25, 26]. However, the complementary theory is criticized by the substitution theory. The researchers argue that the adoption of one control mechanism may reduce the requirement of the other, hence, it would be inefficient to adopt formal control and social control simultaneously [27].

Researchers from the substitution school of thought believe the adoption of one control mechanism obviates the adoption of the other [27]. They argue that social control rests on concrete trust to govern the inter-organization relationship [24], while formal control emphasizes the contract to safeguard against opportunism with high contracting cost [5]. They assume if the trust between the partners is strong enough to govern the inter-organization relationship, the combined adoption of formal control and social control is not economical. In this case, the researchers see formal control and social control as substitutes [5, 27].

However, other scholars disagree, noting that formal control and social control are complements [9, 23, 26] and social control may complement the limitations of formal controls. In a well-designed contract, the partners' behaviors and outcomes are clearly defined, hence a legal framework is provided to govern the relationship [23]. But it is impossible for managers to predict all future contingencies and include them into the contract and difficult to maintain continuous cooperation when unexpected issues arise [24]. Even though trust may exists, ex ante contract costs is hardly reduced [28]. It is through these relationships that [29] view social controls complementing formal controls. Given that the use of social control provides flexibility and fosters bilateralism, social control may interact positively with the use of formal control in explaining cooperation performance [23, 30].

Clearly there are competing views concerning the complementary or substitute view of controls in inter-organizational relationships. The lack of clarity is indicative of a field of academic endeavor which is under-explored. This is particularly pronounced when issues of culture play a part in comparing Western with Eastern outsourcing practices, given "the polarized either/or distinction is a simplification of reality concealing complex interrelationships" [31].

2.3   Guanxi Theory

Hofstede [32] points out that culture influences the individual's thought and behavior in business relationships so it is important to understand the cultural background of the business. Fang et al. [33] points out Chinese culture is considered as "interpersonal-oriented, reciprocal, tactical and network embedded". These characteristics are attributed to Chinese traditional philosophies (i.e. Confucianism, War Stratagem and Taoism). A Chinese businessman who is considered as "Confucian" prefers "win-win" business and cooperation, while the Chinese business man who is considered as Sun Tzu-like strategist prefers "zero-sum" and competition. Trust is considered as the key factor which heavily influences Chinese businessman's business decision [33].

Organizational trust (trust between organizations) in China is associated with "guanxi" which is considered as a critical trait of Chinese society, where "exchanges of favors between people over the long-term are facilitated through a set of interpersonal connexions" [34]. Luo [34] points out Chinese persons prefer to get the things done through "guanxi" way. Guanxi is considered as "door-opener", "gate-keeper" and "peace-maker" in Chinese business context. It can be attributed to Confucian and can be considered as a pragmatic choice to maximize economic benefits. It provides a "moral and ethical framework" [35] within which "transactions could take place appropriately in a weakly regulated society, where inadequacies in both laws and enforcement have weakened professional morality and social responsibility" [36]. Ultimately, guanxi is built up through common attributes such as friendships, clanships, schoolmates and it is cultivated and maintained via social activities.

In sum, guanxi constitutes the fiber woven into every aspect of Chinese society and every Chinese person's social life. It is embedded in Chinese culture deeply and it becomes important in Chinese business context [34]. Luo [23] points out guanxi has been considered as an effective tool in Chinese market and it impacts positively the marketing and accounting performance of the firms. Guanxi is also identified as a source of continuous competence advantage for doing business in China [37, 38].

The term guanxi contains several connotations, however three common definitions are proposed in academic [39]. Generally, guanxi is considered as personal relationships. Luo [40] defines guanxi as "interpersonal linkages with the implication of continued exchanges of favor". Guanxi means implicit mutual obligations, understanding and assurance and leads Chinese attitudes to long-term business and social relationships. The second definition considers guanxi as subsets of relationships which work based on norms and reciprocity. The third definition has a pejorative connotation, meaning to obtain economic or political benefits with the usage of authority by unethical persons. In the study, the author prefers the second definition.

Many contemporary researches study guanxi as the critical tool to do business in China. Lee and Humphreys [41] point out foreign investors have the difficulties to gain knowledge about Chinese domestic market and suggest guanxi networks can be adopted an important source to gain the information on market trend. Guanxi networks also help to attain physical and labor resources, and to build up the relations with local government. Park and Luo [34] propose guanxi plays a critical role in formation sharing with government authorities and business community.

There are few researches on guanxi in outsourcing area. Lee and Humphreys [2] point out that guanxi influences supply management in the area of supplier development, strategic purchasing and outsourcing, and that guanxi helps to develop more integrated and closer supplier relationships. Abramson and Ai [42] propose that "guanxi-based buyer–seller relationships similar to relationship marketing are strongly related to lower levels of perceived uncertainty about the business environment and improved performance outcomes".

Guanxi networks are adopted to overcome the distrust and uncertainty which plague economic transactions [43]. Batjargal and Liu [44] consider guanxi as a risk-mitigating tool in venture capital investments. The author agrees that the buyers build up and maintain guanxi to manage the risk when they deal with supply risk with the suppliers. Transaction Cost Economics is applied to explain why guanxi can mitigate the uncertainty in the environment. Guanxi networks can be adopted to reduce the supplier's opportunism hence decrease transaction costs. This emerges from the nature of guanxi network, which means that if the supplier fails to uphold obligations, then his face is lost and the information is spread to all the members in guanxi network. An underperforming supplier loses the reputation in guanxi network and finds it is difficult to rebuild his image in future. Conversely, guanxi networks help to select the suitable suppliers based on their reputation. Hence, the transaction cost of sourcing and selecting the providers are reduced due to the latent strength of guanxi networks, "which can also reduce the transaction costs associated with environmental uncertainty and opportunistic behavior" [45].

Krause et al. [46] propose that transaction cost economics can be adopted to explain the relationships between the buyers and the suppliers in outsourcing. However, social network theory provides another perspective to study the relationships in outsourcing. Specifically, the author employs social network theory to study how guanxi reduces supply risk and influences outsourcing success. Social network theory is employed since it is "a potent concept to explain inter-organizational processes" [47].

The concept of social capital is one of the key elements in social network theory. There are many definitions of social capital. Coleman [48] defines social capital as "some aspects of social structure, facilitating certain actions in individuals who are within the structure". Social capital is also defined as the opportunities a player obtains through the relationships with others [49]. Putnam [50] considers social capital as "the features of a social organization such as trust, norms, and networks that can improve the efficiency of society by facilitating coordinated actions".

Coleman [48] proposes two benefits of closure cohesive networks for the players in the network during the creation of social capital. Firstly, it facilitates obtain the information since one of important aspects of social capital is the underlying information which is inherent in social relationships. Coleman [48] explains that "a person who is not greatly interested in current events but who is interested in being informed about important developments can save the time required to read a newspaper if he can get the information he wants from a friend who pays attention to such matters". Secondly, within a dense cohesive network, the player's transaction can be detected easily and nobody can escape others' notice. The usage of sanctions is allowed within the closure network, which makes it less risky for the players in the network to trust each other.

Guanxi is considered a type of social capital [51, 52]. Lovett et al. [53] point out that the process of the creation of guanxi is the same as the one of the accumulation of social capital. To cultivate and maintain guanxi is like purchasing the insurance so that one can ask for help when needed. In this sense, it is concluded that guanxi is a type of social capital which can be depend on when the help or support is required. Standifird [54] points out that guanxi can be considered as a form of social capital which is cultivated and maintained between two players through a series of reciprocal exchange. Park and Luo [34] propose the same comment that guanxi is a type of social capital since it consists of the exchange of social obligations and results in the person's face in society. Therefore, in this study guanxi is considered as a form of social capital to influence the success of IT outsourcing.

The perspective of guanxi in the West however is very different, and sometimes viewed as unethical. Li and Wright [55] noted that personal guanxi might lead to corruption and this view is supported by Snell [56]. Since guanxi is based on trust leading to reciprocal obligations that are almost impossible to turn down [51, 57], under conditions of under-developed legal infrastructure, guanxi might result in unethical business practices as render privileged treatments to members within the same guanxi network and under-table dealing [45]. Although some Western authors regard guanxi as simple corruption, most Chinese authors, seeing the phenomenon from their own cultural perspectives, still view it as ethical. To them, a guanxi network may represent the only efficient means of exchange where legal systems are far fully developed [51]. For instance, since China's logistical distribution system is still characterized by complex bureaucracy [58], many foreign invested enterprises, regardless of the products they sell, are faced with challenges at customs clearance. Most importers have to forge close ties with local customs officials and indigenous trading firms in order to secure speedy customs clearance, and efficient delivery [59, 60]. Moreover, given that "China's commercial law has historically been underdeveloped, in part because its inclusion in negotiations is thought to be indicative of bad faith" [61], Chinese executives often rely on personal contacts and friendly discussions to resolve commercial disputes. This unique Chinese way of resolving business conflicts also reminds foreign enterprises of the importance to cultivate guanxi with Chinese officials to protect their corporate interests in the country [62]. Having been further confounded with such Confucian cultural values as emphasizing mutual respect and social harmony [63], it is understandable that the practice of guanxi has different ethical meanings. While Westerners may perceive certain business practices (e.g. gift giving) as bribery, their Chinese counterparts may regard them as totally acceptable and necessary for cultivating mutual trust and long-term relationship. In short, in the eyes of Chinese executives, a guanxi-oriented business system not based on Westerners' ethical standard is not necessarily unethical [53].

3   Conceptual Framework

Based on the theories which are discussed previously, the author proposes the conceptual framework in Fig. 1. The research studies these two questions as below.

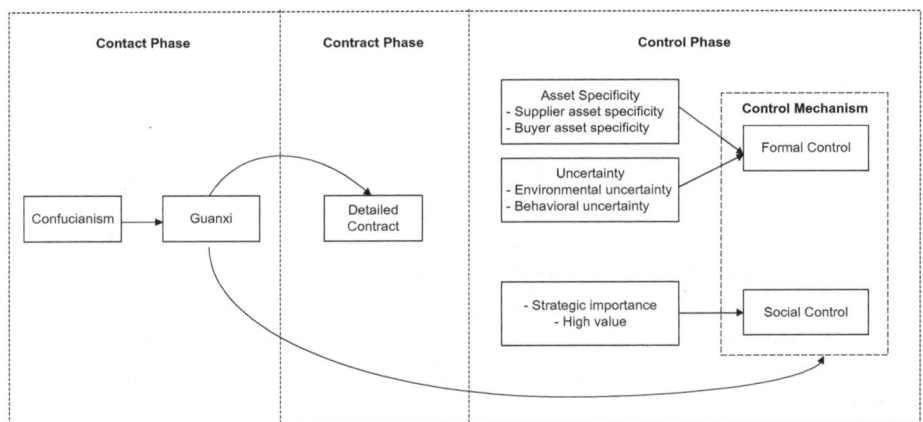

Fig. 1. Conceptual framework

Question 1.

Are social control mechanisms used in the west for strategically important outsourcing contracts which are high value also prevalent in china?

Question 2.

What are the unique characteristics of Guanxi that help (or hinder) outsourcing outcomes in china?

Question 2b.

If Guanxi does not assist outsourcing relations, why not? And in which situations might it (strategically important, high risk situations)?

In China, the corporations prefer social control to govern the inter-organization relationship since they pay attention the social ties in Chinese culture. However, in the recent years, there are some changes of the adoption of control mechanisms in China. The corporation managers increasingly emphasize the formal control. Furthermore, the managers deploy formal control and social control simultaneously as the complements.

In Chinese cultural context, the corporations adopt guanxi to overcome uncertain situation. The greater the environmental uncertainty, the more likely it is that firms will rely on guanxi when entering exchange relationships to deal with an uncertain environment. In contract phase, the buyers prefer the detailed contract to overcome all the uncertainty. However, it is very difficult for the buyer to initiate the detailed contract to cover all the possible issues in the future due to bounded rationality. Hence, they have to execute the incomplete contracts with the risks of adaptation problems and the opportunistic behavior. These incomplete contracts need to be managed by guanxi. In control phase, guanxi influences control mechanism. When the buyers and the providers cultivate and maintain guanxi, social control is increased and formal control is reduced.

4   Contribution and Limitation

The research contributes to academic research in two ways. Firstly, in line with Western literatures, the research investigates whether formal control and social control are prevalent in China. Secondly, the research highlights the different cultural contexts in China hence studies how guanxi influences IT outsourcing projects in China. As a result, the research is helpful for buyers of outsourcing services to implement a wider set of decision-relevant criteria in their IT outsourcing projects in China.

It is very important to acknowledge the limitations of the research which merit future research. Firstly, the research is conducted in China, where the culture context is different from other countries. Guanxi is also adopted in other Eastern countries such as Japan and Korea. It is doubtful whether the findings about guanxi in the research are generalized to these Asian countries. Secondly, the study is conducted from the perspective of the buyers. There is lack of the view of the providers. How do the providers consider formal control, social control and guanxi in IT outsourcing projects? It can be studied in future research.

References

1. Gartner Inc. http://www.gartner.com/newsroom/id/2550615
2. Lee, K.C., Humphreys, P.K.: The role of guanxi in supply management practices. Int. J. Prod. Econ. **106**(2), 450–467 (2007)
3. Gulati, R., Singh, H.: The architecture of cooperation: managing coordination costs and appropriation concerns in strategic alliances. Adm. Sci. Q. **43**, 781–814 (1998)
4. Williamson, O.E.: Comparative economic organization: the analysis of discrete structural alternatives. Adm. Sci. Q. **36**, 269–296 (1991)

5. Gulati, R.: Does familiarity breed trust? The implications of repeated ties for contractual choice in alliances. Acad. Manag. J. **38**, 85–112 (1995)
6. Williamson, O.E.: The Economic Institutions of Capitalism. Free Press, New York (1985)
7. Williamson, O. E.: The modern corporation: origins, evolution, attributes. *Journal of economic literature*, 1537–1568 (1981)
8. Williamson, O.E.: Transaction costs economics. In: Schmalensee, R., Willig, R.D. (eds.) Handbook of Industrial Organization. Elsevier Science (1989)
9. Poppo, L., Zenger, T.R.: Do formal contracts and relational governance act as substitutes or complements? Strateg. Manag. J. **23**(8), 707–725 (2002)
10. Osborn, R.N., Baughn, C.C.: Forms of inter-organizational governance for multinational alliances. Acad. Manag. J. **33**, 503–519 (1990)
11. Osborn, R.N., Hagedoorn, J.: The institutionalization and evolutionary dynamics of inter-organizational alliances and networks. Acad. Manag. J. **40**, 261–278 (1997)
12. Williamson, O.E.: Strategic research: governance and competence perspectives. Strateg. Manag. J. **20**, 1087–1108 (1999)
13. Chiles, T.H., McMackin, J.F.: Integrating variable risk preferences, trust, and transaction cost economics. Acad. Manag. Rev. **21**, 73–99 (1996)
14. Smith, K.G., Carroll, S.J., Ashford, S.J.: Intra- and inter-organizational cooperation: toward a research agenda. Acad. Manag. J. **38**, 7–23 (1995)
15. Ring, P.S., Van de Ven, A.: Structuring cooperative relationships between organizations. Strateg. Manag. J. **13**, 483–498 (1992)
16. Klein, K., Palmer, S.L., Conn, A.B.: Interorganizational relationships: a multilevel perspective. In: Klein, K.J., Kozlowski, S.W.J. (eds.) Multilevel Theory, Research, and Methods in Organizations, pp. 267–307. Jossey-Bass, San Francisco (2000)
17. Anderson, E.: The salesperson as outside agent or employee: a transaction cost analysis. Mark. Sci. **4**, 234–254 (1985)
18. Jaworski, B.J.: Toward a theory of marketing control: Environmental context, control types and consequences. J. Mark. **52**(3), 23–54 (1988)
19. Harmancioglu, N.: Portfolio of controls in outsourcing relationships for global new product development. Ind. Mark. Manage. **38**(4), 394–403 (2009)
20. Peng, M.W., Heath, P.S.: The growth of the firm in planned economies in transition: institutions, organizations, and strategic choice. Acad. Manag. Rev. **21**(2), 492–528 (1996)
21. North, D.C.: Institutions, Institutional Change, and Economic Performance. Norton, New York (1990)
22. Xin, K., Pearce, J.L.: Guanxi: connections as substitutes for formal institutional support. Acad. Manag. J. **39**(6), 1641–1658 (1996)
23. Luo, Y.: Contract, cooperation, and performance in international joint ventures. Strateg. Manag. J. **23**(10), 903–920 (2002)
24. Uzzi, B.: Social structure and competition in interfirm networks: the paradox of embeddedness. Adm. Sci. Q. **42**(1), 37–69 (1997)
25. Peng, M.W.: Institutional transitions and strategic choices. Acad. Manag. Rev. **28**(2), 275–286 (2003)
26. Zhou, X., Li, Q., Zhao, W., Cai, H.: Embeddedness and contractual relationships in China's transition economy. Am. Sociol. Rev. **68**(1), 75–102 (2003)
27. Dyer, J.H., Singh, H.: The relational view: cooperative strategy and sources of Inter-organizational competitive advantage. Acad. Manag. Rev. **23**(4), 660–679 (1998)
28. Dyer, J.H., Chu, W.: The role of trustworthiness in reducing transaction costs and improving performance: empirical evidence from the United Status, Japan, and Korea. Organ. Sci. **14**(1), 57–68 (2003)

29. MacNeil, I.R.: Contracts: adjustment of long-term economic relations under classical, neoclassical, and relational contract law. Northwest. Univ. Law Rev. **72**, 854–905 (1978)
30. Narasimhan, R., Talluri, S., Das, A.: Exploring flexibility and execution competencies of manufacturing firms. J. Oper. Manag. **22**(1), 91–106 (2004)
31. Huber, T.L., Fischer, T.A., Dibbern, J., Hirschheim, R.: A process model of complementarity and substitution of contractual and relational governance in IS outsourcing. J. Manag. Inform. Syst. **30**, 81–114 (2014)
32. Hofstede, G.: Culture's Consequences: International Differences in Work-Related Values. Sage Publications, Beverly Hills (1980)
33. Ghauri, P., Fang, T.: Negotiating with the Chinese: a socio-cultural analysis. J. World Bus. **36**(3), 303–325 (2001)
34. Park, S.H., Luo, Y.: Guanxi and organizational dynamics: organizational networking in Chinese firms. Strateg. Manag. J. **22**, 455–477 (2001)
35. Millington, A., Eberhardt, M., Wilkinson, B.: Gift giving, guanxi and illicit payments in buyer–supplier relations in China: analysing the experience of UK companies. J. Bus. Ethics **57**(3), 255–268 (2005)
36. Griffith, D.A., Harvey, M.G., Lusch, R.F.: Social exchange in supply chain relationships: the resulting benefits of procedural and distributive justice. J. Oper. Manag. **24**(2), 85–98 (2006)
37. Fock, H.K.Y., Woo, K.S.: The China market: strategic implications of guanxi. Bus. Strategy Rev. **9**(3), 33–43 (1998)
38. Tsang, E.W.K.: Can guanxi be a source of sustained competitive advantage for doing business in China? Acad. Manag. Exec. **12**(2), 64–73 (1998)
39. de Pablos, P.O.: Western and Eastern views on social networks. Learn. Organ. **12**(5), 436–456 (2005)
40. Luo, Y.: Guanxi and Business. World Scientific Publishing, Singapore (2000)
41. Lee, J.N., Huynh, M.Q., Kwok, R.C.W., Pi, S.M.: IT outsourcing evolution – past, present and future. Commun. ACM **46**(5), 84–89 (2003)
42. Abramson, N.R., Ai, J.X.: Using guanxi-style buyer–seller relationships in China: Reducing uncertainty and improving performance outcomes. Int. Executive **39**(6), 39–78 (1997)
43. Galaskiewicz, J., Wasserman, S.: Mimetic process within an inter-organizational field: An empirical test. Adm. Sci. Q. **34**(3), 454–479 (1989)
44. Batjargal, B., Liu, M.: Entrepreneurs' access to private equity in China: the role of social capital. Organ. Sci. **15**(2), 159–172 (2004)
45. Standifird, S.S., Marshall, R.S.: The transaction cost advantage of guanxi-based business practices. J. World Bus. **35**(1), 21–42 (2000)
46. Krause, D.R., Handfield, R.B., Tyler, B.B.: The relationships between supplier development, commitment, social capital accumulation and performance improvement. J. Oper. Manag. **25**, 528–545 (2007)
47. Adler, P.S., Kwon, S.W.: Social capital: prospects for a new concept. Acad. Manag. Rev. **27**(1), 17–40 (2002)
48. Coleman, J.S.: Foundations of Social Theory. Harvard University Press, Cambridge (1990)
49. Burt, R.S.: Structural Holes: The Social Structure of Competition. Harvard University Press, Cambridge (1992)
50. Putnam, R.D.: Tuning in, tuning out: the strange disappearance of social capital in America. Polit. Sci. Polit. **28**(4), 664–683 (1995)
51. Luo, Y., Chen, M.: Does guanxi influence firm performance? Asia Pac. J. Manag. **14**, 1–16 (1997)
52. Carlisle, E., Flynn, D.: Small business survival in China: guanxi, legitimacy, and social capital. J. Dev. Entrepreneurship **10**(1), 79–96 (2005)

53. Lovett, S., Simmons, L.C., Kali, R.: Guanxi versus the market: ethics and efficiency. J. Int. Bus. Stud. **30**(2), 231–248 (1999)
54. Standifird, S.S.: Using guanxi to establish corporate reputation in China. Corp. Reputation Rev. **9**(3), 171–178 (2006)
55. Li, J., Wright, P.: The issue of guanxi: discrepancies, reality and implications, BRC Working Paper 99036, September 1999
56. Snell, R.: Obedience to authority and ethical dilemmas in Hong Kong companies. Bus. Ethics Q. **9**(3), 507–526 (1999)
57. Hong, W., Speece, M.: Sales force development in China. J. Int. Selling Sales Manag. **4**(1), 3–20 (1998)
58. Luk, S.T., Xu, Y.Z., Ye, W.C.: Distribution, the Chinese puzzle. Long Range Plann. **31**(2), 295–307 (1998)
59. Forney, M.: WTO may help foreign firms clear China's distribution hurdles. Wall Street J. (12), A12 (1999)
60. Reinganum, J., Helsell, T.: To market, to market. China Bus. Rev., 30–34 (1994)
61. Pearce, J.A., Robinson, R.B.: Cultivating guanxi as a foreign investor strategy. Bus. Horiz. **43**(1), 31–38 (2000)
62. Yau, O.H., Lee, J.S., Chow, R.P., Sin, L.Y., Alan, C.B.: Relationship marketing: the Chinese way. Bus. Horiz. **43**(1), 16–24 (2000)
63. Cragg, C.: Business on the orient (Chinese Business Ethics). Accountancy Age (11), 20–22 (1995)

Author Index